GRAPHIS PHOTO 91

GRAPHIS PHOTO 91

· ·

THE INTERNATIONAL ANNUAL OF PHOTOGRAPHY

DAS INTERNATIONALE JAHRBUCH DER PHOTOGRAPHIE

LE RÉPERTOIRE INTERNATIONAL DE LA PHOTOGRAPHIE

EDITED BY/HERAUSGEGEBEN VON/RÉALISÉ PAR

B. MARTIN PEDERSEN

PUBLISHER AND CREATIVE DIRECTOR: B. MARTIN PEDERSEN
ASSISTANT EDITORS: HEINKE JENSSEN, ANNETTE CRANDALL

GRAPHIS PRESS CORP., ZURICH (SWITZERLAND)

GRAPHIS PUBLICATIONS

GRAPHIS, The International Bi-Monthly Journal Of Visual Communication
GRAPHIS DESIGN, The International Annual Of Design And Illustration
GRAPHIS PHOTO, The International Annual Of Photography
GRAPHIS POSTER, The International Annual Of Poster Art
GRAPHIS PACKAGING, An International Survey Of Packaging Design
GRAPHIS LETTERHEAD 1, An International Survey Of Letterhead Design
GRAPHIS DIAGRAM, The Graphic Visualization Of Abstract, Technical And
    Statistical Facts And Functions
GRAPHIS LOGO 1, An International Survey Of Logos
GRAPHIS PUBLICATION DESIGN, An International Survey Of The Best
    In Magazine Design
GRAPHIS ANNUAL REPORTS, An International Compilation Of The Best Designed
    Annual Reports
GRAPHIS CORPORATE IDENTITY, An International Compilation Of The Best In
    Corporate Identity Design
42 YEARS OF GRAPHIS COVERS, An Anthology Of All GRAPHIS Covers From 1944-86 With Artists'
    Short Biographies And Indexes Of All Graphis Issues
POSTERS MADE POSSIBLE BY A GRANT FROM MOBIL, A Collection Of 250
    International Posters Commissioned by Mobil and Selected By The Poster Society

GRAPHIS PUBLIKATIONEN

GRAPHIS, die internationale Zweimonatszeitschrift der visuellen Kommunikation
GRAPHIS DESIGN, das internationale Jahrbuch über Design und Illustration
GRAPHIS PHOTO, das internationale Jahrbuch der Photographie
GRAPHIS POSTER, das internationale Jahrbuch der Plakatkunst
GRAPHIS PACKAGING, ein internationaler Überblick der Packungsgestaltung
GRAPHIS LETTERHEAD 1, eine internationale Auswahl von Briefpapiergestaltung
GRAPHIS DIAGRAM, die graphische Darstellung abstrakter technischer und
    statistischer Daten und Fakten
GRAPHIS LOGO 1, eine internationale Auswahl von Firmen-Logos
GRAPHIS PUBLICATION DESIGN, eine internationale Zusammenstellung des besten
    Zeitschriften Designs
GRAPHIS ANNUAL REPORT, ein internationaler Überblick über die Gestaltung
    von Jahresberichten
GRAPHIS CORPORATE IDENTITY, eine internationale Auswahl des besten
    Corporate Identity Designs
42 YEARS OF GRAPHIS COVERS, eine Sammlung aller Graphis-Umschläge von 1944-86 mit
    Informationen über die Künstler und Inhaltsübersichten aller Ausgaben der
    Zeitschrift Graphis
POSTERS MADE POSSIBLE BY A GRANT FROM MOBIL, Eine Sammlung von 250 internationalen
    Plakaten, von Mobil in Auftrag gegeben und von der Poster Society ausgewählt

PUBLICATIONS GRAPHIS

GRAPHIS, La Revue Bimestrielle Internationale de la Communication Visuelle
GRAPHIS DESIGN, Le Repertoire International de la Communication Visuelle
GRAPHIS PHOTO, Le Répertoire International de la Photographie
GRAPHIS POSTER, Le Répertoire International de l'Affiche
GRAPHIS EMBALLAGES, Le Repertoire International des Formes de l'Emballage
GRAPHIS LETTERHEAD, Le Répertoire International du Design de Papier à Lettres
GRAPHIS DIAGRAM, Le Repertoire Graphique de Faits et Donnees Abstraits,
    Techniques et Statistiques
GRAPHIS LOGO 1, Le Répertoire International de Logos
GRAPHIS PUBLICATION DESIGN, Le Repertoire International de Couvertures de Revues.
GRAPHIS ANNUAL REPORTS, Panorama International du Meilleur Design de Rapports
    Annuels D'Entreprises
GRAPHIS CORPORATE IDENTITY, Panorama International Du Meilleur Design d'Identité Corporate
42 YEARS OF GRAPHIS COVERS, Recueil de Toutes les Couvertures de GRAPHIS 1944 à 1986
    Avec des Notices Biographiques des Artistes et le Sommaire de Tous les Numéros du
    Magazine Graphis
POSTERS MADE POSSIBLE BY A GRANT FROM MOBIL, Une Collection de 250 Affiches
    Internationales Commandées par Mobil et Choisies par la Poster Society

Contents · Inhalt · Sommaire

AUSTRIA...........................AUT	AUSTRALIEN.......................AUS	AFRIQUE DU SUD ....SAF
AUSTRALIA........................AUS	BELGIEN..........................BEL	ALLEMAGNE ....GER
BELGIUM..........................BEL	DÄNEMARK.........................DEN	AUSTRALIE........................AUS
CANADA ....CAN	DEUTSCHLAND ....GER	AUTRICHE.........................AUT
CZECHOSLOVAKIA...................CSR	FRANKREICH.......................FRA	BELGIQUE ....BEL
DENMARK ....DEN	GROSSBRITANNIEN ....GBR	CANADA ....CAN
FRANCE...........................FRA	HONGKONG ....HKG	DANEMARK.........................DEN
GERMANY ....GER	ISLAND ....ISL	ESPAGNE ....SPA
GREAT BRITAIN....................GBR	ITALIEN ....ITA	ÉTATS-UNIS ....USA
HONG KONG ....HKG	JAPAN............................JPN	FRANCE...........................FRA
ISLAND ....ISL	KANADA ....CAN	GRANDE-BRETAGNE..................GBR
ITALY ....ITA	NIEDERLANDE ....NLD	HONGKONG ....HKG
JAPAN............................JPN	ÖSTERREICH ....AUT	ISLANDE ....ISL
NETHERLANDS ....NLD	POLEN ....POL	ITALIE ....ITA
POLAND...........................POL	SCHWEIZ ....SWI	JAPON............................JPN
SOUTH AFRICA.....................SAF	SPANIEN..........................SPA	PAYS-BAS ....NLD
SPAIN............................SPA	SÜDAFRIKA ....SAF	POLOGNE..........................POL
SWITZERLAND ....SWI	TSCHECHOSLOWAKEI ....CSR	SUISSE...........................SWI
USA..............................USA	USA..............................USA	TCHÉCOSLOVAQUIE..................CSR

REMARKS

WE EXTEND OUR HEARTFELT THANKS TO CON-
TRIBUTORS THROUGHOUT THE WORLD WHO
HAVE MADE IT POSSIBLE FOR US TO PUBLISH
A WIDE AND INTERNATIONAL SPECTRUM OF
THE BEST WORK IN THIS FIELD.

ENTRY INSTRUCTIONS MAY BE REQUESTED AT:
GRAPHIS PRESS CORP., DUFOURSTRASSE 107,
8008 ZURICH, SWITZERLAND

ANMERKUNGEN

UNSER HERZLICHER DANK GILT DEN EIN-
SENDERN AUS ALLER WELT, DIE ES UNS
DURCH IHRE BEITRÄGE MÖGLICH GEMACHT
HABEN, EIN BREITES, INTERNATIONALES
SPEKTRUM DER BESTEN ARBEITEN ZU VERÖF-
FENTLICHEN.

TEILNAHMEBEDINGUNGEN:
GRAPHIS VERLAG AG, DUFOURSTRASSE 107,
8008 ZÜRICH, SCHWEIZ

ANNOTATIONS

TOUTE NOTRE RECONNAISSANCE VA AUX
DESIGNERS DU MONDE ENTIER DONT LES
ENVOIS NOUS ONT PERMIS DE CONSTITUER UN
VASTE PANORAMA INTERNATIONAL DES
MEILLEURS TRAVAUX.

MODALITÉS D'ENVOI DE TRAVAUX:
EDITIONS GRAPHIS SA, DUFOURSTRASSE 107,
8008 ZURICH, SUISSE

ALBERT WATSON

GOLDEN NUDE WITH 15TH CENTURY AZTEC FAN, BY ALBERT WATSON

THE FIRST TIME I SAT BEHIND THE WHEEL OF A CAR I WAS TERRIFIED! AT THE END OF MY FIRST

LESSON I DECIDED THAT IT WOULD BE VIRTUALLY IMPOSSIBLE TO PERFORM ALL THE MANY STEPS

REQUIRED AT ONE TIME TO SAFELY PROPEL THE CAR FORWARD. HOW IS IT POSSIBLE TO CHECK

ONE'S MIRROR, CHANGE GEARS (USING TWO PEDALS), INDICATE, CHECK SPEED, TURN THE WHEEL,

ETC., ETC.? AS WE ALL KNOW, TIME AND PRACTICE TAKE CARE OF ALL THESE PROBLEMS AND AFTER

A WHILE WE CAN PERFORM ALL OF THESE TASKS WITH THE GREATEST OF EASE. THE LEARNING OF

PHOTOGRAPHIC TECHNIQUES PRESENTS ONE WITH SIMILAR PROBLEMS AND FEELINGS. HOWEVER,

EVEN AFTER TWENTY YEARS OF BEING A PHOTOGRAPHER AND DRIVER I AM STILL

MORE COMFORTABLE BEHIND THE WHEEL THAN BEHIND THE CAMERA! PHOTOGRAPHIC

TECHNIQUE SHOULD ALWAYS BE THE MEANS TO THE END AND ONLY THAT. AFTER ALL,

IT IS NOT THE OPERATION OF THE CAR ITSELF THAT IS IMPORTANT BUT WHERE THE CAR CAN TAKE

YOU. IT IS THE SAME WITH PHOTOGRAPHY. MY PASSION FOR PHOTOGRAPHY BEGAN WHILE I WAS

STUDYING TO BE A GRAPHIC DESIGNER. IT CONTINUED THROUGH MY POST-GRADUATE STUDIES IN

FILM AND TELEVISION AT THE ROYAL COLLEGE OF ART AND, EVEN AFTER THOSE YEARS, I ALWAYS

CAME BACK TO STILL PHOTOGRAPHY. THIS PASSION HAS DRIVEN ME IN DIVERSE DIRECTIONS OVER

THE YEARS. I HAVE NOT BEEN ABLE TO SETTLE WITH ONE PARTICULAR FORMAT FOR ANY EXTENDED

PERIOD OF TIME AND CONTINUOUSLY CHANGE FROM 35MM TO 8x10. I HAVE TRIED WHENEVER

POSSIBLE TO GO AGAINST THE NORM—A STILL LIFE ON 35MM, A MOVING FIGURE ON 8x10—NOT

(ABOVE) FROM A FASHION LAYOUT, IN TEXAS, FOR STERN MAGAZINE (OPPOSITE) RAP ARTIST SLICK RICK, FOR DETAILS MAGAZINE.■

always successfully but at least trying to force a change of perspective. Since my vision itself is so diverse, I am just as happy shooting on a beach, in the desert, in urban surroundings, in a studio (preferably my own), in Milan, Paris, Tokyo, London or New York, whether I am using a strobe, tungsten, available light or a mixture of all three. I have kept an avid interest in still life, fashion, beauty, landscape, reportage and portraiture. This diversification does have its problems; as the old saying goes "Jack of all trades, master of none." □ The identity of the photographer is, of course, in his work. The more specialized the photographer, the more assured he is of his identity. For example, some photographers only shoot highly specialized black-and-white fashion stories and never touch color. Others, often due to *business pressures, take a good fashion shot, a not bad still life, an acceptable beauty picture and may even handle a car account. The choice of black-and-white or color may never be theirs to make. □ As we head into the 1990s I intend to become more selfish and aggressively independent. I am never happier than when I am in control and the more control I have, the more responsibility I feel toward the final image. In advertising my feelings of responsibility have shifted away from the art director and designer. While I never ignore the needs and suggestions of these creative and hard-working people, my responsibility is to the company itself. I believe that, for the moment anyway, nothing is more important or desirable than image, and so the end result is that everyone is happy ever after.* ■

ALBERT MACKENZIE WATSON WAS BORN IN SCOTLAND IN 1942. HE ATTENDED THE DUNCAN OF JORDANSTONE COLLEGE OF ART IN DUNDEE AND THE ROYAL COLLEGE OF ART IN LONDON (BA AND MA DEGREES). HIS PHOTOGRAPHS HAVE BEEN ON EXHIBIT IN MANY ONE-MAN-SHOWS. HE HAS BEEN THE OFFICIAL PHOTOGRAPHER FOR THE WEDDING OF PRINCE ANDREW AND SARAH FERGUSON AND ALSO FOR THE VISIT TO CANADA OF THE DUKE AND DUCHESS OF YORK. AMONG HIS CURRENT CLIENTS ARE LIFE MAGAZINE, TIME, NEWSWEEK, ROLLING STONE, STERN, ITALIAN VOGUE, AMERICAN VOGUE, MACY'S, NEW YORK, REVLON, CLAIROL, CHANEL, L'OREAL, INTERVIEW, AND SPORTS ILLUSTRATED. PRESENTLY, HE IS WORKING ON A BOOK OF HIS OWN PERSONAL PHOTOGRAPHY. ■

WETTKAMPFTEILNEHMER BEIM RODEO IN CALGARY, KANADA. ■

Als ich das erste Mal am Steuer eines Autos sass, hatte ich
fürchterliche Angst. Am Ende der ersten Fahrstunde kam ich
zu dem Schluss, dass es schlicht unmöglich sei, all die vielen
Schritte gleichzeitig auszuführen, die nötig sind, um das
Gefährt sicher zu steuern. Wie kann man in den Rückspiegel
schauen, zwei Pedale bedienen, um den Gang zu wechseln,
den Blinker betätigen, die Geschwindigkeit beachten und das
Auto lenken, usw., usw.? Wie wir alle wissen, lösen Zeit und
Erfahrung all diese Probleme, und nach einer Weile haben
wir alles mühelos im Griff. Beim Erlernen der Phototechnik
hat man ähnliche Probleme und Gefühle. Nach 20 Jahren
Erfahrung als Photograph und Autofahrer fühle ich mich
allerdings hinter dem Steuerrad wesentlich sicherer als
hinter der Kamera! Phototechnik sollte immer nur ein Mittel
zum Zweck sein, nichts weiter. Beim Autofahren kommt es
schliesslich auch nicht auf das Fahren als solches an,
sondern darauf, wohin man mit dem Auto fährt. Das gleiche
gilt für die Photographie. Ich entdeckte die Photographie,
als ich Graphik-Design studierte. Meine Begeisterung für die
unbewegten Bilder verlor ich während des anschliessenden
Film- und Fernsehstudiums am Royal College of Art nicht,

und auch danach bin ich immer wieder zur Photographie
zurückgekehrt. Diese Vorliebe hat mich mit der Zeit in
verschiedene Richtungen geführt. Ich habe mich auf kein
Format festgelegt, sondern wechsle ständig zwischen 35mm
und 8x10. Wenn immer möglich, habe ich mich bemüht,
etwas anderes als das Standardformat – z.B. Stilleben auf
35mm, sich bewegende Objekte auf 8x10 – zu machen, nicht
immer mit Erfolg, aber immerhin waren es Versuche, die
Perspektive zu verändern. Mir kommt es nicht darauf an, ob
ich am Strand, in der Wüste, in städtischer Umgebung oder
im Studio (am liebsten in meinem eigenen), in Mailand,
Paris, Tokio, London oder New York photographiere oder
ob ich mit Strobe, Tungsten, dem vorhandenen Licht oder
einer Kombination aus allen drei Lichtquellen arbeite. Mich
interessieren Stilleben ebenso wie Mode, Beauty,
Landschaften, Reportage und Porträts. Diese Vielseitigkeit
bringt auch Probleme mit sich, es wird ja behauptet, dass
die, die alles können, nichts wirklich beherrschen. Die
Identität eines Photographen ist natürlich in seiner Arbeit
zu suchen. Je mehr sich ein Photograph spezialisiert hat,
desto sicherer fühlt er sich hinsichtlich seiner Identität.
Einige Photographen machen z.B. ausschliesslich
Modeaufnahmen in Schwarzweiss. Farbe kommt für sie nicht
in Frage. Andere machen eine gute Modeaufnahme, ein recht
gutes Stilleben, eine annehmbare Beauty-Aufnahme, und
vielleicht haben sie noch einen Auftrag für Autoaufnahmen.
Meistens stecken wirtschaftliche Gründe dahinter. Sie haben
nicht die Wahl zwischen Schwarzweiss und Farbe. Wenn man
die Photographie liebt und einen breiten Horizont hat, ist
das Bild das, was wirklich zählt. Man muss versuchen, eine
neue Art des Sehens zu finden, man muss seine Energie
darauf konzentrieren, damit auch das Publikum die Dinge
mit anderen (mit Deinen) Augen sehen kann. □ Ich habe
beschlossen, dass ich in diesem neuen Jahrzehnt
egoistischer und bewusst freier sein will. Nie bin ich
glücklicher, als wenn ich das Sagen habe, und je mehr auf
mich gehört wird, desto mehr fühle ich mich für das
entstehende Bild verantwortlich. Natürlich berücksichtige
ich die Bedürfnisse und höre mir die Vorschläge der hart
arbeitenden kreativen Leute an. Ich bin aber fest davon
überzeugt, dass schliesslich nichts wichtiger als das Bild
selbst ist, und dass das Endergebnis zählt. Wie im Märchen
ist es wichtig, dass am Schluss alle glücklich sind. ■

ALBERT MACKENZIE WATSON WURDE 1942 IN SCHOTTLAND GEBOREN. ER BESUCHTE DAS DUNCAN OF JORDANSTONE COLLEGE
OF ART IN DUNDEE UND DAS ROYAL COLLEGE OF ART IN LONDON. SEINE PHOTOS WURDEN IN VIELEN EINZELAUSSTELLUNGEN
GEZEIGT. ZU SEINEN GEGENWÄRTIGEN KUNDEN GEHÖREN DIE ZEITSCHRIFTEN LIFE, TIME, NEWSWEEK, ROLLING STONE, STERN,
VOGUE ITALIA, DIE AMERIKANISCHE VOGUE, INTERVIEW UND SPORTS ILLUSTRATED SOWIE DAS KAUFHAUS MACY'S IN NEW YORK,
REVLON, CLAIROL, CHANEL UND L'ORÉAL. ZUR ZEIT ARBEITET ER AN EINEM BUCH ÜBER SEINE EIGENE ARBEIT, DAS 1991 ERSCHEINT. ■

La première fois que je me suis retrouvé au volant d'une voiture, j'ai été absolument terrifié! A la fin de ma première leçon de conduite, j'étais persuadé qu'il me serait pratiquement impossible d'exécuter en même temps tous les gestes qu'il faut pour faire fonctionner une voiture. Comment pouvait-on à la fois regarder dans le rétroviseur, changer de vitesse (en utilisant deux pédales), mettre le clignotant, contrôler la vitesse et manier le volant? Nous le savons tous, le temps et l'expérience viennent à bout de ces problèmes et très vite, on peut accomplir toutes ces tâches le plus aisément du monde. L'apprentissage des techniques photographiques pose le même genre de problèmes et suscite les mêmes sensations. Et pourtant, après 20 ans de pratique de la photo et de la conduite, je me sens toujours plus à l'aise derrière un volant que derrière mon appareil photo! La technique de la photographie devrait être un moyen pour arriver à ses fins, et rien de plus. Après tout, ce qui importe, ce n'est pas la conduite de la voiture en soi, mais le lieu où elle peut nous transporter. Il en est de même avec la photographie. ▫ Ma passion pour la photo s'est éveillée alors que je faisais des études de graphisme. Elle s'est poursuivie pendant tout le temps de mes études supérieures de cinéma et de télévision au Royal College of Art; finalement, après toutes ces années, j'étais toujours attiré par la photographie. Cette passion m'a poussé dans les directions les plus diverses au fil des ans. Je n'ai jamais pu me limiter à un format particulier pendant très longtemps, j'ai constamment changé, passant du 35 mm au 8x10. Je me suis efforcé, toutes les fois que c'était possible, d'aller contre cette norme qui veut qu'on photographie une nature morte en 35 mm et une personne en mouvement en 8x10. Ce n'était pas toujours une réussite, mais au moins, j'essayais de me contraindre à un changement de perspective. Etant donné que ma vision est aussi diversifiée, j'éprouve autant de plaisir à prendre des photos sur la plage, dans le désert ou dans les banlieues des grandes villes, en studio (le mien de préférence), à Milan, Paris, Tokyo, Londres ou New York, que j'utilise un éclairage stroboscopique, des lampes tungstène, la lumière naturelle, ou les trois à la fois. J'ai gardé un intérêt prodigieux pour la nature morte, la photo de mode, de cosmétiques, le paysage, le reportage et le portrait. Cette diversification n'est pas sans poser quelques problèmes; comme l'exprime un vieux dicton, «Qui trop embrasse mal étreint». L'identité du photographe

(EN HAUTE) PHOTOGRAPHIE DE MODE POUR VOGUE ITALIA. ■

fait une avec son œuvre: plus le photographe est spécialisé et plus il est assuré de son identité. Certains photographes par exemple ne prennent que des photos de mode en noir et blanc hyper-sophistiquées et ils ne touchent jamais à la couleur. D'autres, souvent à cause de la pression du marché, vont réaliser une belle photo de mode, une nature morte passable, des pages beauté acceptables, il se peut aussi qu'ils photographient des voitures. Il ne leur appartient pas de faire le choix du noir et blanc ou de la couleur. ▫ Au seuil des années 90, j'ai décidé d'être plus indépendant et plus agressif. Mon grand plaisir, c'est de pouvoir tout contrôler et plus j'ai de possibilités de contrôle, plus je me sens responsable de l'image finale. Dans la publicité, je délègue mes sentiments de responsabilité au directeur artistique, au designer et au conseil en publicité. Bien que je ne néglige jamais les besoins et les suggestions de ces gens créatifs et travailleurs, ma responsabilité est plutôt engagée envers l'agence elle-même. Je suis fermement convaincu que, pour le moment du moins, rien n'est plus important ni désirable que l'image et en définitive, ce qui compte, c'est que, comme dans tous les contes qui finissent bien, tout le monde soit heureux. ■

ALBERT MACKENZIE WATSON EST NÉ EN ECOSSE EN 1942. IL A FRÉQUENTÉ LE DUNCAN OF JORDANSTONE COLLEGE OF ART DE LONDRES. SES PHOTOS ONT ÉTÉ PRÉSENTÉES DANS DE NOMBREUSES EXPOSITIONS PERSONNELLES. PARMI SES CLIENTS, ON PEUT DITER LES MAGAZINES LIFE, TIME, NEWSWEEK, ROLLING STONE, STERN, VOGUE ITALIA, LE VOGUE AMÉRICAIN, INTERVIEW ET SPORTS ILLUSTRATED, AINSI QUE LE GRAND MAGASIN MACY'S À NEW YORK, REVLON, CLAIROL, CHANEL ET L'ORÉAL. ACTUELLEMENT, IL PRÉPARE UN LIVRE SUR SON ŒUVRE PERSONNELLE QUI DOIT PARAITRE EN 1991. ■

EBERHARD GRAMES

THE SPECIAL THING ABOUT THE MEDIA BUSINESS IN THE 1980S WAS THE ALMOST ENDLESS OVERFEEDING WITH PICTURES OF ANY KIND–TO WHICH WE CONTRIBUTED EXTENSIVELY. AND WE WILL SPEED THROUGH THE 1990S, OVER-INFORMED TO THE POINT OF A MENTAL BREAKDOWN. THE FLOODS OF PICTURES, WHICH OUR POOR BRAIN MUST SEE, EVALUATE AND STORE IN THE EVERYDAY CONSUMPTION, WOULD OVERTAX MANY A SOPHISTICATED COMPUTER. BUT WE MANAGE! STARTING WITH THE PAPER AT BREAKFAST AND FINISHING OFF WITH THE EVENING MULTI-CHANNEL PROGRAM, WE STUFF OUR BRAIN WITH PICTURES AND INFORMATION AS IF OUR MODERN ORGANISM NEEDED IT TO SURVIVE. INFORMATION PACKAGED INTO PICTURES BECOMES THE PERMANENT ENTERTAINMENT IN OUR UNEVENTFUL LIVES, WHERE EVEN WORK HAS DEGENERATED INTO BORING MOTOR ACTIVITY. ☐ A GIGANTIC ARMY OF ART DIRECTORS, EDITORS, AND PHOTOGRAPHERS ARE INCESSANTLY BUSY, TRYING TO TASTEFULLY PROCESS THE ALLEGED REALITY ACCORDING TO THE ZEITGEIST. THEY ALWAYS STICK TO THE RIGID LAWS OF THE MARKET, WHICH ARE VERY SIMPLE: RATING AND IMPROVED CIRCULATION. PRECISELY SCHEDULED PHOTOGRAPHERS ARE RUSHED AROUND THE WORLD ON ASSIGNMENT, IN PANIC LOOKING FOR THE NEVER-SEEN-BEFORE. IT MUST BE PECULIAR AT LEAST, BUT EXOTIC IN ANY CASE. PORTRAIT PHOTOGRAPHERS FORCE THEIR MODELS INTO MORE AND MORE ECCENTRIC POSES, THEY EVEN HAVE SERIOUS LYRIC POETS MAKE PIROUETTES OVER DOUBLE PAGES— REALITY AS DISNEYLAND OF STRAINED SURPRISES, EVERY DAY, EVERY WEEK, EVERY MONTH ANEW. ☐

(OPPOSITE PAGE) FROM A PHOTOGRAPHIC ESSAY ON AN ELDERLY RESIDENT OF THE IRISH COUNTRYSIDE, WHOSE LIFE IS UNAFFECTED BY CHANGES THAT HAVE OCCURRED IN THE LAST 100 YEARS. (ABOVE) STILL-LIFES BY THE PHOTOGRAPHER. ▪

If, by chance, the photography turns out to be a bit too realistic in this continuous battle for better entertainment, typography and doctored details will bend it straight. We'll experience the Gulf war in magazine style, casually leaned back, chewing chips and drinking coffee; always hanging on to the reality of the war, perhaps making the critical objection that the corpses in Coppola's Appocalypse Now *looked somewhat more real. ▫ To be part of the army of photographing adventurers who always experience life first-hand has become a dubious pleasure. The zig-zag course through editorial offices caused many to acquire an occupational disease which rather prevents than fosters good photography. Too often, journalism is deliciously presented like food photography, hard to distinguish from the perfectly presented advertisement page. The photographer not only goes along in this levelling-down, he even becomes an accomplice since he is the first link in the chain of picture procurers. For a healthy self-awareness, the photographer sometimes needs a slap in the face to mess up a little bit the smooth way in which he sees himself. This actually happened to me when I was doing a photo-series in Bulgaria on 100-year-olds. ▫ When, in the first Balkan village, we set up the tripod in ankle-deep muck, surrounded by a handful of tousled, filthy children, we knew: this trip was different. Here the pleasantness— sometimes quickly transformed into smugness—of Western behavior is stripped of importance. Bluntly and directly, bold guys looked into our faces, calloused hands were stretched out. Here, in the absolute East of Europe, the usual take and go of photograpehrs was out of the question. And we learned to appreciate it. I seldom slept better,*

invited by strangers who stuffed me with all edible things they could find. I seldom handed out Polaroid pictures with such joy. What a unique moment, when the 110-year-old man and his 92-year-old son experienced an unforgettable day in front of my cameras: decrying as they saw their ghost pictures come to life due to chemistry. For a change, the photographer had something to give too. The most exciting thing the people possessed were their faces. We listened to stories that were still life-stories. When I repeatedly aske the hunter where he had his trophies, he answered with a smile that hunting alone was the aim. ▫ We were brooding a lot about such basic and wise statement, uttered by people who, according to our Western standards, are uninformed, poor ignorants, who are the deplorable target group of a media society to come (and that's only a question of time). After two weeks among people who daily routine is set by domestic animals we just started to discover what freedom inside your head could be. The straightness of their simple life was so appealing and inviting that the deadlines became unimportant and the office a faraway factory in a different world. In fact, photographing itself turned into quite an experience. Figuring that tourist busses will spit out their passengers in these villages one day to show Western consumers the pure life like an outdated object in a museum made us shiver. Here in the Balkan, environmental protection is in high demand, also in front of photo-graphers, that was clear. And even if our story about the one-hundred-year-olds will never be published, we have experienced it. And this can be a precious piece of photo-graphy. I wish all my colleagues that they will photograph what they like most—without cheap showmanship. ▪

EBERHARD GRAMES IS KNOWN FOR HIS PHOTOGRAPHIC ESSAYS ON ETHNIC CULTURES THAT ARE THREATENED WITH EXTINCTION IN EUROPE, THE UNITED STATES AND ASIA. HIS REPORTS HAVE BEEN PUBLISHED IN THE MAGAZINES STERN, GEO, FAZ-MAGAZIN, AND OTHERS. MR. GRAMES HAS ALSO PUBLISHED SEVERAL BOOKS ON JAPAN AND IS A MEMBER OF THE BILDERBERG AGENCY. ▪

Das eigentlich Besondere an der Medienlandschaft der achtziger Jahre war die schier grenzenlose Überfütterung mit Bildern aller Art, wozu wir ausgiebig beigetragen haben. Und auch die neunziger werden wir über-informiert bis zum geistigen Kollaps zurücklegen. Die Bilderfluten, die unser armes Gehirn im alltäglichen Rasterkonsum sortieren, bewerten und speichern soll, würde so manchen Grossrechner überfordern. Doch wir schaffen's! Von der Frühstückszeitung bis zum abendlichen Multi-Kanal-Programm schaufeln wir Bilder und Informationen in uns rein, als würde unser moderner Organismus sie zum Durchhalten brauchen. Die bebilderte Information wird zur Dauerunterhaltung in unserem ereignislosen Leben, wo selbst die Arbeit zur langweiligen Motorik verkommen ist. □ Ein gigantisches Heer von Art Direktoren, Redakteuren und Photographen ist unentwegt damit beschäftigt, die angebliche Wirklichkeit geschmackvoll im Zeitgeist aufzubereiten. Stets streng nach den Gesetzen des Marktes, die da lauten: Einschaltquoten und Auflagensteigerung. Genau terminierte Photographen werden «on assignment» über den Globus getrieben, in panischer Suche nach dem noch nie Gesehenen, schrill muss es mindestens sein, exotisch auf jeden Fall. Porträt-Photographen zwängen ihre Modelle in immer abwegigere Posen, lassen auch den ernsten Lyriker die doppel-seitenschwangere Pirouette schlagen. Die Wirklichkeit als Disneyland der gequälten Überraschungen, jeden Tag, jede Woche, jeden Monat neu. Sollte in der Dauerschlacht um die bessere Unterhaltung die Photographie mal etwas zu realistisch geraten sein, werden Typo oder frisierter Ausschnitt es schon richten. Lässig zurückgelehnt erleben wir den Golf-Krieg im Illustrierten-Stil, Chips kauend, rauchend und Kaffee trinkend. Immer dran an der Wirklichkeit des Krieges, vielleicht mit dem kritischen Einwand, dass die Leichen in Coppolas Apokalypse irgendwie echter aussehen. □ Es ist ein durchaus zweifelhaftes Vergnügen geworden, zum Heer der photographierenden Abenteurer zu gehören, die das Leben immer aus erster Hand erleben dürfen. Der Slalom durch die Redaktionszwänge hat bei vielen zu einer Berufskrankheit geführt, die gute Photographie eher verhindert als fördert. Allzuoft wird auch Journalismus so lecker wie Food-Photographie dargeboten, kaum noch zu unterscheiden von der perfekt moderierten Werbeseite. □ Bei dieser Gleichmacherei ist der Photograph nicht nur Mitmacher, sondern auch Mittäter, denn er ist immerhin das erste Glied in der Kette der Bildbeschaffer. So braucht der Photograph zur Nabelschau gelegentlich eine schallende Ohrfeige, damit sein glattes Selbstverständnis ein wenig in Unordnung gerät. So mir geschehen bei meiner letzten Arbeit über die Hundertjährigen in Bulgarien. □ Schon als wir im ersten Balkandorf das Stativ in den knöcheltiefen Schlamm stellten und die zerzauste, dreckstarrende Kinderschar uns umlagerte, war klar: Dieser Trip war anders. Hier hatte das gefällige bis selbstgefällige Westler-Auftreten keine Bedeutung mehr. Frank und frei schauten verwegene Typen uns ins Gesicht, schwielige Hände streckten sich uns entgegen. Hier, im absoluten Osten Europas war das übliche «take-and-go» des Photographen nicht drin. Und wir lernten es zu schätzen. Selten schlief ich besser, eingeladen von wildfremden Menschen, abgefüllt mit allem Essbaren, das sie auftreiben konnten. Selten habe ich mit solcher Freude Sofort-Bilder verschenkt. Welch ein Augenblick, als der 110jährige Alte und sein 92jähriger Sohn vor meiner Kamera einen der denkwürdigsten Tage ihres Lebens erlebten: Weinend sahen sie ihr Geisterbild aus der Chemie auftauchen. Endlich einmal hatte auch der Photograph etwas zu geben. Das Aufregendste, was diese Leute besassen, waren ihre Gesichter. Wir hörten Geschichten, die noch Lebensgeschichten sind. Als ich den Jäger wiederholt gefragt hatte, wo er denn seine Trophäen habe, antwortete er lächelnd, nur die Jagd selbst sei das Ziel. □ Wir gerieten ins Grübeln über so grundlegende Weisheiten, ausgesprochen von Menschen, die nach unseren West-Massstäben absolut uninformiert sind, arme Unwissende, die bedauernswerte Zielgruppe einer Mediengesellschaft, die da kommen wird. (Das ist nur eine Zeitfrage.) Nach zwei Wochen unter den Menschen, deren Tagesablauf von den Haustieren bestimmt wurde, nicht von der Informationsaufnahme, bekamen wir eine leise Ahnung, was Freiheit im Kopf sein kann. Die Schnörkellosigkeit dieses einfachen Lebens war so ansteckend, dass meine Termine gleichgültig wurden und die Redaktion zu einer fernen Fabrik in einer anderen Welt. Tatsächlich wurde das Photographieren selbst Erlebnis. Die Vorstellung, dass in diesen Dörfern irgendwann die Touristenbusse ausgekippt werden, um dem Westkonsumenten das pure Leben wie ein verstaubtes Museumsstück vorzuführen, liess uns schaudern. Hier im Balkan ist Umweltschutz gefragt, auch vor Photographen, das wurde uns klar. Und auch wenn die Geschichte über die Hundertjährigen nie erscheinen sollte, haben wir sie doch erlebt. Und das kann ein wertvolles Stück Photographie sein. ■

EBERHARD GRAMES PHOTOGRAPHIERT ESSAYS ÜBER AUSSTERBENDE KULTURFORMEN IN EUROPA, DEN USA UND ASIEN. SEINE GESCHICHTEN ERSCHIENEN IN STERN, GEO, FAZ-MAGAZIN ETC. GRAMES IST MITGLIED DER AGENTUR BILDERBERG. ■

Ce qui aura sans doute caractérisé le plus le monde des médias dans les années 80, c'est ce gavage en images de toutes sortes auquel nous aurons été soumis - nous y avons du reste amplement contribué. Les années 90 risquent, elles aussi, d'être une époque de surinformation, et ce jusqu'à l'indigestion. Ce flot d'images que notre pauvre petit cerveau doit trier, évaluer et emmagasiner quotidiennement donnerait du fil à retordre à plus d'un super-ordinateur. Et pourtant, nous y arrivons! Du journal du petit déjeuner aux programmes des multiples chaînes de télévision du soir, nous ingurgitons force images et informations, comme si notre organisme en avait besoin pour tenir le coup. L'information illustrée est en passe de devenir une distraction permanente dans nos existences monotones où même le travail se réduit à un train-train ennuyeux. □ Une gigantesque armée de directeurs artistiques, de rédacteurs et de photographes travaille sans relâche à rendre la soi-disant réalité plus attrayante, à la mettre au goût du jour. Mais toujours en respectant les lois du marché, à savoir les taux d'écoute et l'accroissement des tirages. Des photographes auxquels ont fixe des délais bien précis sont envoyés en mission de par le monde, dans une quête désespérée du jamais vu. Il faut du tape-à-l'œil, de l'exotisme en tout cas. Les photographes de portrait contraignent leurs modèles à prendre des poses de plus en plus extravagantes et ils n'hésitent pas à faire faire au poète le plus respectable des entrechats sur double page. La réalité présentée tel un Disneyland, du sensationnel à tout prix, de la nouveauté chaque jour, chaque semaine, chaque mois. Et si dans cette lutte perpétuelle pour produire le meilleur spectacle possible, la photographie est devenue par trop réaliste, la typo ou un fragment bien retouché y remédieront. Confortablement installés, nous vivrons la guerre du Golf comme dans les illustrés, en dégustant des chips, fumant et buvant notre café. Toujours au plus près de la réalité de la guerre, avec toutefois cette réserve que les cadavres de l'Apocalypse de Coppola avaient en quelque sorte l'air plus authentiques. □ Faire partie de la meute des aventuriers-photographes qui ont le privilège de vivre les événements en direct est devenu un plaisir plutôt sujet à caution. A force de slalomer entre les contraintes imposées par les rédactions, de nombreux photographes ont été contaminés par cette maladie professionnelle qui empêche de faire de la bonne photographie. Trop souvent, le journalisme est présenté de manière aussi appétissante que de la photographie culinaire, c'est à peine si on peut la distinguer des pages de publicité parfaitement commentées. □ Avec ce nivellement, le photographe n'est pas seulement un participant, il est aussi un complice car, ne l'oublions pas, il est le premier maillon de la chaîne de ceux qui font l'image. Une bonne gifle est parfois salutaire au photographe pour que la haute idée qu'il se fait de sa personne soit un peu remise en question. C'est ce qui m'est arrivé lors de mon dernier travail sur les centenaires de Bulgarie. □ Dans le premier village des Balkans, à peine avions-nous posé le pied de l'appareil dans une boue qui nous arrivait à la cheville, entourés d'une ribambelle d'enfants crasseux, que déjà une chose était claire: ce voyage allait être différent des autres. Ici, l'attitude complaisante et prétentieuse de l'Occidental n'avait plus aucune signification. Des types pleins d'audace nous regardaient carrément dans les yeux, des mains calleuses se tendaient vers nous. Là, au cœur de l'Europe de l'Est, l'habituel «take and go» du photographe était absolument hors de question. J'ai rarement dormi aussi bien, invité par des gens qui m'étaient absolument inconnus, gavé de toute la nourriture qu'ils avaient pu dénicher. J'ai rarement offert avec autant de joie des photos Polaroïd. Quel moment inoubliable que celui où ce vieillard de 110 ans et son fils de 92 ans vécurent devant mon appareil l'un des jours les plus mémorables de leur vie! Ils regardaient en pleurant leur visage apparaître, émerger de l'émulsion chimique. Finalement, pour une fois, le photographe avait aussi quelque chose à donner. La chose la plus fascinante que ces gens possèdent, c'est leur visage. Nous avons écouté des histoires qui sont encore l'histoire d'une vie. □ Après avoir passé deux semaines parmi ces gens dont l'emploi du temps était déterminé par les animaux domestiques, et non par l'absorption d'informations, nous commencions à avoir une légère idée de ce que c'est que d'avoir l'esprit libre. Cette vie simple, sans fioritures, était si contagieuse que les délais imposés pour mes photos m'étaient devenus indifférents; la rédaction n'était plus qu'une usine lointaine quelque part dans un autre monde. De fait, photographier était devenu une expérience en soi. Nous avions le frisson rien que de penser que tôt ou tard, les cars de touristes allaient se déverser dans ces villages, pour montrer aux consommateurs occidentaux la vie à l'état pur comme une pièce de musée poussiéreuse. Ici, dans les Balkans, la protection de l'environnement est nécessaire; il faut aussi le protéger des photographes, nous en avons pris conscience. Et même si l'histoire sur les centenaires ne paraît jamais, nous l'aurons vécue. Cela sera peut être un morceau d'anthologie. ■

EBERHARD GRAMES A RÉALISÉ DES PHOTOGRAPHIES POUR ILLUSTRER DES ESSAIS SUR LES CULTURES EN VOIE D'EXTINCTION EN EUROPE, AUX USA ET EN ASIE. SES RÉCITS ONT PARU DANS STERN, GEO, LE FRANKFURTER ALLGEMEINE MAGAZIN, ETC. GRAMES EST MEMBRE DE L'AGENCE BILDERBERG. ■

ROBERT IMHOFF

PORTRAIT OF ROBERT IMHOFF BY STEPHEN JENNINGS

SHOCK FROM DOWN UNDER: I FEEL LIKE THE WAITER AT THE LAST SUPPER BEING ASKED TO WRITE THE INTRODUCTION TO THE BIBLE. □ IN THE LATE 60S AND EARLY 70S, I WAS LED TO BELIEVE THAT TO BE A SUCCESSFUL PHOTOGRAPHER, ONE HAD TO MOVE TO LONDON, PARIS OR NEW YORK. IN 1975 I SET OFF TO SEE WHERE I WOULD SETTLE. HAVING WORKED IN SOUTH EAST ASIA FOR CREATIVE TALENT FROM THESE CITIES, I WAS ABLE TO JUMP THE QUEUE AND MEET TOP PHOTOGRAPHERS AND ART DIRECTORS, ALL OF WHOM WERE IMPRESSED BY THE BROAD SCOPE OF MY PORTFOLIO. IN AUSTRALIA, YOU DON'T HAVE TO SPECIALIZE IN ONE AREA. THIS HAS ALWAYS PLEASED ME, AS I THRIVE ON NEW CHALLENGES, AND HAVE BEEN FORTUNATE TO WORK FOR UNINHIBITED, LATERAL THINKERS. WHY SHOULDN'T A FASHION EDITOR USE A FOOD PHOTOGRAPHER TO SHOOT A FASHION SERIES? WHY SHOULDN'T AN ART DIRECTOR USE A FASHION PHOTOGRAPHER TO SHOOT A STILL LIFE SUBJECT? USUALLY BECAUSE OF THE INHIBITIONS AND LIMITATIONS OF PHOTOGRAPHERS AND BUYERS OF PHOTOGRAPHY. □ TO MY SURPRISE I FOUND AN ENORMOUS AMOUNT OF BAD PHOTOGRAPHY IN BRITAIN, EUROPE AND AMERICA, AND I CAME TO REALIZE THAT IT WAS A MATTER OF RATIOS: THE LARGER THE POPULATION, THE GREATER THE NUMBER OF GOOD AND BAD PHOTOGRAPHERS. IT WAS NOT WHERE, BUT HOW YOU PHOTOGRAPHED THAT MATTERED, AND I REALIZED I COULD COMPETE INTERNATIONALLY FROM AUSTRALIA. □ I RETURNED TO OPEN MY OWN STUDIO IN 1976 WITH A WEALTH OF INFORMATION AND INSPIRATION. TO BE A SUCCESSFUL STILLS PHOTOGRAPHER IS NOT UNLIKE BEING A FILM DIRECTOR. YOU ARE ONLY AS GOOD AS THE TEAM YOU

select to support each project. A simple recipe for good photography: use only the best (or most appropriate) camera, lighting, assistant, processing laboratory, stylist, talent, make-up artist, set constructor, model maker etc. etc. Too often we see the inferior results of compromise □ Photography is an endless art, its horizons are broad encompassing objects that are moving and/or static; sharp and/or blurred: far and/or close; black-and-white and/or color; its only limitations are the artists and their naiveté, inhibitions, laziness and lack of vision. □ Graphis Photo offers a great window into professional photography. Over the years we have seen innovative masters leading the way. Where are the photographers of the future? Come forward and show us your work! Don't just look and plagiarize the past, don't be shy, inhibited or lazy. Don't hide your work under the banner of "Art." Come forward and compete in the international arena. Don't be scared of being plagiarized, for if your talent is good, you should be able to show your currrent work and move on to future challenges.

Too many photographers are insular; they work to premeditated systems that don't allow for the adventure of further development. I have not been one to reproduce my work details, such as type of camera, lens, lighting positions, filters, film, etc., for I like the challenge of variety and not the boring safety of the production line. Photography should express the mood of the artist, be guided by emotion, not by text book rules. □ Great names have disappeared from recent annuals, where have they gone. Villas in the South of France? Farms in Wales, vineyards in Tuscany, skiing in Aspen? No! Names such as Bailey, Bookbinder and Moon are now prominent in movies, directing TV commercials, pop clips and films. Why the move? Certainly the challenge of new horizons, but could it be as well that the electronic medium is the future, and the supply-and-demand principle guides good photographers into this very creative area, where movement and music help enhance their art? Who knows, perhaps we will view Graphis Photo on our monitors in the future? ■

ROBERT IMHOFF ATTENDED THE ART-ORIENTED BITHAM HIGH SCHOOL AND RMIT PHOTOGRAPHY COLLEGE IN MELBOURNE, AUSTRALIA. HE HAS WORKED LOCALLY AND INTERNATIONALLY FOR MANY AUTOMOTIVE, AIRLINE AND PRODUCT CLIENTS. HE CURRENTLY OWNS THE LIGHTHOUSE PHOTOGRAPHIC CENTRE IN MELBOURNE, WHICH HOUSES PHOTOGRAPHERS' OFFICES, STUDIOS AND THE RESPECTED LIGHTHOUSE GALLERY, EXHIBITING LOCAL AND INTERNATIONAL SHOWS. HIS PASSION FOR SHARING HIS KNOWLEDGE HAS LED TO SPEAKING ENGAGEMENTS AT MANY AUSTRALASIAN CONVENTIONS AND ART COLLEGES; CURRENTLY HE HAS ELEVEN FORMER ASSISTANTS IN THE REGION COMPETING AGAINST HIM, IN BOTH STILLS AND MOVIE WORK. TODAY HIS WORK IS MAINLY PORTRAITURE, LANDSCAPE AND DIRECTING TV COMMERCIALS. A GREAT BELIEVER IN THERAPEUTIC ACTIVITY, HE SHARES AS MUCH TIME AS POSSIBLE WITH HIS FAMILY IN THEIR HISTORIC FARM PROPERTY AND IS CURRENTLY RESTORING HIS 1925 LANCIA LAMBDA FOR RALLY COMPETITION. ■

Es ist ein eigenartiges Gefühl: Es kommt mir vor, als sei ich ein Kellner beim Abendmahl und man verlange von mir, die Einführung zur Bibel zu schreiben. □ In den späten sechziger und frühen siebziger Jahren glaubte ich, man müsse in London, Paris oder New York leben, um ein erfolgreicher Photograph zu werden. 1975 sah ich mich nach einem geeigneten Wohnort um. Ich hatte im südostasiatischen Raum für Kreative aus diesen Städten gearbeitet und hatte deshalb keine Mühe, Kontakt zu Top-Photographen und Art Direktoren aufzunehmen. Sie zeigten sich alle von dem breiten Spektrum, das mein Portfolio aufwies, beeindruckt. In Australien muss man sich nicht auf ein Gebiet spezialisieren. Das hat mir immer gefallen, weil es neue Herausforderungen bedeutet, und ich hatte das Glück, für Leute zu arbeiten, die Mut und Phantasie hatten. Warum sollte ein Photo Editor nicht einmal einen Food Photographen für die Modeaufnahmen nehmen? Warum sollte ein Art Direktor nicht einen Modephotographen für ein Stilleben einsetzen? Normalerweise geht das nicht wegen der Ängstlichkeit und Beschränktheit der Photographen und Art Buyer. □ Zu meinem Erstaunen fand ich in Grossbritannien wie auf dem europäischen Festland und in Amerka eine enorme Menge schlechter Photographie, und ich begriff, dass es eine Frage des Verhältnisses ist: je grösser die Bevölkerung desto grösser die Anzahl von guten und schlechten Photographen. Es kam nicht darauf an, wo, sondern wie man photographiert und mir wurde klar, dass ich auch von Australien aus mit der internationalen Konkurrenz Schritt halten kann. □ So kehrte ich 1976 in mein Atelier zurück, erfüllt von Ideen und Erkenntnissen. Es ist egal, ob man photographiert oder filmt, man darf nur das Beste (oder Geeignetste) wählen: Kamera, Beleuchtung, Assistent, Entwicklungslabor, Stylist, Modelle, Make-up-Spezialist, Dekorateur, Requisiteur etc. Nur allzuhäufig sehen wir, wieviel Kompromisse verderben können. □ Photographie hat fast unendliche Möglichkeiten: sie befasst sich mit Dingen, die sich bewegen und/oder bewegungslos sind; scharf und/oder verzerrt; fern und/oder nah; schwarzweiss und/oder farbig; ihre einzigen Grenzen liegen bei den Künstlern selbst, in ihrer Naivität, Faulheit oder Phantasielosigkeit. □ Graphis Photo bietet einen umfassenden Einblick in die professionelle Photographie. In all den Jahren haben wir innovative Meister gesehen, die zu Wegbereitern wurden. Wo sind die Photographen der Zukunft? Zeigt Euch und zeigt was Ihr könnt! Schaut nicht nur auf die Vergangenheit und kopiert sie nicht, seid nicht schüchtern, ängstlich oder faul. Versteckt Eure Arbeit nicht unter dem Mantel der «Kunst». Kommt heraus und stellt Euch der internationalen Konkurrenz. Habt keine Angst davor, kopiert zu werden. Wenn Ihr talentiert seid, könnt Ihr Eure jetzige Arbeit ruhig zeigen und Neues wagen. Zu viele Photographen kapseln sich ab, sie arbeiten nach vorgefassten Konzepten, die ihnen keinen Raum für eine Weiterentwicklung lassen, für das Abenteuer neuer Herausforderungen. Ich habe mich nie auf eine bestimmte Kamera, ein Objektiv, Beleuchtungspositionen, Filter, Filmmaterial etc. verlassen, mir gefällt es auszuprobieren; ich kann auf Vorhersehbares, auf Sicherheit verzichten. Photographie soll die Stimmung des Künstlers ausdrücken, soll von Gefühlen, nicht von den Regeln der Lehrbücher bestimmt werden. □ Aus den Jahrbüchern der letzten Jahre sind einige grosse Namen verschwunden. Wo sind sie geblieben? In Villen in Südfrankreich? Auf Landsitzen in Wales, in den Weinbergen der Toskana oder beim Skivergnügen in Aspen? Nein! Namen wie Bailey, Bookbinder und Moon tauchen jetzt im Vorspann von Filmen auf, sie machen TV-Spots, Pop Video-Clips und -Filme. Warum ein solcher Wechsel? Natürlich reizen die neuen Erfahrungen, aber es könnte auch sein, dass das elektronische Medium die Zukunft ist, dass das Prinzip von Angebot und Nachfrage gute Photographen veranlasst, sich mit diesem sehr kreativen Bereich zu befassen, in dem sie sich der Bewegung und der Musik bedienen können, um ihre künstlerische Aussage zu unterstützen. □ Werden wir uns Graphis Photo in Zukunft auf unserem Monitor anschauen können? ∎

ROBERT IMHOFF BESUCHTE DIE KUNSTORIENTIERTE BITHAM HIGH SCHOOL UND DAS RMIT PHOTOGRAPHY COLLEGE IN MELBOURNE. ER HAT IM IN- UND AUSLAND FÜR VIELE AUTOFIRMEN, LUFTFAHRTGESELLSCHAFTEN UND HERSTELLER VON KONSUMARTIKELN GEARBEITET. IHM GEHÖRT DAS LIGHTHOUSE PHOTOGRAPHIC CENTRE IN BELBOURNE, IN DEM PHOTOGRAPHEN BÜROS UND ATELIERS HABEN, UND WO SICH DIE ANGESEHENE LIGHTHOUSE GALERIE BEFINDET, IN DER REGIONALE UND INTERNATIONALE AUSSTELLUNGEN STATTFINDEN. SEIN ANLIEGEN, SEIN WISSEN MIT ANDEREN ZU TEILENM HAT DAZU GEFÜHRT, DASS ER BEI KONFERENZEN UND AN KUNSTSCHULEN IN AUSTRALLEN UND ASIEN ZAHLREICHE VORTÄGE GEHALTEN HAT. ZUR ZEIT MACHEN IHM SIEBEN EHEMALIGE ASSISTENTEN IN SEINER REGION KONKURRENZ, SOWOHL IM PHOTO- ALS AUCH IM FILMBEREICH. HEUTE MACHT ER VOR ALLEM PORTRÄT- UND LANDSCHAFTSAUFNAHMEN SOWIE TV-SPOTS. ER IST VON DER THERAPEUTISCHEN WIRKUNG AKTIVER FREIZEITGESTALTUNG ÜBERZEUGT UND VERBRINGT SOVIEL ZEIT WIE MÖGLICH MIT SEINER FAMILIE AUF IHREM HISTORISCHEN LANDSITZ. ∎

C'est sans doute le choc des Antipodes, mais je me sens comme le serveur de la Cène, auquel on aurait demandé d'écrire une introduction de la Bible. □ A la fin des années 60 et début 70, je croyais que pour devenir un photographe à succès, il fallait s'exiler à Londres, Paris ou New York. En 1974, je me mis en route pour trouver un lieu où me fixer. J'avais travaillé en Asie du Sud-Est pour des créateurs de talent venant de ces villes, cela me permit de brûler les étapes et de rencontrer les photographes et les directeurs artistiques les plus prestigieux. Tous furent impressionnés par le large rayon d'action de mon portfolio. En Australie, vous n'avez pas besoin de vous spécialiser dans un domaine particulier. Cela m'a toujours plu car les nouveaux enjeux me stimulent; j'ai eu ainsi la chance de travailler pour des gens plutôt marginaux, sans inhibitions. Pourquoi un éditeur de mode ne demanderait-il pas à un spécialiste de la photographie culinaire de prendre une série de photos de mode? Pourquoi un directeur artistique ne chargerait-il pas un photographe de mode de photographier une nature morte? Généralement à cause des inhibitions et des limites des photographes et des acheteurs. □ A ma grande surprise, je découvris une quantité énorme de mauvaise photographie en Grande-Bretagne et dans les autres pays européens, ainsi qu'en Amérique. J'en conclus que c'était une question de proportions: plus la population est nombreuse, plus grand sera le nombre des mauvais et des bons photographes. Ce qui importe, ce n'est pas où, mais comment vous photographiez, et je me rendis compte que je pourrais concourir pour l'Australie sur le plan international. □ J'y retournai pour ouvrir mon propre studio en 1976, riche d'une profusion d'informations et bouillant d'inspiration. Etre un photographe à succès, c'est la même chose que d'être un réalisateur de films. Le résultat dépendra de l'équipe que vous choisirez pour réaliser chacun de vos projets. C'est une recette élémentaire si vous voulez faire de la bonne photographie: utilisez le meilleur appareil photo (ou celui qui convient le mieux), le meilleur éclairage, le meilleur assistant, le meilleur laboratoire de développement, les meilleurs stylistes, maquilleurs, décorateurs, la meilleure agence de modèles, etc.

Nous voyons trop souvent des photographies médiocres qui sont dues à des compromis. □ La photographie est un art aux possibilités illimitées, ses horizons sont vastes. Elle comprend des objets qui bougent et/ou sont statiques, précis et/ou flous, lointains et/ou proches, noir et blanc et/ou en couleurs. Ses seules limitations sont les artistes eux-mêmes et leur naïveté, leurs inhibitions, leur paresse et leur vision restreinte. □ Graphis Photo, c'est une fenêtre grande ouverte sur la photographie professionnelle. Au cours des années, nous avons vu des maîtres particulièrement innovateurs, qui montraient la voie. Où sont les photographes du futur? Faites-vous connaître et montrez-nous votre travail! Ne vous contentez pas de regarder et de plagier les œuvres du passé; ne soyez ni timide, ni inhibé, ni paresseux. Ne cachez pas votre travail sous la bannière de l'Art. Faites-vous connaître et lancez-vous dans l'arène internationale. Trop de photographes sont insulaires, ils élaborent des systèmes trop prémédités qui ne leur permettent pas de s'aventurer par la suite dans de nouvelles directions. Je n'ai jamais été quelqu'un qui se répète dans les moindres détails, qui utilise toujours le même genre d'appareil photo, d'objectifs, les positions de la lumière, les filtres, les pellicules, etc. J'aime la variété et j'abhorre la sécurité ennuyeuse de la production à la chaîne. La photographie devrait exprimer l'humeur de l'artiste, être guidée par l'émotion, et non par les règles écrites dans les livres. □ Les grands noms ont disparu des plus récents annuaires de la photographie. Où sont-ils donc? dans des villas du sud de la France? dans des manoirs du Pays de Galles, des vignobles de Toscane, sur les pentes de ski d'Aspen? Pas du tout. Des noms tels que ceux de Bailey, Bookbinder et Moon font maintenant la une des cinémas; ils réalisent des émissions publicitaires pour la télévision, des clips et des films. Pourquoi ce changement? Certainement à cause du défi que constituent ces nouveaux horizons; mais se pourrait-il que les médias de l'électronique soient le futur? Le principe de l'offre et de la demande entraîne les bons photographes dans cette voie éminemment créative où le mouvement et la musique les aident à se dépasser. □ Verrons-nous à l'avenir Graphis Photo sur nos écrans de télévision? ■

ROBERT IMHOFF A REÇU UNE FORMATION ARTISTIQUE À LA ELTHAM HIGH SCHOOL AVANT D'ENTRER AU RMIT PHOTOGRAPHY COLLEGE DE MELBOURNE. IL A TRAVAILLÉ POUR L'INDUSTRIE AUTOMOBILE, DES COMPAGNIES D'AVIATION ET DE NOMBREUX FABRICANTS DE PRODUITS EN AUSTRALIE ET À L'ÉTRANGER. IL EST À LA TETE DU LIGHTHOUSE PHOTOGRAPHIC CENTRE DE MELBOURNE, QUI HÉBERGE DES BUREAUX DE PHOTOGRAPHES, DES STUDIOS ET LA VÉNÉRABLE LIGHTHOUSE GALLERY, UNE SALLE D'EXPOSITIONS ET DES MANIFESTATIONS INTERNATIONALES. TOUJOURS SOUCIEUX DE PARTAGER SES CONNAISSANCES, IL A FAIT DES CONFÉRENCES DANS DE NOMBREUX CONGRES ET DES ÉCOLES D'ART EN AUSTRALIE. ACTUELLEMENT, ONZE DE SES ANCIENS ASSISTANTS SONT DEVENUS SES CONCURRENTS, AUSSI BIEN DANS LA PHOTO QUE DANS LE CINÉMA. AUJOURD'HUI, IL SE CONSACRE PRINCIPALEMENT AU PORTRAIT, AU PAYSAGE ET À LA MISE EN SCENE D'ÉMISSIONS TÉLÉVISÉES COMMERCIALES. ADEPTE CONVAINCU DES ACTIVITÉS THÉRAPEUTIQUES, IL PASSE AUTANT DE TEMPS QUE POSSIBLE AVEC SA FAMILLE DANS LEUR FERME CLASSÉE ET IL EST EN TRAIN DE RESTAURER SA LANCIA LAMBDA 1925 POUR FAIRE DES COURSES DE RALLYE..■

MADE POSSIBLE BY THE PROFESSIONAL PHOTOGRAPHY
DIVISION OF THE EASTMAN KODAK COMPANY

THE GRAPHIS PHOTO 91 AWARDS

PORTRAITS OF THE JUDGES BY WILLIAM COUPON

(CLOCKWISE FROM TOP LEFT)

WALTER BERNARD, HOWARD CHAPNICK,

PETER HOWE AND JOHN JAY

THIS YEAR, GRAPHIS PRESS CORP. HAS BEEN ABLE TO PRESENT A SERIES OF AWARDS WITH THE GENEROUS SUPPORT OF THE PROFESSIONAL PHOTOGRAPHY DIVISION OF THE EASTMAN KODAK COMPANY. A DISTINGUISHED JURY, COMPRISED OF WALTER BERNARD, WORLD-REKNOWNED DESIGNER; HOWARD CHAPNICK, PRESIDENT OF BLACKSTAR PICTURES; PETER HOWE, DIRECTOR OF PHOTOGRAPHY, LIFE MAGAZINE; JOHN JAY, DIRECTOR OF ADVERTISING, BLOOMINGDALE'S DEPARTMENT STORE; AND B. MARTIN PEDERSEN, PUBLISHER AND CREATIVE DIRECTOR OF GRAPHIS PRESS; HAVE SELECTED THE PHOTOGRAPHS THAT APPEAR ON THE FOLLOWING PAGES—AND THE PHOTOGRAPHERS BEHIND THEM—TO BE THE RECIPIENTS OF THE BRONZE SCULPTURE "G,"DESIGNED BY TAKENOBU IGARASHI AND SELECTED BY GRAPHIS FROM HIS "ALUMINUM ALPHABET." OUR CONGRATULATIONS TO ALL THE PHOTOGRAPHERS AND OUR THANKS TO ALL WHO HAVE CONTRIBUTED. ■

DIESES JAHR KONNTE GRAPHIS DANK DER GROSSZÜGIGEN UNTERSTÜTZUNG DER PROFESSIONAL PHOTOGRAPHY DIVISION VON EASTMAN KODAK EINE REIHE VON SONDERPREISEN VERGEBEN. WALTER BERNARD, EIN WELTBEKANNTER DESIGNER; HOWARD CHAPNICK, PRÄSIDENT VON BLACKSTAR PICTURES; PETER HOWE, DIRECTOR OF PHOTOGRAPHY VOM LIFE MAGAZINE; JOHN LAY, DIRECTOR OF ADVERTISING DES KAUFHAUSES BLOOMINGDALE'S, UND B. MARTIN PEDERSEN, VERLAGER UND CREATIVE DIRECTOR DES GRAPHIS VERLAG, GEHÖRTEN DER JURY AN, DIE DIE PREISTRÄGER ERMITTELTE. DIE PRÄMIERTEN AUFNAHMEN WERDEN AUF DEN FOLGENDEN SEITEN VORGESTELLT. DIE PHOTOGRAPHEN WERDEN MIT DER VON TAKENOVU IGARASHI ENTWORFENEN BRONZE-SKULPTUR «G» AUS SEINEM «ALUMINIUM ALPHABET» AUSGEZEICHNET. WIR GRATULIEREN DEN GEWINNERN UND DANKEN ALLEN BETEILIGTEN. ■

CETTE ANNÉE, LES ÉDITIONS GRAPHIS ONT PU DÉCERNER UNE SÉRIE DE PRIX GRACE AU SOUTIEN GÉNÉREUX DE LA SECTION PHOTOGRAPHIE PROFESSIONNELLE DE LA FIRME EASTMAN KODAK. UN JURY DISTINGUÉ, COMPOSÉ DE WALTER BERNARD, DESIGNER DE RENOMMÉE MONDIALE, HOWARD CHAPNICK, PRÉSIDENT DE BLACKSTAR PICTURES, PETER HOWE, DIRECTEUR DE LA PHOTO AU MAGAZINE LIFE, JOHN JAY, DIRECTEUR DE LA PUBLICTÉ DES GRANDS MAGASINS BLOMMINGDALE'S, ET B. MARTIN PEDERSEN, ÉDITEUR ET DIRECTEUR CRÉATIF DES ÉDITIONS GRAPHIS, A SÉLECTIONNÉ LES PHOTOGRAPHIES QUI SONT PRÉSENTEEES DAN LES PAGES SUIVANTES: LEURS AUTEURS RECEVRONT LA SCULPTURE EN BRONZE «G», CRÉÉE PAR TAKENOBU IGARASHI ET CHOISIE DANS SON «ALPHABET EN ALUMINIUM» PAR GRAPHIS. NOUS ADRESSONS NOS MEILLEURS COMPLIMENTS À TOUS LES PHOTOGRAPHES ET NOS REMERCIEMENTS À TOUS CEUX QUI ONT CONTRIBUÉ À CET OUVRAGE. ■

AWARD RECIPIENTS

BEST OF SHOW

TITLE: SURVIVORS

PHOTOGRAPHER: JAMES BALOG

CLIENT: HARRY N. ABRAMS

BEST PEOPLE

TITLE: EVA JESSYE

PHOTOGRAPHER: BRIAN LANKER

CLIENT: STEWART, TABORI & CHANG INC.

BEST SPORTS

TITLE: STEPHANIE ORTWIG

PHOTOGRAPHER: LACI PERÉNI

CLIENT: SPORTS MAGAZINE

BEST STILL LIFE

TITLE: FLOWERS

PHOTOGRAPHER: KLAUS FRAHM

CLIENT: SELBST

BEST FASHION

TITLE: L'OREAL CALENDAR

PHOTOGRAPHER: FABRIZIO FERRI

CLIENT: VOGUE

BEST OUTDOOR

TITLE: FANTASIA

PHOTOGRAPHER: JOHN ISAAC

CLIENT: MINOLTA CAMERA CO., LTD.

BEST WILDLIFE

TITLE: A SNOWDRIFT OF SWANS

PHOTOGRAPHER: TEIJI SAGA

CLIENT: LIFE MAGAZINE

FASHION

MODE

MODE

FASHION

PHOTOGRAPHER:
ALBERT WATSON
PHOTO EDITOR:
JODI NAKATSUKA
CLIENT:
L.A. STYLE
ART DIRECTOR:
MARILYN BABCOCK
DESIGNER:
NEVILLE BURTIS/
HOLLY CAPORALE
◄■ 1

PHOTOGRAPHER:
STEVE HIETT
CLIENT:
MARIE CLAIRE
ART DIRECTOR:
WALTER ROSPERT
■ 2

PHOTOGRAPHER:
CHRISTIAN MOSER
REPRESENTATIVE:
FRAME
CAMERA:
HASSELBLAD
FILM:
KODAK
CLIENT:
MALISY
ART DIRECTOR:
NANDO MIGLIO
■ 3

■ 1 (PRECEDING SPREAD) FROM A SERIES OF FASH-
ION PHOTOGRAPHS APPEARING IN *LA STYLE* UNDER
THE HEADLINE "SEEING RED." THE PLEATED WOOL
TOP AND SKIRT ARE BY GIANNI VERSACE. (USA)

■ 2 THE CELEBRATION OF THE FRENCH BASTILLE
DAY (JULY 14TH) CREATES THE THEME FOR THIS
FASHION LAYOUT IN FRENCH MAGAZINE *MARIE
CLAIRE.* THE SILK SUIT IN THE COLORS OF THE
"TRICOLORE" IS BY KENZO. (FRA)

■ 3 EXAMPLE FROM A SERIES OF HYPERREALISTIC
CLOSE-UP PHOTOGRAPHS FOR A MALISY FASHION
CATALOG. (ITA)

● 1 (VORHERGEHENDE SEITE) AUFNAHME AUS
EINER SERIE FÜR EINEN MODEBEITRAG IN *LA STYLE*
MIT DEM TITEL «WIR SEHEN ROT»: PLISSIERTES
OBERTEIL UND ROCK VON GIANNI VERSACE. (USA)

● 2 DER FRANZÖSISCHE NATIONALFEIERTAG AM 14.
JULI WAR DAS THEMA EINER MODEREPORTAGE IN
MARIE CLAIRE. DEM ANLASS ENTSPRECHEND TRÄGT
DAS MODELL EINEN SEIDENANZUG (KENZO) IN DEN
FARBEN DER TRIKOLORE. (FRA)

● 3 BEISPIEL AUS EINER REIHE HYPERREALISTI-
SCHER NAHAUFNAHMEN FÜR EINEN MODEKATALOG
VON MALISY. (ITA)

▲ 1 (PAGE PRÉCÉDENTE) PHOTO D'UNE SÉRIE DE
PAGES DE MODE INTITULÉES «NOUS VOYONS
ROUGE», PARUES DANS *LA STYLE*: HAUT PLISSÉ ET
JUPE DE GIANNI VERSACE. (USA)

▲ 2 LA FÊTE NATIONALE DU 14 JUILLET ÉTAIT LE
THÈME DE CE REPORTAGE DE MODE PARU DANS
MARIE CLAIRE. LE MODÈLE PORTE À CETTE OCCA-
SION UN ENSEMBLE TRICOLORE EN SOIE AUX COU-
LEURS DU DRAPEAU FRANÇAIS. (FRA)

▲ 3 EXEMPLE D'UNE SÉRIE DE GROS PLANS D'INS-
PIRATION HYPERRÉALISTE POUR UN CATALOGUE DE
MODE DE MALISY. (ITA)

BEST FASHION

PHOTOGRAPHER:
FABRIZIO FERRI
CLIENT:
L'ORÉAL
ART DIRECTOR:
CIRO FALAVIGNA
STYLIST:
MONICA COPPOLA/
ALDO COPPOLA
■ 4-6

■ 4-6 THIS SERIES OF BLACK-AND-WHITE PHOTO-GRAPHS GRACES L'ORÉAL'S 1989/1990 CALENDAR. THE DESIRE WAS TO EMPHASIZE GLOBAL BEAUTY, FEATURING WOMEN FROM ALL OVER THE WORLD WITHOUT DIRECTLY ADDRESSING THEIR ETHNIC BACKGROUND. HAIRSTYLES ARE BY ALDO COPPOLA AND HIS DAUGHTER. FABRIZIO FERRI HAS RECEIVED THE BEST IN CATEGORY, FASHION, AWARD FOR THE GRAPHIS PHOTO 91 COMPETITION, WHICH IS SPONSORED BY EASTMAN KODAK. (ITA)

● 4-6 DIESE SCHWARZWEISS-AUFNAHMEN STAMMEN AUS DEM KALENDER 1989/90 DER KOSMETIKFIRMA L'ORÉAL. DIE AUFNAHMEN SOLLTEN FRAUEN AUS ALLER WELT ZEIGEN, OHNE ETHNISCH ZU WIRKEN. DER POPULÄRE ITALIENISCHE HAARKÜNSTLER ALDO COPPOLA UND SEINE TOCHTER KREIERTEN DIE FRISUREN. FABRIZIO FERRI WURDE FÜR DIESE AUFNAHME MIT DEM «BEST OF CATEGORY AWARD» FÜR DIE KATEGORIE MODE VON GRAPHIS PHOTO 91 AUSGEZEICHNET. (ITA)

▲ 4-6 CES PHOTOS EN NOIR ET BLANC ONT ÉTÉ RÉALISÉES POUR LE CALENDRIER 1989/90 DE L'ORÉAL. L'OBJECTIF ÉTAIT DE PRÉSENTER DES FEMMES DU MONDE ENTIER EN ÉVITANT DE TOMBER DANS LE LOOK ETHNOLOGIQUE. LE CÉLÈBRE COIFFEUR-STYLISTE ALDO COPPOLA ET SA FILLE ONT CRÉÉ LES COIFFURES. FABRIZIO FERRI A REÇU LE «BEST OF CATEGORY AWARD/FASHION» DU CONCOURS GRAPHIS PHOTO 91 SPONSORISÉ PAR EASTMAN KODAK. (ITA)

PHOTOGRAPHER:
ALBERT WATSON
PHOTO EDITOR:
JODI NAKATSUKA
CLIENT:
L.A. STYLE
ART DIRECTOR:
MICHAEL BROCK
DESIGNER:
MICHAEL BROCK
STYLIST:
KATE HARRINGTON
■ 7

PHOTOGRAPHER:
DEBORAH TURBEVILLE
PHOTO EDITOR:
JODI NAKATSUKA
CLIENT:
L.A. STYLE
ART DIRECTOR:
MICHAEL BROCK
DESIGNER:
MICHAEL BROCK
▶■ 8, 9

■ 7 GIORGIO DI SANT ANGELO USED A NEW FABRIC—A STRETCH SILK GAUZE—FOR THIS BUSTER AND SHORTS OUTFIT. THE PHOTOGRAPH SERVES AS THE OPENING OF A FASHION SPREAD, ENTITLED "SHOULDER TO SHOULDER." IN *LA STYLE*. (USA)

■ 8, 9 FASHION RETURNS TO ROMANCE, ACCORDING TO *LA STYLE* IN THE FEATURE ENTITLED "ROMANTIC REPRISE." SHOWN ARE A CHOCOLATE-BROWN, WOOL CREPE JACKET BY ANGEL ESTRADA; SILK CREPE BLOUSE BY CHANEL, AND BLACK FLOOR-LENGTH CASHMERE SKIRT BY YVES ST. LAURENT. (USA)

● 7 GIORGIO DI SANT ANGELO VERWENDETE EINEN NEUEN STOFF, STRETCH-SEIDENGAZE, FÜR DEN BUSTIER UND DIE SHORTS. DIE AUFNAHME DIENTE ALS AUFMACHER FÜR EINEN MODEBEITRAG IN DER ZEITSCHRIFT *LA STYLE*. (USA)

● 8, 9 «ROMANTISCHE REPRISE» WAR DAS THEMA UND DIE STIMMUNG DES MODEBEITRAGS IN *LA STYLE*. DIE SCHOKOLADENBRAUNE, GERAFFTE JACKE IST VON ANGEL ESTRADA; DIE SEIDENCRÊPE-BLUSE VON CHANEL UND DER BODENLANGE KASCHMIR-ROCK VON YVES SAINT LAURENT. (USA)

▲ 7 GIORGIO DI SANT ANGELO A EMPLOYÉ UNE NOUVELLE ÉTOFFE, UNE GAZE DE SOIE STRETCH, POUR LE BUSTIER ET LE SHORT. CETTE PHOTO INTRODUIT UN REPORTAGE DE MODE DANS *LA STYLE*. (USA)

▲ 8, 9 PHOTO RÉALISÉE POUR UN ARTICLE DE MODE PUBLIÉ DANS *LA STYLE* INTITULÉ «REPRISE ROMANTIQUE». VESTE DRAPÉE CHOCOLAT EN CRÊPE DE LAINE D'ANGEL ESTRADA, BLOUSE EN CRÊPE DE SOIE CHANEL, JUPE LONGUE EN CACHEMIRE D'YVES SAINT LAURENT. (USA)

PHOTOGRAPHER:

BARBARA BORDNICK

DESIGNER:

JOHN BORDNICK

STYLIST:

CHINA MACHADO

■ 10

PHOTOGRAPHER:

FRANK HERHOLDT

REPRESENTATIVE:

NIALL HORTON

STEVENS

CAMERA:

ROLLEIFLEX 6006

FILM:

KODAK EPN 120

CLIENT:

COTTON COUNCIL

INTERNATIONAL

ART DIRECTOR:

JOHN MCKEEVER

STYLIST:

SUE ROWLANDS

►■ 11

■ 10 THE FAMOUS PLEATS AND SCULPTURAL LOOK THAT TYPIFIES THE DESIGN OF ISSEY MIYAKE IS THE SUBJECT OF THIS PHOTOGRAPH, ORIGINATED AS PART OF AN EDITORIAL LAYOUT AND USED AS SELF-PROMOTION FOR THE PHOTOGRAPHER, BARBARA BORDNICK. (USA)

■ 11 THE ROOM SET FOR THIS PHOTOGRAPH WAS DESIGNED BY SUE ROWLANDS AND THE PHOTOGRAPHER FRANK HERHOLDT. THE BACKDROP EMPLOYED IS A COPY OF A VICTORIAN PAINTING; BY COINCIDENCE, THE MODEL FOLLOWED THE POSE OF THE ORIGINAL. THE PIECE WAS COMMISSIONED BY THE COTTON COUNCIL INTERNATIONAL. (GBR)

● 10 DER TYPISCHE SKULPTURARTIGE CHARAKTER EINES PLISSIERTEN KLEIDUNGSSTÜCKS DES MODESCHÖPFERS ISSEY MIYAKE IST THEMA DIESER AUFNAHME FÜR EINEN MODEBEITRAG, DIE AUCH ALS EIGENWERBUNG DER PHOTOGRAPHIN BARBARA BORDNICK DIENT. (USA)

● 11 DER RAUM FÜR DIESE AUFNAHME IM AUFTRAG DES COTTON COUNCIL INTERNATIONAL WURDE VON SUE ROWLANDS UND DEM PHOTOGRAPHEN FRANK HERHOLDT ENTWORFEN. DAS BILD IST EINE KOPIE EINES VIKTORIANISCHEN GEMÄLDES. GANZ VON SELBST NAHM DAS MODELL DIE POSE DER FRAU AUF DEM BILD EIN. (GBR)

▲ 10 LA PHOTO MET EN VALEUR LE CARACTÈRE SCULPTURAL DE CE VÊTEMENT D'ÉTOFFE PLISSÉE CARACTÉRISTIQUE DU COUTURIER ISSEY MIYAKE. CONÇUE POUR UN REPORTAGE DE MODE, ELLE EST UTILISÉE COMME AUTOPROMOTION PAR LA PHOTOGRAPHE, BARBARA BORDNICK. (USA)

▲ 11 LE DÉCOR DE CETTE PHOTO RÉALISÉE POUR COTTON COUNCIL INTERNATIONAL A ÉTÉ IMAGINÉ PAR SUE ROWLANDS ET LE PHOTOGRAPHE FRANK HERHOLDT. LA PEINTURE EST UNE COPIE D'UNE ŒUVRE DE L'ÉPOQUE VICTORIENNE. SPONTANÉMENT, LE MODÈLE ADOPTA LA MÊME POSE QUE LA FEMME REPRÉSENTÉE SUR CETTE PEINTURE. (GBR)

PHOTOGRAPHER:
DARRELL PETERSON
REPRESENTATIVE:
STACIE HAMILTON
CAMERA:
NIKON F2
FILM:
KODAK PLUS-X
CLIENT:
SOUND MIND AND
BODY HEALTH CLUB
ART DIRECTOR:
DARRELL PETERSON
DESIGNER:
WILLIAM ALLEN AND
ASSOCIATES
■ 12

■ 12 PHOTO USED FOR AN IMAGE POSTER TO PRO-
MOTE THE OPENING OF A NEW HEALTH AND FITNESS
CLUB. (USA)

■ 13-16 PHOTOGRAPHS TAKEN ON HAWAII AND IN
THE BAHAMAS FOR SWIMWEAR SPREADS IN *ELLE*
REPRESENT A RANGE OF STYLES: THE UNITARD FOR
THE SERIOUS SWIMMER; NEW NAUTICAL FASHIONS
IN BLACK-AND-WHITE; BEAUTIFUL BODYSUITS FOR
BATHING BEAUTIES, AND SUITS WITH SCALES FOR
SIRENS OF THE SURF. (USA)

● 12 MIT DIESER AUFNAHME – IN FORM EINES
PLAKATES – WURDE DIE ERÖFFNUNG EINES NEUEN
FITNESS-CLUBS ANGEKÜNDIGT. (USA)

● 13-16 AUF HAWAII UND DEN BAHAMAS ENTSTAN-
DENE PHOTOS FÜR EINEN BADEMODEBEITRAG IN
DER ZEITSCHRIFT *ELLE*. DAS EINTEILIGE MODELL
IST NUR FÜR ERNSTE SCHWIMMERINNEN GEDACHT;
DER NEUE MARINE-LOOK PRÄSENTIERT SICH IN
SCHWARZWEISS; DIE SCHÖNSTEN BODYSUITS UND
PAILLETTEN FÜR STRANDSIRENEN. (USA)

▲ 12 PHOTO PUBLIÉE SOUS FORME DE POSTER AFIN
D'ANNONCER L'OUVERTURE D'UN NOUVEAU FIT-
NESS-CLUB. (USA)

▲ 13-16 PHOTOS PRISES À HAWAÏ ET AUX BAHAMAS
POUR UN ARTICLE SUR LES MAILLOTS DE BAIN PARU
DANS *ELLE*. MODÈLE UNE PIÈCE DESTINÉ AUX
VÉRITABLES CHAMPIONNES DE NATATION; LE
NOUVEAU LOOK MARIN, EN NOIR ET BLANC; LES
MAILLOTS LES PLUS ÉLÉGANTS ET LES SIRÉNES
REVÊTUES DE PAILLETTES. (USA)

 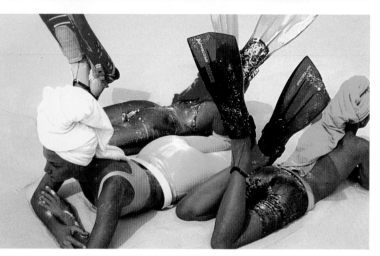

PHOTOGRAPHER:
GILLES BENSIMON
REPRESENTATIVE:
YASUKO AUSTIN
CAMERA:
NIKON
FILM:
FUJI RFP
PUBLICATION DIRECTOR:
RÉGIS PAGNIEZ
CLIENT:
ELLE MAGAZINE
ART DIRECTOR:
OLIVIA BADRUTT-
GIRON
STYLIST:
LOREN LANEY 13,
15, 16
FANNY PAGNIEZ 14
■ 13-16

■ 18 FINE ART PHOTOGRAPHER SALLY GALL TOOK THIS PHOTOGRAPH IN CORPUS CHRISTI, TEXAS, FOR A FASHION PHOTO ESSAY IN *TEXAS MONTHLY* ON SWIMSUITS INFLUENCED BY THE STYLE OF THE THIRTIES. (USA)

■ 19 "BEAUTY AND NATURE" IS THE SUBJECT OF THIS PHOTOGRAPH TAKEN IN ARIZONA AND USED FOR A DIRECT MAIL PIECE BY A CLOTHING BOUTIQUE INTRODUCING THEIR SUMMER LINE. (USA)

● 18 SALLY GALL, AUF KÜNSTLERISCHE PHOTO-GRAPHIE SPEZIALISIERT, MACHTE DIESE AUFNAHME IN CORPUS CHRISTI, TEXAS, FÜR EINEN PHOTO-ESSAY IN *TEXAS MONTHLY* ÜBER BADEANZÜGE IM STIL DER DREISSIGER JAHRE. (USA)

● 19 «SCHÖNHEIT UND NATUR» IST DAS THEMA DIESER AUFNAHME, DIE IN ARIZONA ENTSTAND UND ALS DIRECT MAIL-WERBUNG FÜR DIE SOMMERMODE EINER BOUTIQUE VERWENDET WURDE. (USA)

▲ 18 SPÉCIALISÉE DANS LA PHOTOGRAPHIE D'ART, SALLY GALL A RÉALISÉ CE CLICHÉ À CORPUS CHRISTI, AU TEXAS, POUR UN ARTICLE SUR LES MAILLOTS DE BAIN DE STYLE 1930 PARU DANS LE *TEXAS MONTHLY*. (USA)

▲ 19 «BEAUTÉ ET NATURE»: TEL EST LE THÈME DE CETTE PHOTO, PRISE EN ARIZONA ET UTILISÉE COMME PUBLICITÉ DIRECTE PAR LA POSTE POUR LA NOUVELLE MODE ESTIVALE D'UNE BOUTIQUE. (USA)

PHOTOGRAPHER:
SALLY GALL
CAMERA:
HASSELBLAD
FILM:
KODAK TRI-X
PHOTO EDITOR:
D.J. STOUT
CLIENT:
TEXAS MONTHLY
ART DIRECTOR:
D.J. STOUT
DESIGNER:
D.J. STOUT
◀■ 18

PHOTOGRAPHER:
RICK RUSING
CAMERA:
HASSELBLAD
FILM:
FUJI
EXPOSURE:
F 11, 1/125
CLIENT:
UH OH CLOTHING
BOUTIQUE
ART DIRECTOR:
STEVE DITKO
DESIGNER:
STEVE DITKO
■ 19

PHOTOGRAPHER:

JOHN DUGDALE

REPRESENTATIVE:

CARLA GRANDE

CLIENT:

DAYTON'S

ART DIRECTOR:

AMY QUINLIVAN

DESIGNER:

AMY QUINLIVAN

◀■ 20-23

PHOTOGRAPHER:

STEPHEN WILKES

CAMERA:

NIKON 28MM

FILM:

FUJI 50

EXPOSURE:

F 4.5, 1/125

CLIENT:

NIKE

ART DIRECTOR:

ANN SCHWEIBINGER

■ 24

■ 20-23 A SERIES OF COUTURE FASHION PHOTOS USED IN A BOOKLET FOR DAYTON'S DEPARTMENT STORE. THE SUBJECT TO INTERPRET WAS "QUIET PLACES." (USA)

■ 24 THIS PHOTOGRAPH FOR NIKE WAS TAKEN ON A BLACK SAND-BEACH IN KONA, HAWAII. THIS BEACH NO LONGER EXISTS—THE SMOKE IN THE BACK-GROUND WAS CAUSED BY ACTUAL LAVA FLOWING INTO THE WATER. MOST OF THE FORTY VOLCANOS OF THIS GROUP OF ISLANDS ARE EXTINGUISHED. THE RAINBOW WAS A LUCKY COINCIDENCE. (USA)

● 20-23 AUFNAHMEN VON DESIGNER-MODE, DIE FÜR EINE BROSCHÜRE DES KAUFHAUSES DAYTON'S VERWENDET WURDEN. DAS THEMA HIESS »RUHIGE ORTE«. (USA)

● 21 DIESES PHOTO FÜR NIKE ENTSTAND AM IN-ZWISCHEN VERSCHWUNDENEN SCHWARZEN SAND-STRAND VON KONA, HAWAII. DIE URSACHE DES RAUCHS IM HINTERGRUND IST LAVA, DIE INS WASSER FLIESST. DIE MEISTEN DER 40 VULKANE DER INSELGRUPPE SIND ERLOSCHEN. DER REGEN-BOGEN WAR EINE GLÜCKLICHE FÜGUNG. (USA)

▲ 20-23 CES PHOTOS REPRÉSENTENT DES MODÈLES DE COUTURIERS ONT ÉTÉ UTILISÉES POUR UNE BROCHURE DU MAGASIN DAYTON'S. LE SUJET DONNÉ S'INTITULAIT: »LIEUX TRANQUILLES«. (USA)

▲ 21 CETTE PHOTO POUR NIKE A ÉTÉ RÉALISÉE SUR LA PLAGE DE SABLE NOIR DE KONA, À HAWAÏ, DEPUIS LORS SUBMERGÉE. LA FUMÉE À L'HORIZON EST OCCASIONNÉE PAR UNE COULÉE DE LAVE QUI SE JETTE DANS LA MER. LA PLUPART DES 40 VOLCANS DE L'ARCHIPEL SONT ÉTEINTS. L'ARC-EN-CIEL EST UNE HEUREUSE COÏNCIDENCE. (USA)

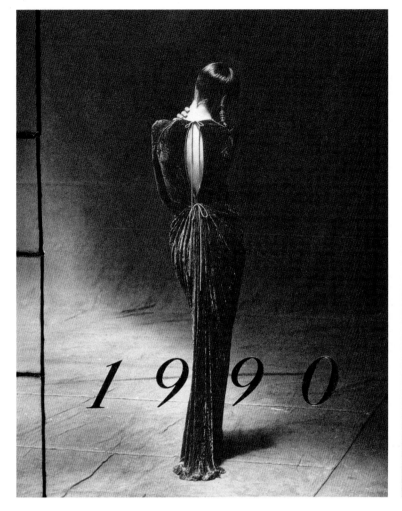

PHOTOGRAPHER:
STEVEN MEISEL
REPRESENTATIVE:
ART + COMMERCE
CLIENT:
BLOOMINGDALE'S
ART DIRECTOR:
JOHN C. JAY
DESIGNER:
JOHN C. JAY
■ 25

PHOTOGRAPHER:
FABRIZIO FERRI
PHOTO EDITOR:
JODI NAKATSUKA
CLIENT:
L.A. STYLE
ART DIRECTOR:
MICHAEL BROCK
DESIGNER:
NEVILLE BURTIS
■ 26

PHOTOGRAPHER:
JOACHIM MAGREAN
CAMERA:
NIKON FE2
▶■ 27

■ 25 PHOTOGRAPH USED FOR THE COVER OF A SMALL-FORMAT "1990" BLOOMINGDALE'S BOOKLET INTRODUCING THE LATEST LADIES FASHIONS. (USA)

■ 26 THE SARONG, A DRAPED PIECE OF TRADITIONAL MALAYAN CLOTHING USUALLY MADE OF A COLORFUL COTTON FABRIC, WAS THE SUBJECT OF THE FEATURE IN *LA STYLE* FOR WHICH THIS PHOTOGRAPH WAS TAKEN. (USA)

■ 27 THE PHOTOGRAPH WAS TAKEN IN SUMMER AT A CORSICAN BEACH. MODEL AND STYLIST FOR THIS PERSONAL STUDY WAS ANNETT MONHEIM. THE FILM WAS PUSHED AT MAXIMUM, ONE COLOR WAS ADDED IN THE DEVELOPMENT PROCESS. (FRA)

● 25 DIE AUFNAHME WURDE FÜR EINEN KLEINFORMATIGEN KATALOG MIT DER NEUESTEN MODE DES KAUFHAUSES BLOOMINGDALE'S VERWENDET. (USA)

● 26 DER SARONG, EIN GEWICKELTES KLEIDUNGSSTÜCK DER MALAIEN, MEISTENS AUS FARBENPRÄCHTIGEM BAUMWOLLSTOFF, ALS THEMA EINES BEITRAGS IN *LA STYLE*, FÜR DEN DIESE AUFNAHME GEMACHT WURDE. (USA)

● 27 DIESE STUDIE VON JOACHIM MAGREAN ENTSTAND AM STRAND VON KORSIKA. MODELL UND STYLISTIN WAR ANNETT MONHEIM. DER FILM WURDE GESTOSSEN UND BEIM ENTWICKELN WURDE IHM EINE FARBE HINZUGEFÜGT. (FRA)

▲ 25 PHOTO POUR UN CATALOGUE DES GRANDS MAGASINS BLOOMINGDALE'S PRÉSENTANT DES MODÈLES 1990 DE GRANDS COUTURIERS. (USA)

▲ 26 LE SARONG, SORTE DE JUPE DE COTON TRADITIONNELLE, NORMALEMENT DE COULEUR CHATOYANTE, PORTÉE PAR LES MALAIS, ÉTAIT LE SUJET DE L'ARTICLE PUBLIÉ DANS LE MAGAZINE *LA STYLE* QU'ILLUSTRAIT CETTE PHOTO. (USA)

▲ 27 CETTE ÉTUDE PERSONNELLE DE JOACHIM MAGREAN A ÉTÉ PHOTOGRAPHIÉE SUR UNE PLAGE CORSE. ANNETT MONHEIM ÉTAIT À LA FOIS RESPONSABLE DU STYLISME ET MANNEQUIN. LE FILM A ÉTÉ POUSSÉ ET VIRÉ AU TIRAGE. (FRA)

■ 28 PORTRAIT OF FAMOUS SINGER MILVA. (USA)

■ 29 PHOTOGRAPH FOR A FASHION FEATURE IN BLACK AND WHITE IN *VOGUE ITALIA*. THE DRESS SHOWN IS BY GAZAR. (ITA)

■ 30 COVER PHOTOGRAPH FOR *LA STYLE* MAGAZINE FEATURING "FALL FASHION—THE VALUE OF TRADITION." (USA)

● 28 PORTRÄT DER SÄNGERIN MILVA. (USA)

● 29 AUFNAHME FÜR EINEN MODEBEITRAG IN SCHWARZWEISS IN *VOGUE ITALIA*. DAS KLEID IST VON GAZAR. (ITA)

● 30 TITELAUFNAHME FÜR DIE ZEITSCHRIFT *LA STYLE* ZUM THEMA «HERBSTMODE – DER WERT DER TRADITION». (USA)

▲ 28 PORTRAIT DE LA CHANTEUSE MILVA. (USA)

▲ 29 PHOTO D'UN REPORTAGE DE MODE EN NOIR ET BLANC SUR LE THÈME DE L'ÂME GITANE, PUBLIÉ DANS *VOGUE ITALIA*. ROBE DE GAZAR. (ITA)

▲ 30 PHOTO DE COUVERTURE DE *LA STYLE* SUR LE THÈME «LA MODE AUTOMNALE – LA VALEUR DE LA TRADITION». (USA)

PHOTOGRAPHER:
ALBERT WATSON
CLIENT:
VOGUE ITALIA
ART DIRECTOR:
FABIEN BARON
■ 28

PHOTOGRAPHER:
STEVEN MEISEL
REPRESENTATIVE:
ART + COMMERCE
CLIENT:
VOGUE ITALIA
ART DIRECTOR:
JUAN GATTI
■ 29

PHOTOGRAPHER:
DEBORAH TURBEVILLE
PHOTO EDITOR:
JODI NAKATSUKA
CLIENT:
L.A. STYLE
ART DIRECTOR:
MICHAEL BROCK
DESIGNER:
MICHAEL BROCK
▶■ 30

THE MOST BEAUTIFUL WOMEN IN TOWN

PHOTOGRAPHER:
STEVEN MEISEL
REPRESENTATIVE:
ART + COMMERCE
CLIENT:
BLOOMINGDALE'S
ART DIRECTOR:
JOHN C. JAY
DESIGNER:
JOHN C. JAY/
KIRSTI KROENER
▲
◀■ 31

PHOTOGRAPHER:
SHEILA METZNER
PHOTO EDITOR:
JODI NAKATSUKA
CLIENT:
L.A. STYLE
ART DIRECTOR:
MICHAEL BROCK
DESIGNER:
MICHAEL BROCK
◀■ 32

PHOTOGRAPHER:
HARRY DE ZITTER
CAMERA:
FUJI 6X9
FILM:
KODAK EPR 120
EXPOSURE:
F 16, 1/30
CLIENT:
NIKE
ART DIRECTOR:
CHRISTY ROBERTS
■ 33

■ 31 PHOTOGRAPH USED FOR THE FRONT (NEGA-TIVE) AND BACK COVER (POSITIVE) OF A 1990 SPRING FASHION BLOOMINGDALE'S CATALOG, WHICH WAS PRINTED IN BLACK-AND-WHITE. THE THEME WAS "A NEW COOL." (USA)

■ 32 "A DIFFERENT STRIPE" IS THE THEME OF THE FASHION AND SETTING SHOWN ON THIS PHOTO-GRAPH FOR LA STYLE. (USA)

■ 33 MEMBERS OF THE SAMBURU TRIBE WEARING NIKE LAVADOME WALKING BOOTS PHOTOGRAPHED ON LOCATION IN NORTHERN KENYA FOR A NATIONAL US PRINT CAMPAIGN FOR NIKE. (USA)

● 31 DIESE AUFNAHME WURDE FÜR DEN UMSCHLAG (VORDERSEITE NEGATIV) EINES KATALOGS IN SCHWARZWEISS MIT DER FRÜHJAHRSMODE 1990 DES KAUFHAUSES BLOOMINGDALE'S VERWENDET. DAS THEMA WAR: »DIE NEUE KÜHLE.« (USA)

● 32 »EINE ANDERE ART VON STREIFEN« SIND DAS THEMA DER MODE UND DES DEKORS DIESER AUF-NAHME FÜR LA STYLE. (USA)

● 33 MITGLIEDER DES SAMBURU STAMMES, NIKE-LAUFSCHUHE TRAGEND. DIE AUFNAHME ENTSTAND IM NORDEN KENYAS UND WURDE FÜR EINE NIKE-KAMPAGNE IN DEN USA VERWENDET. (USA)

▲ 31 PHOTO REPRODUITE EN POSITIF ET EN NÉGA-TIF (AU RECTO) SUR LA COUVERTURE D'UN CATA-LOGUE EN NOIR ET BLANC DE BLOOMINGDALE'S, PRÉSENTANT LA MODE PRINTEMPS 1990. LE THÈME ÉTAIT: «LA NOUVELLE DÉCONTRACTION». (USA)

▲ 32 LE LEITMOTIV DES RAYURES A INSPIRÉ LE DÉCOR DE CETTE PHOTO DE MODE RÉALISÉE POUR LA STYLE. (USA)

▲ 33 CES MEMBRES DE LA TRIBU DES SAMBURU PORTENT DES CHAUSSURES DE SPORTS NIKE. LA PHOTO, PRISE AU NORD-KENYA, A ÉTÉ UTILISÉE POUR UNE CAMPAGNE D'ANNONCES DE NIKE. (USA)

PHOTOGRAPHER:

JAVIER VALLHONRAT

CLIENT:

VOGUE ITALIA

ART DIRECTOR:

ALBERTO NODOLINI

■ 34

PHOTOGRAPHER:

JAVIER VALLHONRAT

■ 35

■ 34 A FASHION PHOTOGRAPH BY SPANISH PHOTOGRAPHER JAVIER VALLHONRAT WHICH WAS PUBLISHED IN *VOGUE ITALIA*. IT IS MARKED BY THE SAME PASSION AND DRAMATICS THAT THE GREATEST SPANISH PAINTERS HAVE UTILIZED TO HIGHLIGHT BEAUTY. (ITA)

■ 35 PHOTO FROM A SERIES OF PERSONAL WORK ("ANIMAL-VEGETAL") BY SPANISH PHOTOGRAPHER JAVIER VALLHONRAT. (SPA)

■ 36 THE DESIGN OF THIS PHOTOGRAPH WAS INSPIRED BY VELAZQUES'S PAINTING "THE ROKEBY VENUS." THE IMAGE WAS USED TO COMMUNICATE THE WIDE RANGE OF SERVICES OFFERED BY THE BACKDROP SOLUTION. (USA)

● 34 EINE MODEAUFNAHME DES SPANISCHEN PHOTOGRAPHEN JAVIER VALLHONRAT, DIE IN *VOGUE ITALIA* ERSCHIENEN IST. SIE IST VON DER GLEICHEN LEIDENSCHAFT GEPRÄGT, MIT DER DIE GROSSEN SPANISCHEN MALER SCHÖNHEIT DARZUSTELLEN PFLEGTEN. (ITA)

● 35 AUS EINER SERIE FREIER ARBEITEN DES PHOTOGRAPHEN JAVIER VALLHONRAT MIT DEM TITEL «TIERISCH-PFLANZLICH». (SPA)

● 36 VELAZQUES' BILD «DIE ROKEBY VENUS» DIENTE ALS VORLAGE FÜR DIESE AUFNAHME. SIE WURDE ALS WERBUNG FÜR EINE FIRMA EINGESETZT, DIE DEKORATIONEN UND AUFBAUTEN ALLER ART ANBIETET. (USA)

▲ 34 PHOTO DE MODE DU PHOTOGRAPH ESPAGNOL JAVIER VALLHONRAT, PUBLIÉE DANS *VOGUE ITALIA*. IL A MIS DANS CETTE PHOTO LA MÊME PASSION ET DRAMATURGIE QUE LES PLUS GRANDS PEINTRES ESPAGNOLS ONT UTILISÉES POUR METTRE EN VALEUR LA BEAUTÉ. (ITA)

▲ 35 «ANIMAL-VÉGÉTAL» – PHOTO TIREÉ D'UNE SÉRIE D'ŒUVRES PERSONNELLES DU PHOTOGRAPHE JAVIER VALLHONRAT. (SPA)

▲ 36 LA «VÉNUS AU MIROIR» DE VÉLASQUEZ A INSPIRÉ CETTE PHOTOGRAPHIE. ELLE A ÉTÉ UTILISÉE COMME PUBLICITÉ D'UNE FIRME SPÉCIALISÉE DANS LA DÉCORATION ET LES DÉCORS EN TROMPE-L'ŒIL. (USA)

PHOTOGRAPHER:
PAUL MARSHALL
REPRESENTATIVE:
DOLLY MARSHALL
CAMERA:
MAMIYA RB 67
FILM:
EKTACHROME 100
EXPOSURE:
F 8, 1/60 WITH
DIFFUSION FILTER

PHOTO EDITOR:
SY SAJID
CLIENT:
THE BACKDROP
SOLUTION
ART DIRECTOR:
SY SAJID
DESIGNER:
SY SAJID
■ 36

■ 37 A STYLISH SKIER, PRESENTED ON THE PAGES OF *MARIE CLAIRE*, HAS ADAPTED A VERY FEMININE VERSION OF THE JUMPSUIT (BY YOHJI YAMAMOTO) FOR HER DAILY WEAR. (FRA)

■ 38 ONE FROM A SERIES THAT MADE UP THE LARGEST PRINT CAMPAIGN EVER CREATED FOR THE MAGAZINE PUBLISHERS OF AMERICA, THE HIGH VANTAGE POINT OF THIS PHOTOGRAPH WAS OBTAINED BY RAISING THE PHOTOGRAPHER UP IN A "CHERRY-PICKER" TRUCK. THE CAMPAIGN SUBTLY PLUGGED THE PERVASIVE NATURE OF THE AMERICAN MAGAZINE WITH ITS TAGLINE: "SHE SHOWS UP IN ALL THE BEST PLACES." (USA)

■ 39 IT WAS WILLIAM LAXTON'S FIRST ASSIGNMENT FOR *VOGUE PARIS*. AFTER TRYING DESPERATELY TO SHOOT THE DIAMONDS IN THE SHADOW, THE PHOTOGRAPHER CAUGHT THE MODEL (CHARLOTTE PLOSSANT-PELLÉ) IN A MOMENT OF REST IN THE SUN. (USA)

● 37 ALS STILVOLLE SKILÄUFERIN TRÄGT MAN AUCH IM ALLTAG EINEN OVERALL, ALLERDINGS IN EINER SEHR FEMININEN VERSION VON YOHJI YAMAMOTO. DIE AUFNAHME ERSCHIEN IN *MARIE CLAIRE*. (FRA)

● 38 DIESES PHOTO WURDE FÜR DIE GRÖSSTE DRUCKWERBEKAMPAGNE DES ZEITSCHRIFTENVERLEGER-VERBANDES DER USA VERWENDET. DIE PERSPEKTIVE WURDE MIT HILFE EINES KRANWAGENS ERREICHT, VON DEM AUS DER PHOTOGRAPH DIE AUFNAHME MACHTE. DIE KAMPAGNE LIEF UNTER DEM SLOGAN: »MAN FINDET SIE AN DEN BESTEN ORTEN,« WOMIT DIE WEITE VERBREITUNG VON ZEITSCHRIFTEN GEMEINT IST. (USA)

● 39 ES WAR DER ERSTE AUFTRAG FÜR WILLIAM LAXTON FÜR *VOGUE PARIS*. NACHDEM ER VERZWEIFELT VERSUCHT HATTE, DIE DIAMANTEN IM SCHATTEN AUFZUNEHMEN, ÜBERRASCHTE ER DAS MODELL (CHARLOTTE PLOSSANT-PELLÉ) IN EINEM MOMENT DER ENTSPANNUNG IN DER SONNE. (FRA)

▲ 37 «SKIEUSE DE STYLE»: LE MANNEQUIN PORTE UNE VERSION RAFFINÉE ET TRÈS FÉMININE DE LA COMBINAISON-PANTALON. MODÈLE DE YOHJI YAMAMOTO, PRÉSENTÉ DANS *MARIE CLAIRE*. (FRA)

▲ 38 PHOTO POUR LA PLUS GRANDE CAMPAGNE DE PUB QUI AIT JAMAIS ÉTÉ PUBLIÉE PAR L'ASSOCIATION DES ÉDITEURS DE MAGAZINES AMÉRICAINS. CE TAXI NEW-YORKAIS, VU EN PERSPECTIVE PLONGEANTE, A ÉTÉ PRIS DU HAUT D'UN CAMION-GRUE. CETTE CAMPAGNE ÉTAIT BASÉE SUR LE SLOGAN: «ON LA TROUVE DANS LES MEILLEURS ENDROITS», QUI SOULIGNAIT LA LARGE DIFFUSION DONT JOUISSENT LES MAGAZINES. (USA)

▲ 39 IL S'AGISSAIT DE LA PREMIÈRE COMMANDE DE WILLIAM LAXTON POUR *VOGUE PARIS*. APRÈS AVOIR VAINEMENT ESSAYÉ DE PHOTOGRAPHIER LE BRACELET DE DIAMANT DANS L'OMBRE, IL SURPRIT LE MODÈLE, CHARLOTTE PLOSSANT-PELLÉ, DANS UN MOMENT DE DÉTENTE AU SOLEIL. (FRA)

PHOTOGRAPHER:
STEPHEN WILKES
CAMERA:
NIKON F3 180MM
FILM:
FUJI 50
EXPOSURE:
F 8, 1/125
CLIENT:
PUBLISHERS OF
AMERICA

PHOTOGRAPHER:
WILLIAM LAXTON
REPRESENTATIVE:
YANNICK MORISOT
CAMERA:
HASSELBLAD
PHOTO EDITOR:
MARIE-AMELIE
SAUVET
CLIENT:
VOGUE PARIS
ART DIRECTOR:
MARY SHANAHAN

PHOTOGRAPHER:
PAOLO ROVERSI
CLIENT:
MARIE CLAIRE
ART DIRECTOR:
WALTER ROSPERT

◀■ 37

■ 38

■ 39

■ 40 THIS SHOT FOR AN ARTICLE IN *AVENUE* ON SUN-BATHING WAS DONE IN THE PHOTOGRAPHER'S STUDIO. (NLD)

■ 41 PHOTOGRAPH FOR AN ARTICLE IN GERMAN *VOGUE* PRESENTING NEW IDEAS FOR VERY LIGHT WEIGHT SUMMER WEAR MADE OF ARTISTIC NETLIKE FABRICS. (GER)

■ 42 WHETHER IN AN EVENING DRESS OR A SWIM SUIT, HOLLYWOOD'S FILM DIVAS PLAYED OUT ROLES THAT WERE IMITATED BY WOMEN EVERY-WHERE. THIS PHOTOGRAPH WAS USED FOR A FEATURE ON HOLLYWOOD IN *FRANKFURTER ALLGE-MEINE MAGAZIN*. (GER)

● 40 DIESE AUFNAHME FÜR EINEN BEITRAG IN *AVENUE* ÜBER SONNENBADEN WURDE IM STUDIO DES PHOTOGRAPHEN GEMACHT. (NLD)

● 41 AUFNAHME FÜR EINEN ARTIKEL IN DER DEUT-SCHEN *VOGUE*, IN DEM KUNSTVOLL GEKNÜPFTES FÜR DEN SOMMER VORGESTELLT WIRD – UND DAS, WAS MAN DARUNTER TRÄGT. (GER)

● 42 OB IM ABENDKLEID ODER IM BADEANZUG, HOLLYWOODS VERFÜHRERISCHE FILMDIVAS SPIEL-TEN SICH SELBST UND WURDEN ANDEREN ZUM VORBILD. DIE AUFNAHME STAMMT AUS EINEM BEI-TRAG ÜBER HOLLYWOOD IM *FRANKFURTER ALLGE-MEINE MAGAZIN*. (GER)

▲ 40 CETTE PHOTO ILLUSTRANT UN ARTICLE DU MAGAZINE *AVENUE* SUR LES BAINS DE SOLEIL A ÉTÉ RÉALISÉE EN STUDIO. (NLD)

▲ 41 PHOTO POUR UN ARTICLE DE L'ÉDITION ALLE-MANDE DE *VOGUE*, QUI PRÉSENTE DES VÊTEMENTS TRESSÉS POUR L'ÉTÉ – ET CE QUI SE PORTE DESSOUS, BODY, SLIP OU RIEN DU TOUT. (USA)

▲ 42 EN ROBE DU SOIR OU EN MAILLOT DE BAIN, LES STARS D'HOLLYWOOD JOUÈRENT LES SÉDUC-TRICES ET ELLES FURENT IMITÉES PAR UN GRAND NOMBRE DE FEMMES. CETTE PHOTO EST TIRÉE D'UN ARTICLE SUR HOLLYWOOD, PARU DANS LE *FRANK-FURTER ALLGEMEINE MAGAZIN*. (GER)

PHOTOGRAPHER:
ALAN DAVID-TU
REPRESENTATIVE:
SANDEE ASHTON
ASSOCIATION
CAMERA:
SINAR
FILM:
KODAK 6118
CLIENT:
AVENUE MAGAZINE
ART DIRECTOR:
HANS VAN
BLOMMESTEIN
■ 40

PHOTOGRAPHER:
ANDREW
MACPHERSON
REPRESENTATIVE:
KIM SION/
SMILE MANAGEMENT
CLIENT:
VOGUE
ART DIRECTOR:
ALESJANDRO
GONZALES
■ 41

PHOTOGRAPHER:
SARAH MOON
CLIENT:
*FRANKFURTER ALL-
GEMEINE MAGAZIN*
ART DIRECTOR:
HANS-GEORG
POSPISCHIL
■ 42

PHOTOGRAPHER:
KAREN LEVY
CAMERA:
HASSELBLAD 150MM
FILM:
VPS 3, 80 ASA
PHOTO EDITOR:
DIDI KATONA

CLIENT:
ELVIRA VALI
ART DIRECTOR:
DIDI KATONA/
JOHN PYLYPCZAK
DESIGNER:
DIDI KATONA
■ 43-46

PHOTOGRAPHER:
LAUREN SOROKIN
CAMERA:
NIKON F3
FILM:
TX-135MM

CLIENT:
YOUNG FASHIONS
ART DIRECTOR:
SARA FELDMANN
DESIGNER:
TAMARA KOPPER
■ 47

■ 43-46 PHOTOGRAPHS FROM A SMALL BROCHURE FOR AN EXCLUSIVE CHILDREN'S CLOTHING DESIGNER. A LARGE VINTAGE PAINTED STAGE CANVAS WAS USED AS A BACKDROP IN THE STUDIO. (CAN)

■ 47 HAND-COLORED PHOTOGRAPH FROM AN EDITORIAL ON CHILDREN'S NAUTICAL FASHIONS IN *YOUNG FASHIONS MAGAZINE.* (USA)

● 43-46 AUFNAHMEN AUS EINER KLEINEN BROSCHÜRE FÜR EXKLUSIVE KINDERMODE. EIN GROSSER, ALTER BÜHNENPROSPEKT DIENTE ALS HINTERGRUND IM STUDIO. (CAN)

● 47 HANDKOLORIERTE SCHWARZWEISS-AUFNAHME AUS *YOUNG FASHION MAGAZINE.* DAS THEMA: MARINE-LOOK FÜR KINDER. (USA)

▲ 43-46 PHOTOS D'UNE PETITE BROCHURE PRÉSENTANT UNE MODE ENFANTS EXCLUSIVE. UN GRAND RIDEAU DE SCÈNE PEINT A SERVI DE DÉCOR POUR CES PHOTOS PRISES EN STUDIO. (CAN)

▲ 47 PHOTO NOIR ET BLANC COLORÉE MAIN PARUE DANS *YOUNG FASHION MAGAZINE,* SUR LE THÈME DU STYLE MARIN. (USA)

PHOTOGRAPHER:
ALBERT WATSON
CAMERA:
HASSELBLAD
FILM:
KODAK
CLIENT:
BYBLOS
ART DIRECTOR:
NANDO MIGLIO
■ 48

PHOTOGRAPHER:
AMYN NASSER
REPRESENTATIVE:
REPOSSI, MILAN/
LINKE, MUNICH
CAMERA:
NIKON
FILM:
KODAK EES 800/1600
PHOTO EDITOR:
KAREEN HECHTER/
DOROTHA FLANDRIN
(PUBLICIS AGENCY)
CLIENT:
DANIEL HECHTER
ART DIRECTOR:
DOROTHA FLANDRIN
▲
▶■ 49

PHOTOGRAPHER:
NADAV KANDER
REPRESENTATIVE:
DAVID BURNHAM, UK/
STOCKLAND
MARTEL, USA/
VERONIQUE PERES
DOMERGUE, FRANCE
CLIENT:
SPEEDO
ART DIRECTOR:
MARCUS VINTON
▶■ 50

■ 48 PHOTOGRAPH FOR THE SPRING/SUMMER 1990 CAMPAIGN FOR BYBLOS FASHION, SHOT AT VENICE BEACH (CALIFORNIA). (ITA)

■ 49 "WHAT A GOOD LIFE YOU HAVE WHEN YOU LEAD THE LIFE YOU WANT." SUCH WAS THE LEADING THEME FOR THE DANIEL HECHTER SPRING/SUMMER 1990 FASHION CATALOG FROM WHICH THIS PHOTOGRAPH WAS TAKEN. (FRA)

■ 50 "JUST ADD WATER" WAS THE SLOGAN OF A CAMPAIGN FOR SPEEDO SWIMWEAR, FOR WHICH NADAV KANDER CHOSE TO PHOTOGRAPH THE MODELS WITHOUT WATER. (GBR)

● 48 PHOTO FÜR DIE FRÜHJAHR/SOMMER-1990-KAMPAGNE FÜR BYBLOS-MODE, AUFGENOMMEN AN DER VENICE BEACH (KALIFORNIEN). (ITA)

● 49 «WAS FÜR EIN GUTES LEBEN MAN HAT, WENN MAN DAS LEBEN FÜHRT, DAS MAN SICH WÜNSCHT.» DAS WAR DER LEITSPRUCH FÜR DEN DANIEL-HECHTER-KATALOG MIT DER FRÜHJAHRS-/SOMMERMODE 1990, AUS DEM DIESE AUFNAHME STAMMT. (FRA)

● 50 «MAN FÜGE NUR WASSER HINZU» WAR DER SLOGAN EINER KAMPAGNE FÜR SPEEDO-BADEMODE, DIE NADAV KANDER GANZ OHNE WASSER PHOTOGRAPHIERTE. (GBR)

▲ 48 CETTE PHOTO D'UNE CAMPAGNE POUR LA MODE PRINTEMPS/ÉTÉ 1990 DE BYBLOS A ÉTÉ RÉALISÉE À VENICE BEACH, EN CALIFORNIE. (ITA)

▲ 49 «AH LA BELLE VIE QU'ON VIT QUAND ON VIT LA VIE QU'ON VEUT.» TEL ÉTAIT LE LEITMOTIV DU CATALOGUE DE LA MODE PRINTEMPS/ÉTÉ 1990 DU COUTURIER DANIEL HECHTER D'OÙ EST TIRÉE CETTE IMAGE. (FRA)

▲ 50 NADAV KANDER A RÉALISÉ CES PHOTOS POUR LES MAILLOTS DE BAIN SPEEDO DONT LE SLOGAN ÉTAIT: «IL NE MANQUE PLUS QUE L'EAU» SANS MONTRER UNE GOUTTE D'EAU. (USA)

PHOTOGRAPHER:
SUE BENNETT
CAMERA:
NIKON
FILM:
KODAK HIGH SPEED
INFRARED

CLIENT:
LITTLE LAURA OF
CALIFORNIA
STYLIST:
JANINE HESS
■ 51, 52

■ 51, 52 A HUMOROUS WAY OF PRESENTING MEN'S SPORTSWEAR BY LITTLE LAURA OF CALIFORNIA. THE BLACK-AND-WHITE PHOTOS WERE DONE IN FRONT OF A HAND-PAINTED BACKGROUND, WITH A LIGHTING COMBINATION OF STROBE AND TUNGSTEN USING SLOW SHUTTER SPEED. THEY WERE USED FOR TRADE SHOW BOOTHS AND AS POINT-OF-PURCHASE DISPLAYS. (USA)

● 51, 52 SPORTKLEIDUNG VON LITTLE LAURA OF CALIFORNIA, HUMORVOLL PRÄSENTIERT. DIE SCHWARZWEISS-BILDER WURDEN VOR EINEM HAND-GEMALTEN HINTERGRUND MIT EINER KOMBINATION VON STROBE- UND TUNGSTEN-BELEUCHTUNG BEI LANGEN BELICHTUNGSZEITEN AUFGENOMMEN. SIE WURDEN FÜR MESSESTÄNDE UND ALS LADENAUF-STELLER VERWENDET. (USA)

▲ 51, 52 UNE MANIÈRE HUMORISTIQUE DE PRÉSEN-TER LA MODE SPORTS DE LITTLE LAURA OF CALI-FORNIA. CES PHOTOS EN NOIR ET BLANC ONT ÉTÉ PRISES SUR UN FOND DE DÉCOR PEINT ET ILLUMI-NÉES AVEC DES LAMPES STROBOSCOPIQUES ET TUNGSTÈNE. ELLES ONT ÉTÉ EXPOSÉES DANS DES STANDS DE GRANDES FOIRES ET SUR LES POINTS DE VENTE. (USA)

PHOTOGRAPHER:
BRUCE WEBER
REPRESENTATIVE:
NAN BUSH
CAMERA:
PENTAX 6 BY 7
CLIENT:
CALVIN KLEIN
COSMETICS
ART DIRECTOR:
SAM SHAHID

◀■ 53

PHOTOGRAPHER:
JÜRGEN KRIEWALD
CAMERA:
HASSELBLAD
FILM:
KODAK EPN 6012
CLIENT:
MC GREGOR
ART DIRECTOR:
WERNER WÜRDINGER

■ 54

PHOTOGRAPHER:
GEORGE PETRAKES
REPRESENTATIVE:
MARY JANE JOYCE
CAMERA:
NIKON F3
FILM:
EKTACHROME PLUS
EXPOSURE:
F 11, 1/250

PHOTO EDITOR:
TYLER SMITH
CLIENT:
LOUIS, BOSTON
ART DIRECTOR:
TYLER SMITH
DESIGNER:
TYLER SMITH

■ 55

■ 53 THE FRAGRANCE "OBSESSION" BY CALVIN KLEIN COSMETICS INTERPRETED IN A BLACK-AND-WHITE PHOTOGRAPH. (USA)

■ 54 THE ANGLOPHILE CHARACTER OF THE FALL/WINTER COLLECTION BY MCGREGOR WAS TO BE CONVEYED IN THIS PHOTOGRAPH (ONE OF SIX) PRESENTING HIGHSTYLE COUNTRY LIFE. IT WAS TAKEN IN A STUDIO USING A BACKGROUND PREPARED BY A STAGE PAINTER. (GER)

■ 55 "WHEN IN TLAQUEPAQUE, DO AS THE TLAQUEPAQUIANS DO". THE MODEL ADOPTING THE POSE OF THE "MEXICAN" FIGURE REMINISCENT OF THE SMALL CLAY FIGURES OF MEXICAN FOLK ART. THIS PHOTOGRAPH WAS USED IN A CATALOG OF LOUIS, BOSTON, SHOWING A WARM WEATHER COLLECTION IN THE COLORS OF MEXICO. (USA)

● 53 DAS PARFUM «OBSESSION» VON CALVIN KLEIN COSMETICS, INTERPRETIERT IN EINER SCHWARZ-WEISS-AUFNAHME. (USA)

● 54 DER ANGLOPHILE CHARAKTER DER HERBST-/WINTERKOLLEKTION VON MCGREGOR SOLLTE IN DIESER AUFNAHME, DIE COUNTRY LIFE AUF HOHEM NIVEAU DARSTELLT, ZUM AUSDRUCK KOMMEN. DER HINTERGRUND FÜR DIE ATELIERAUFNAHMEN WURDE VON EINEM BÜHNENMALER GESTALTET. (GER)

● 55 «IN TLAQUEPAQUE WIE DIE TLAQUEPAQUE-NENSER.» DAS MODELL NIMMT DIE POSE DER AN DIE KLEINEN TONFIGUREN DER MEXIKANISCHEN VOLKSKUNST ERINNERNDEN GESTALT EIN. DIESE AUFNAHME STAMMT AUS EINEM KATALOG VON LOUIS, BOSTON, MIT DER KOLLEKTION FÜR HEISSE TAGE, IN DEN FARBEN MEXIKOS. (GER)

▲ 53 LE PARFUM «OBSESSION» DE CALVIN KLEIN COSMETICS, INTERPRÉTÉ DANS UNE PHOTO EN NOIR ET BLANC. (USA)

▲ 54 CETTE PHOTO QUI MET EN SCÈNE LA VERSION CITADINE DU GENTLEMAN-FARMER ILLUSTRE L'ÉLÉGANCE TRÈS BRITISH DE LA COLLECTION AUTOMNE/HIVER DE MC GREGOR. LE FOND DE CES PHOTOS PRISES EN STUDIO A ÉTÉ PEINT PAR UN DÉCORATEUR DE THÉÂTRE. (GER)

▲ 55 «À TLAQUEPAQUE, SOYEZ COMME LES TLAQUEPAQUIENS.» LE MODÈLE REPREND LA MÊME POSE QUE LA FIGURINE EN TERRE, TYPIQUE DE L'ART POPULAIRE MEXICAIN. CETTE PHOTO EST TIRÉE DU CATALOGUE PRÉSENTANT LA COLLECTION DE VÊTEMENTS POUR LES JOURS CHAUDS DE LOUIS, BOSTON, AUX COULEURS DE MEXICO. (USA)

■ 56 STUDIO SHOT FOR AN EDITORIAL ON MEN'S FASHION IN *DETAILS* MAGAZINE. THE VELVET SUIT AND SILK CREPE DE CHINE MARBLEIZED SHIRT ARE BY CHRISTIAN KENTH. (USA)

■ 57 THIS IS HOW *SPY* MAGAZINE PICTURES VINCENT VAN GOGH, HAD HE LIVED IN 1990: AS A WELL DRESSED, CELEBRATED DOWNTOWN PAINTER. PHOTOGRAPH FOR A FASHION FEATURE ON THE SUBJECT OF WHAT HISTORICAL PERSONALITIES WOULD WEAR AND WHAT THEY WOULD DO WERE THEY ALIVE TODAY. (USA)

■ 58 PHOTO FROM A SERIES OF FOUR USED AS SELF-PROMOTION FOR GEORGE WHITESIDE PHOTOGRAPHY. (CAN)

● 56 STUDIO-AUFNAHME FÜR EINEN MODEBEITRAG IN *DETAILS*. DER BLAUE SAMTANZUG UND DAS MARMORIERTE HEMD AUS CRÊPE DE CHINE SIND VON CHRISTIAN KENTH. (USA)

● 57 SO STELLT SICH DIE ZEITSCHRIFT *SPY* VINCENT VAN GOGH VOR, WÜRDE ER HEUTE LEBEN: ALS GUT GEKLEIDETER, ERFOLGREICHER MALER IM NEW YORKER KÜNSTLERVIERTEL. DIE AUFNAHME GEHÖRT ZU EINEM MODEARTIKEL, IN DEM ES DARUM GEHT, WAS HISTORISCHE PERSÖNLICHKEITEN IN UNSERER ZEIT TRAGEN WÜRDEN. (USA)

● 58 BEISPIEL AUS EINER SERIE VON VIER AUFNAHMEN, DIE ALS EIGENWERBUNG VON GEORGE WHITESIDE DIENEN. (CAN)

▲ 56 PHOTO DE STUDIO POUR UN ARTICLE DE MODE DU MAGAZINE *DETAILS*. VESTE DE VELOURS BLEU ET CHEMISE EN CRÊPE DE CHINE AVEC EFFET DE MARBRURE DE CHRISTIAN KENTH. (USA)

▲ 57 UN PEINTRE HABITANT NEW YORK, BIEN HABILLÉ ET COURONNÉ DE SUCCÈS: C'EST AINSI QUE *SPY* S'IMAGINE VINCENT VAN GOGH, S'IL VIVAIT À NOTRE ÉPOQUE. LA PHOTO PROVIENT D'UN ARTICLE DE MODE OÙ L'ON IMAGINE QUELS VÊTEMENTS ET QUEL STYLE DE VIE CERTAINES PERSONNALITÉS ADOPTERAIENT AUJOURD'HUI. (USA)

▲ 58 EXEMPLE D'UNE SÉRIE DE QUATRE PHOTOGRAPHIES SERVANT D'AUTOPROMOTION À GEORGE WHITESIDE. (CAN)

PHOTOGRAPHER:
JOHN CHAN
CAMERA:
ROLLAFLAN
FILM:
EKTACHROME, 64, 120
EXPOSURE:
F 8.5, 1/60
CLIENT:
DETAILS MAGAZINE
ART DIRECTOR:
DEBBIE SMITH
DESIGNER:
JOHN CHAN
■ 56

PHOTOGRAPHER:
JOSEF ASTOR
REPRESENTATIVE:
BARBARA VON
SCHREIBER
CAMERA:
HASSELBLAD
FILM:
FUJICHROME 64T
CLIENT:
SPY MAGAZINE
ART DIRECTOR:
ROSEMARIE TURK
CREATIVE DIRECTOR:
STEPHEN DOYLE
■ 57

PHOTOGRAPHER:
GEORGE WHITESIDE
CLIENT:
GEORGE WHITESIDE
PHOTOGRAPHY
ART DIRECTOR:
ANNA HARASYM
DESIGNER:
ANNA HARASYM
▶■ 58

PHOTOGRAPHER:

JOST WILDBOLZ

CAMERA:

PENTAX 607

FILM:

EKTACHROM 200

CLIENT:

SCHNEIDER'S

BEKLEIDUNG

ART DIRECTOR:

FRANZ MERLICEK

DESIGNER:

JANNA THÜR

■ 59

PHOTOGRAPHER:

ALBERT WATSON

CAMERA:

HASSELBLAD

FILM:

KODAK

CLIENT:

BYBLOS

ART DIRECTOR:

NANDO MIGLIO

■ 60, 61

■ 59 PHOTOGRAPH FOR AN AUSTRIAN FASHION HOUSE. THE HIGH VOLTAGE WARNING IS A HUMOROUS CONTRAST TO THE INDIFFERENT EXPRESSION OF THE MODELS. (AUT)

■ 60 MEN'S NAUTICAL FASHIONS PRESENTED BY MEANS OF A TIE IN THIS BLACK-AND-WHITE PHOTOGRAPH FOR BYBLOS. (ITA)

■ 61 THE MEN'S COAT BY BYBLOS PHOTOGRAPHED AGAINST THE DRAMATIC GRAY COLORS OF THE SEA AND THE SKY FOR A CATALOG. (ITA)

● 59 AUFNAHME FÜR EIN ÖSTERREICHISCHES MODEHAUS. DIE STARKSTROMWARNUNG DIENT ALS HUMORVOLLER KONTRAST ZU DEN UNBETEILIGTEN MIENEN DER MODELLE. (AUT)

● 60 MARINE-LOOK FÜR MÄNNER, IN DIESER AUFNAHME FÜR EINEN BYBLOS-KATALOG ANHAND EINER KRAWATTE DEMONSTRIERT. (ITA)

● 61 EIN HERRENMANTEL VON BYBLOS, AUFGENOMMEN GEGEN DIE DRAMATISCHEN GRAUTÖNE DES MEERES UND DES HIMMELS. (ITA)

▲ 59 POUR UN MAGASIN DE MODE AUTRICHIEN. L'AIR INDIFFÉRENT DES MODÈLES CONTRASTE IRONIQUEMENT AVEC LE PANNEAU «DANGER DE HAUTE TENSION» DU POTEAU ÉLECTRIQUE. (AUT)

▲ 60 MARIN DE CHARME CRAVATÉ SUR UNE PHOTO EN NOIR ET BLANC D'UN CATALOGUE DE MODE HOMMES DE BYBLOS. (ITA)

▲ 61 MANTEAU POUR HOMMES DE BYBLOS, PHOTOGRAPHIÉ AU BORD DE LA MER, DANS UNE ATMOSPHÈRE NOCTURNE ET DRAMATIQUE. (ITA)

■ 62, 63 MEN'S FASHION BY CROSSINGS PHOTO-
GRAPHED IN THE LIGHT OF THE WINTER SUN ON AN
OLD PRIVATE AIRPORT. (USA)

■ 64 "NEW WEST FRAGRANCE" BY ARAMIS INTER-
PRETED BY THE CALIFORNIAN COLORS IN THIS PHO-
TOGRAPH, SHOT IN LOS ANGELES. (USA)

● 62, 63 MÄNNERMODE VON CROSSINGS, IM LICHT
DER WINTERSONNE AUF EINEM ALTEN PRIVATFLUG-
HAFEN AUFGENOMMEN. (USA)

● 64 DAS PARFUM «NEW WEST» VON ARAMIS,
DARGESTELLT DURCH DIE FARBEN KALIFORNIENS.
DIE AUFNAHME ENTSTAND IN LOS ANGELES. (USA)

▲ 62, 63 LA MODE MASCULINE DE CROSSINGS,
PHOTOGRAPHIÉE PAR UNE BELLE JOURNÉE D'HIVER
SUR UN VIEIL AÉROPORT PRIVÉ. (USA)

▲ 64 COULEURS CALIFORNIENNES POUR LE
NOUVEAU PARFUM «NEW WEST» D'ARAMIS. LA
PHOTO A ÉTÉ PRISE À LOS ANGELES. (USA)

PHOTOGRAPHER:

JOHN GOODMAN

REPRESENTATIVE:

MICHAEL ASH

CAMERA:

DEARDORFF 4X5

FILM:

FUJI 100D

CLIENT:

CROSSINGS

ART DIRECTOR:

MICHAEL TOTH

DESIGNER:

MICHAEL TOTH

◀■ 62, 63

PHOTOGRAPHER:

STEPHEN WILKES

REPRESENTATIVE:

BETTE WILKES

CAMERA:

NIKON F4

FILM:

FUJI 50

EXPOSURE:

F 5.6, 1/125

CLIENT:

ARAMIS, INC.

ART DIRECTOR:

ANELLE MILLER

■ 64

JOURNALISM

JOURNALISMUS

JOURNALISME

PHOTOGRAPHER:
DEBORAH MEYERS
CAMERA:
TOYO VIEW CAMERA
8X10
FILM:
POLAROID COLOR,
ORIGINAL, 8X10
EXPOSURE:
F 11, 1/250
CLIENT:
CARE PARTNERS
ART DIRECTOR:
JILL STONE/
HEDDE YAMADA
DESIGNER:
JILL STONE/
HEDDE YAMADA

◀■ 65

PHOTOGRAPHER:
JIM SIMS
REPRESENTATIVE:
FRIEND AND JOHNSON
CAMERA:
NIKON F4
FILM:
KODACHROME 64
■ 66-68

■ 65 (PRECEDING SPREAD) THE ASSIGNMENT WAS TO DESCRIBE A COMMUNITY BASED NURSING SERVICE FOR CANCER PATIENTS. THE PHOTOGRAPHER CHOSE A REAL PATIENT IN ORDER TO REALLY COMMUNICATE THE PHYSICAL AND SPIRITUAL IMPACT OF THE DISEASE. (USA)

■ 66, 67 SELECTIONS FROM A SERIES OF PERSONAL WORK BY JIM SIMS OF HOUSTON ON THE SUBJECT OF VICTIMS OF THE POLITICAL STRIFE IN EL SALVADOR. SHOWN HERE ARE TWO CHILDREN WHO SUFFER THE EFFECTS OF THE CIVIL WAR. (USA)

■ 68 FURTHER EXAMPLE OF JIM SIMS'S DOCUMENTARY WORK IN EL SALVADOR: AN ADOLESCENT GIRL WHO FIGHTS WITH THE REBEL FORCES PHOTOGRAPHED WITH A YOUNG CHILD FROM AN IMPOVERISHED VILLAGE. (USA)

● 65 (VORHERGEHENDE SEITE) DER AUFTRAG FÜR DIESE AUFNAHME KAM VON EINEM GEMEINDE-PFLEGEDIENST FÜR KREBSPATIENTEN. DIE PHOTO-GRAPHIN ENTSCHLOSS SICH, EINE ECHTE PATIEN-TIN ZU ZEIGEN, UM DIE PHYSISCHE UND PSYCHI-SCHE BELASTUNG SICHTBAR ZU MACHEN. (USA)

● 66, 67 ZWEI SCHWARZWEISS-PORTRÄTS VON KINDERN IN EL SALVADOR, DEN OPFERN DES BÜR-GERKRIEGS. ES SIND PERSÖNLICHE STATEMENTS DES PHOTOGRAPHEN JIM SIMS AUS HOUSTON ZUR POLITISCHEN LAGE IN EL SALVADOR. (USA)

● 68 EINE WEITERE AUFNAHME AUS DER SERIE DES PHOTOGRAPHEN JIM SIMS ÜBER DIE OPFER DER POLITIK: EIN HALBWÜCHSIGES MÄDCHEN, DAS ZU DEN REBELLEN GEHÖRT, MIT EINEM KIND AUS EINEM DORF IN EL SALVADOR. (USA)

▲ 65 (PAGE PRÉCÉDENTE) CETTE PHOTO ÉTAIT UNE COMMANDE D'UN SERVICE MUNICIPAL D'ASSIS-TANCE AUX CANCÉREUX. LA PHOTOGRAPHE DEBO-RAH MEYERS A CHOISI DE MONTRER UNE MÈRE MALADE POUR METTRE EN RELIEF LES SOUFFRANCES PHYSIQUES ET PSYCHIQUES ENDURÉES. (USA)

▲ 66, 67 PORTRAITS NOIR ET BLANC D'ENFANTS DU SALVADOR, VICTIMES DE LA GUERRE CIVILE. CES TÉMOIGNAGES PERSONNELS DU PHOTOGRAPHE JIM SIMS DE HOUSTON SONT UN PLAIDOYER EN FAVEUR DE LA PAIX. (USA)

▲ 68 UNE AUTRE PHOTO DU REPORTAGE SUR LES ENFANTS DU SALVADOR, RÉALISÉE PAR JIM SIMS: UNE ADOLESCENTE, MEMBRE DES COMMANDOS REBELLES, PHOTOGRAPHIÉE AVEC UN PETIT VILLAGEOIS. (USA)

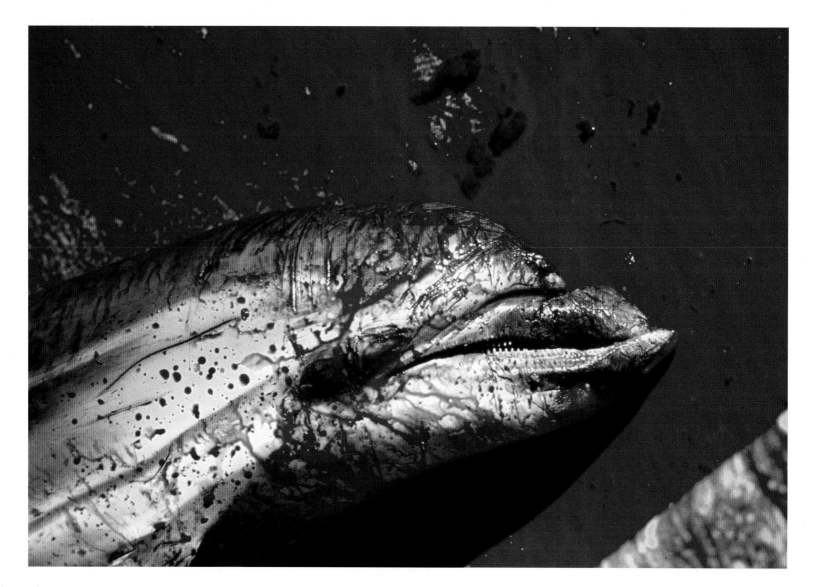

PHOTOGRAPHER:
STEVE HART
CLIENT:
PENTHOUSE
MAGAZINE/GENERAL
MEDIA INC.
ART DIRECTOR:
RICHARD BLEIWEISS
CREATIVE DIRECTOR:
FRANK DEVINO
■ 69

■ 69 PHOTOGRAPH USED TO ILLUSTRATE A *PENT-HOUSE* MAGAZINE ARTICLE ON THE KILLING OF DOLPHINES IN THE SEASIDE.COMMUNITY OF TAIJI, JAPAN. ONCE A WHALING TOWN IT CAN NOW BE REFERRED TO AS DOLPHIN TOWN AS INTER-NATIONAL PRESSURE TO SAVE THE WHALES FORCED THE WHALERS TO SEEK THEIR LIVELYHOOD FROM THE WHALE'S CLOSEST RELATIVE, THE DOLPHIN. THEY ARE CAUGHT WITH GIANT NETS THAT ARE PULLED INTO THE COVE. (USA)

■ 70-73 PHOTOGRAPHS OF HOMELESS PEOPLE TAKEN IN THE STREETS AND SUBWAYS OF NEW YORK CITY FOR THE ROBIN HOOD FOUNDATION, A GROUP THAT RAISES MONEY FOR THE NEEDY. (USA)

● 69 AUFNAHME AUS EINEM ARTIKEL IN *PENT-HOUSE*, IN DEM ES UM DAS ABSCHLACHTEN VON DELPHINEN IN DER JAPANISCHEN STADT TAIJI GEHT. DIESE EHEMALIGE WALFÄNGERSTADT IST ZU EINER DELPHIN-STADT GEWORDEN, NACHDEM IN-TERNATIONALER DRUCK DIE WALFÄNGER ZWANG, IHREN LEBENSUNTERHALT ANDERS ZU VERDIENEN. SIE WÄHLTEN DEN NÄCHSTEN ARTVERWANDTEN DES WALS, DEN DELPHIN, DEN SIE IN RIESIGEN NETZEN IN IHRE BUCHT ZIEHEN. (USA)

● 70-73 AUFNAHMEN VON OBDACHLOSEN IN DEN STRASSEN UND U-BAHNSCHÄCHTEN VON NEW YORK FÜR DIE ROBIN HOOD FOUNDATION, DIE SICH UM DIESE MENSCHEN KÜMMERT. (USA)

▲ 69 CETTE PHOTO IMPRESSIONNANTE QUI MONTRE LE MASSACRE DES DAUPHINS DANS LA BAIE DE TAIJI A ÉTÉ RÉALISÉE POUR UN ARTICLE DU MAGAZINE *PENTHOUSE*. DEPUIS QUE LA PRESSION INTERNATIONALE A CONTRAINT LES BALEINIERS D'ABANDONNER LA CHASSE À LA BALEINE, POUR GAGNER LEUR VIE, LES PÊCHEURS ON DÉCIDÉ DE CHASSER L'ANIMAL QUI LUI RESSEMBLAIT LE PLUS, LE DAUPHIN, QU'ILS ATTRAPENT DANS D'IMMENSES FILETS. (USA)

▲ 70-73 CES PHOTOS DE SANS-ABRI DANS LES RUES ET LE MÉTRO DE NEW YORK ONT ÉTÉ PRISES POUR LA ROBIN HOOD FOUNDATION, UNE ORGANI-SATION CARITATIVE AMÉRICAINE. (USA)

PHOTOGRAPHER:
WILLIAM COUPON
CAMERA:
ROLLEI 2 1/4
FILM:
TRI-X 120
CLIENT:
ROBIN HOOD
FOUNDATION
ART DIRECTOR:
DAVID SALZMAN
■ 70-73

PHOTOGRAPHER:
TADEUSZ
CZERNIAWSKI
CAMERA:
NIKON F3, NIKKOR
24MM
FILM:
TRI-X 135/36
EXPOSURE:
F 8, 1/125
CLIENT:
MORZE I ZIEMIA
■ 74-77

PHOTOGRAPHER:
WALTER SCHMITZ
REPRESENTATIVE:
BILDERBERG ARCHIV
DER FOTOGRAFEN
CAMERA:
NIKON F3
FILM:
KODAKCHROME 64
EXPOSURE:
F 4, 1/125
CLIENT:
GRUNER + JAHR
VERLAG/*STERN*
ART DIRECTOR:
WOLFGANG BEHNKEN
▶■ 78, 79

■ 74-77 EDITORIAL COVERAGE IN A POLISH WEEKLY MAGAZINE ON THE EVENTS SURROUNDING THE DISMANTLING OF THE BERLIN WALL. *74, 77:* THE OPENING OF THE BORDER AT POTSDAMER PLATZ, NOVEMBER 12, 1989; *75:* THE WALL IN FEBRUARY 1990; *76:* AT THE WALL, NOVEMBER 12, 1989. (POL)

■ 78, 79 PHOTOGRAPHS FROM AN ARTICLE IN *STERN* ON THE STRONG EMOTIONS PRESENT AT ITALIAN SOCCER MATCHES. OPPOSITE TOP: SMOKE BOMBS EXPLODE ON THE FIELD AT THE SOCCER STADION IN NAPLES. BOTTOM: SAN SIRO STADIAN IN MILAN AFTER A SOCCER GAME. (GER)

● 74-77 FÜR EINEN ARTIKEL IN EINER POLNISCHEN WOCHENZEITSCHRIFT ÜBER DIE BERLINER MAUER NACH DEM 9. NOVEMBER 1989. *74, 77:* ÖFFNUNG DES GRENZÜBERGANGES AM POTSDAMER PLATZ, 12. NOVEMBER 1989; *75:* DIE MAUER IM FEBRUAR 1990; *76:* AN DER MAUER, 12. NOVEMBER 1989. (POL)

● 78, 79 GEGENÜBER OBEN: RAUCHPATRONEN IM FUSSBALLSTADION VON NEAPEL. SOBALD SICH DER NEBEL LICHTET, WIRD ANGEPFIFFEN. UNTEN: MAILANDS SAN SIRO-STADION NACH EINEM SPIEL. BEIDE AUFNAHMEN STAMMEN AUS EINEM BEITRAG IM *STERN* ÜBER FUSSBALL-FANS IN ITALIEN. (GER)

▲ 74-77 PHOTOS PUBLIÉES DANS UN HEBDOMADAIRE POLONAIS SUR LES JOURS QUI SUIVIRENT L'OUVERTURE DU MUR DE BERLIN. *74, 77:* L'OUVERTURE DU POSTE FRONTIÈRE DE LA POTSDAMER PLATZ LE 12 NOVEMBRE; *75:* LE MUR EN FÉVRIER 1990; *76:* DEVANT LE MUR, LE 12 NOVEMBRE 1989. (POL)

▲ 78, 79 PHOTOS D'UN REPORTAGE SUR LES SUPPORTERS DES ÉQUIPES DE FOOTBALL EN ITALIE, PUBLIÉ DANS LE MAGAZINE *STERN*. EN HAUT: LA FUMÉE DES PÉTARDS ENVAHIT LE STADE DE NAPLES. EN BAS: LES GRADINS DU STADE SAN SIRO À MILAN APRÈS UN MATCH. (GER)

PHOTOGRAPHER:
FRANCINE BAJANDE
CLIENT:
MARIE CLAIRE
■ 80-83

PHOTOGRAPHER:
CHRIS SATTLBERGER
REPRESENTATIVE:
REGINA MARIA
ANZENBERGER
CAMERA:
NIKON F3
FILM:
EKTACHROME EPN
100 ASA
PHOTO EDITOR:
CORNELIA BARTSCH
CLIENT:
STERN JAHRBUCH
1989
DESIGNER:
JAN GÖRLICH/
WERNER RICK
▶■ 84

■ 80-83 A DOCUMENTARY REPORT IN *MARIE CLAIRE* ON THE CONDITIONS OF HOSPITAL NURSERIES IN ROMANIA. THE BABIES ARE KEPT IN OVER-CROWDED CONDITIONS AND THEIR MOTHERS, FORCED TO STAY IN THE HOSPITAL TO NURSE THE CHILDREN BECAUSE THEY ARE SICK, ONLY SEE THEIR BABIES WHEN NURSING UNDER STRICT HYGIENIC CONDITIONS. THE BOTTOM SHOWS THE ROOM BEFORE THE MOTHERS ARRIVE FOR THEIR ALLOTTED TIME, THE BAGS AT THE WALL CONTAIN PROTECTIVE MASKS AND GARMENTS. ALSO SHOWN IS A SICK BABY IN AN ORPHANAGE, ISOLATED BECAUSE OF THE FEAR OF AIDS CONTAMINATION. (FRA)

■ 84 ROMANIA IN WINTER 1989. THE PHOTO, PUBLISHED IN THE *STERN* ANNUAL 1989, WAS TAKEN ON THE 24TH OF DECEMBER AT THE CEMETARY OF TEMESVAR. WHILE THE FIGHT GOES ON IN THE CITY, THE VICTIMS OF THE CEAUCESCU TERROR LIE HERE IN THE OPEN, COVERED ONLY WITH WHITE CLOTH. CHAINED WITH BARBED WIRE, THEY HAD BEEN TORTURED TO DEATH BY THE SECURITATE. (GER)

● 80-83 AUFNAHMEN AUS EINEM BERICHT IN DER ZEITSCHRIFT *MARIE CLAIRE* ÜBER EINE SÄUGLINGS-STATION IN EINEM RUMÄNISCHEN KRANKENHAUS. DIE BABIES SIND IN EINE ART SACK VERPACKT. DER EINZIGE AUGENBLICK, IN DEM DIE MÜTTER IHRE KINDER SEHEN, IST BEIM STILLEN UNTER STRENGSTEN HYGIENEVORSCHRIFTEN. DAS PHOTO UNTEN ZEIGT DEN RAUM VOR DEM EINTREFFEN DER MÜTTER. DIE SÄCKE AN DER WAND ENTHALTEN SCHUTZKLEIDUNG. MÜTTER KRANKER KINDER MÜSSEN IM SPITAL BLEIBEN, UM SIE ZU STILLEN. EIN KIND IN EINEM WAISENHAUS WIRD ISOLIERT AUS ANGST VOR AIDS-ÜBERTRAGUNG. (FRA)

● 84 RUMÄNIEN, WINTER 1989. DAS PHOTO, DAS IM *STERN*-JAHRBUCH 1989 VERÖFFENTLICHT WURDE, ENTSTAND AM 24. DEZEMBER AUF DEM FRIEDHOF VON TEMESVAR. HIER LIEGEN DIE OPFER DES CEAUCESCU TERRORS, AUFGEBAHRT AUF EINFACHEM, WEISSEM TUCH UNTER FREIEM HIMMEL. MIT STACHELDRAHT GEFESSELT, WURDEN SIE VON DER SECURITATE ZU TODE GEFOLTERT. (GER)

▲ 80-83 PHOTOS TIRÉES D'UN REPORTAGE SUR LA MATERNITÉ D'UN HÔPITAL ROUMAIN, PARU DANS *MARIE CLAIRE*. LES BÉBÉS SONT ENCORE LANGÉS COMME AU SIÈCLE DERNIER. L'HEURE DE LA TÉTÉE EST LE SEUL MOMENT OÙ MÈRES ET ENFANTS SONT RÉUNIS: LA SÉANCE D'ALLAITEMENT COLLECTIF SE FAIT DANS DES CONDITIONS D'HYGIÈNE DRACONIENNES. LA PHOTO DU BAS MONTRE LA SALLE D'ALLAITEMENT AVANT L'ARRIVÉE DES MÈRES. LES SACS ACCROCHÉS AU MUR CONTIENNENT LA BLOUSE ET LE MASQUE DE GAZE. UN ENFANT MALADE DU SIDA A ÉTÉ ISOLÉ DANS UNE SALLE PAR CRAINTE DE LA CONTAMINATION. (FRA)

▲ 84 ROUMANIE, HIVER 1989. CETTE PHOTO, PUBLIÉE DANS LES ANNALES 1989 DE *STERN*, A ÉTÉ PRISE AU CIMETIÈRE DE TIMISOARA LE 24 DÉCEMBRE. LES VICTIMES DU RÉGIME DE CEAUCESCU FURENT EXPOSÉES EN PLEIN AIR SUR DE SIMPLES DRAPS BLANCS. LIGOTÉES AU MOYEN D'UN FIL DE FER BARBELÉ, ELLES ONT ÉTÉ TORTURÉES À MORT PAR LA SECURITATE. (GER)

PHOTOGRAPHER:
JOHN VINK
REPRESENTATIVE:
AGENCE VU
CAMERA:
LEICA
FILM:
KODAK TRI-X 400
CLIENT:
PHOTO REPORTER
ART DIRECTOR:
J.P. ALDEBERT
■ 85

PHOTOGRAPHER:
PETER TURNLEY
REPRESENTATIVE:
NEWSWEEK/
BLACK STAR
CLIENT:
NEWSWEEK/STERN
▶■ 86

■ 85 THE CIRCUMSTANCES SURROUNDING THIS PHOTOGRAPH ARE SOLEMN, BUT NOT AS TRAGIC AS THE PHOTO MIGHT SUGGEST. THE HANGING FEET BELONG TO A CHILD PLAYFULLY HANGING FROM A BAR, WHILE THE GIRL MAKES ROPE FOR A HAMMOCK. THE CHILDREN ARE REFUGEES FROM EL SALVADORAN POLITICAL TURMOIL, LIVING IN THE CAMP OF MESA GRANDE IN SAN MARCOS, HONDURAS. THE PHOTO WAS PUBLISHED IN THE MAGAZINE *PHOTO REPORTER*. (FRA)

■ 86 A CHILD FROM THE ERITREAN REGION OF ETHIOPIA, LIVING IN THE TUG-WAJALE REFUGEE CAMP IN SOMALIA, A COUNTRY UNABLE TO PROVIDE SUBSTANTIAL RELIEF DUE TO THEIR OWN CIVIL WAR. THE GIRL IS SO WEAK FROM HUNGER THAT SHE HAS NOT THE STRENGTH TO BRUSH AWAY FLIES COVERING HER BODY. PUBLISHED IN BOTH *NEWSWEEK* AND *STERN* MAGAZINES. (USA/GER)

● 85 DIE UMSTÄNDE DIESER AUFNAHME SIND ERNST, ABER NICHT SO TRAGISCH, WIE MAN ANNEHMEN KÖNNTE. DIE HERABHÄNGENDEN FÜSSE GEHÖREN EINEM KIND, DAS SICH VON EINER STANGE HÄNGEN LÄSST, WÄHREND DAS MÄDCHEN EIN SEIL FÜR EINE HÄNGEMATTE ANFERTIGT. DIE KINDER SIND FLÜCHTLINGE AUS EL SALVADOR, DIE IM LAGER MESA GRANDE IN SAN MARCOS, HONDURAS, UNTERGEBRACHT SIND. DAS PHOTO WURDE IN DER ZEITSCHRIFT *PHOTO REPORTER* VERÖFFENTLICHT. (FRA)

● 86 EIN FLÜCHTLINGSKIND AUS ERITREA IM TUG-WAJALE-FLÜCHTLINGSLAGER IN SOMALIA, WO WEGEN DES DORT HERRSCHENDEN BÜRGERKRIEGS EBENFALLS HUNGER HERRSCHT, SO DASS MAN DEN FLÜCHTLINGEN KAUM HELFEN KANN. DAS MÄDCHEN IST ZU SCHWACH, UM DIE FLIEGEN AUF SEINEM KÖRPER ABZUSCHÜTTELN. DAS PHOTO ERSCHIEN IN *NEWSWEEK* UND IM *STERN*. (USA/GER)

▲ 85 PHOTO PRISE AU CAMP DE RÉFUGIÉS SALVADORIENS DE MESA GRANDE À SAN MARCOS, AU HONDURAS. BIEN QU'ASSEZ DRAMATIQUES, LES CIRCONSTANCES NE SONT PAS AUSSI TRAGIQUES QUE L'IMAGE LE SUGGÈRE: PENDANT QUE LA JEUNE FILLE TORD DES FILS POUR CONFECTIONNER DES CORDES DE HAMACS, UN ENFANT S'AMUSE À SE SUSPENDRE PAR LES BRAS DANS LE VIDE. CETTE PHOTOGRAPHIE A ÉTÉ PUBLIÉE DANS LE MAGAZINE *PHOTO REPORTER*. (FRA)

▲ 86 UNE FILLETTE DANS LE CAMP DE RÉFUGIÉS ÉRYTHRÉENS DE TUG-WAJALE EN SOMALIE OÙ, À CAUSE DE LA GUERRE CIVILE, RÈGNE AUSSI LA FAMINE. LA SITUATION REND TOUT SECOURS IMPOSSIBLE. LA FILLETTE EST TROP FAIBLE POUR CHASSER LES MOUCHES SUR SON CORPS. CETTE PHOTO A ÉTÉ PUBLIÉE DANS LES MAGAZINES *NEWSWEEK* ET *STERN*. (USA/GER)

STILL LIFE

STILLEBEN

NATURE MORTE

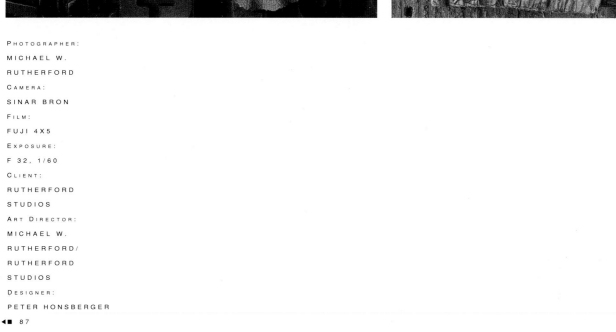

PHOTOGRAPHER:
MICHAEL W.
RUTHERFORD
CAMERA:
SINAR BRON
FILM:
FUJI 4X5
EXPOSURE:
F 32, 1/60
CLIENT:
RUTHERFORD
STUDIOS
ART DIRECTOR:
MICHAEL W.
RUTHERFORD/
RUTHERFORD
STUDIOS
DESIGNER:
PETER HONSBERGER

◄■ 87

PHOTOGRAPHER:
EBERHARD GRAMES
CAMERA:
WISTA 8X10
FILM:
FUJI CHROME
DESIGNER:
EBERHARD GRAMES
■ 88-91

■ 87 (PRECEDING SPREAD) THIS PHOTOGRAPH IS ONE OF A SERIES WHICH PHOTOGRAPHER MICHAEL W. RUTHERFORD TOOK OF HIS COLLECTION OF ANTIQUE TOYS. (USA)

■ 88-91 FOUR EXAMPLES OF STILL LIFES FROM A CALENDAR ENTITLED "MUSCHELHERZ UND FINKEN-SCHLAG" ("MUSSEL HEART AND FINCH'S SONG"). FROM LEFT TO RIGHT: A COMPOSITION WITH WOODEN CASE AND BLOSSOMS OF HOLLYHOCK; A COMPOSITION WITH THE SKETCHBOOK OF HOKUSAI, AUTUMN FRUIT, MARTEN'S SKULL AND JAPANESE BIRD; COMPOSITION WITH BRASILIAN BIRD FETISH, SILVER FOX FURS, KNIT WORK AND AMTURIA (FLOWER); COMPOSITION WITH IRIS, SKELETON OF A KORMORAN (BIRD), ELDER BLOSSOMS, WEATH-ERED WOOD AND LEAVES. (GER)

● 87 (VORHERGEHENDE SEITE) DIESE AUFNAHME GEHÖRT ZU EINER SERIE, DIE DER PHOTOGRAPH MICHAEL W. RUTHERFORD VON SEINER ANTIKEN SPIELZEUGSAMMLUNG MACHTE. (USA)

● 88-91 VIER BEISPIELE VON STILLEBEN AUS EINEM KALENDER MIT DEM TITEL «MUSCHELHERZ UND FINKENSCHLAG». VON LINKS NACH RECHTS: KOM-POSITION MIT HÖLZERNEM SETZKASTEN UND MALVENBLÜTEN; KOMPOSITION MIT SKIZZENBUCH DES HOKUSAI, HERBSTLICHEM FRUCHTSTAND, MARDERSCHÄDEL UND JAPANISCHEM KELCHENBALG; KOMPOSITION MIT BRASILIANISCHEM PFEFFERFRES-SERFETISCH, SILBERFUCHSFELLEN, GESTRICKTEM BUND UND ANTURIE; KOMPOSITION MIT SCHWERT-LILIE, KORMORANGERIPPE, HOLUNDERBLÜTEN, VER-WITTERTEN HOLZPLATTEN UND BLÄTTERN. (GER)

▲ 87 (PAGE PRÉCÉDENTE) CETTE NATURE MORTE EST TIRÉE D'UNE SÉRIE DE PHOTOGRAPHIES DE SA COLLECTION DE JOUETS ANCIENS QUE MICHAEL W. RUTHERFORD A PRISES DANS SON STUDIO. (USA)

▲ 88-91 QUATRE EXEMPLES D'UN CALENDRIER INTITULÉ «MUSCHELHERZ UND FINKENSCHLAG» («CŒUR DE MOULE ET CHANT DU PINSON»). 88: COMPOSITION AVEC CARACTÈRES TYPOGRAPHIQUES EN BOIS ET FLEURS DE MAUVE; 89: COMPOSITION AVEC LE LIVRE D'ESQUISSES DE HOKUSAÏ, FRUIT AUTOMNAL, CRÂNE DE MARTRE ET CORPS DE ROUGE-GORGE; 90: COMPOSITION AVEC TOUCAN, FOURRURE DE RENARD ARGENTÉ, BANDE DE TRICOT ET ANTURIUM; 91: COMPOSITION AVEC IRIS, SQUE-LETTE DE CORMORAN, FLEURS DE SUREAU ET FEUILLES MORTES. (GER)

PHOTOGRAPHER:
MICHAEL
MOLKENTHIN
REPRESENTATIVE:
ANITA GREEN
CAMERA:
8X10
FILM:
KODAK
ART DIRECTOR:
RICHARD DANNE
DESIGNER:
RICHARD DANNE
■ 92

PHOTOGRAPHER:
GREGOR SCHUSTER
CAMERA:
TOYO VIEW 45
FILM:
KODAK EPR 4X5
EXPOSURE:
FLASH LIGHT

CLIENT:
IKEA 93, 98/
PULS-DESIGN 94/
GRIGAT + NEU 96/
BSF 95, 97
ART DIRECTOR:
GREGOR SCHUSTER
►■ 93-98

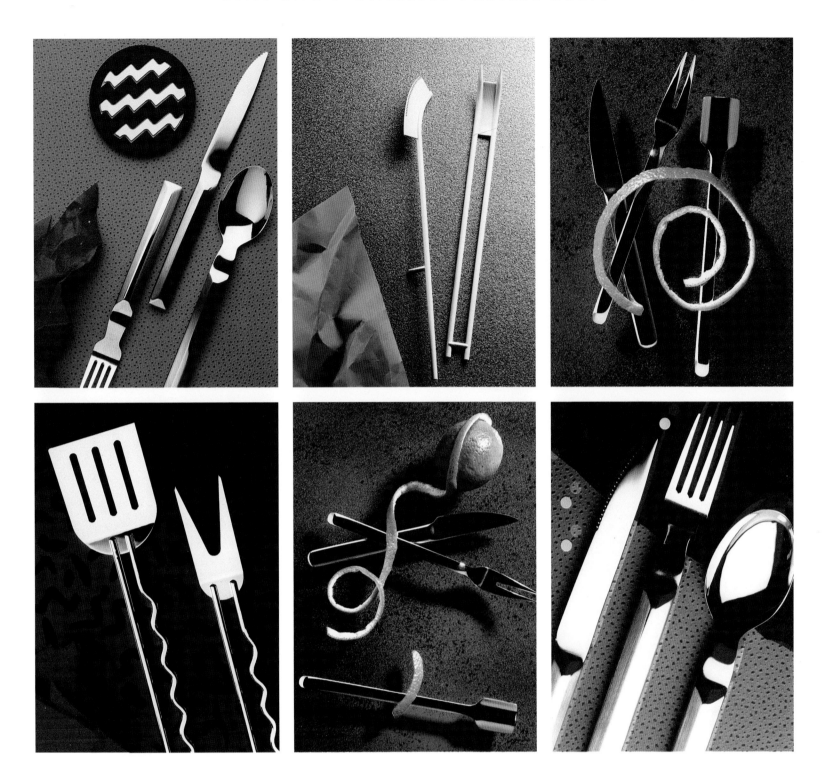

■ 92 STILL LIFE AS SELF-PROMOTION OF THE MOLKENTHIN STUDIOS IN NEW YORK. (USA)

■ 93-98 STILL LIFES WITH CUTLERY. THIS PAGE FROM LEFT TO RIGHT AND FROM TOP TO BOTTOM: FREE STUDY OF A SET DESIGNED FOR THE IKEA STORES PHOTOGRAPHED ON A SHEET OF GLASS; HAND-MADE PROTOTYPES MADE BY PULS DESIGN; A SET OF CUTLERY MADE BY BSF; HAND-MADE PROTOTYPES BY GRIGAT + NEU DESIGN; A SET MADE BY BSF; FREE STUDY OF A SET (ON A SHEET OF GLASS) DESIGNED FOR IKEA. (GER)

● 92 STILLEBEN ALS EIGENWERBUNG DER MOLKEN-THIN STUDIOS AUS NEW YORK. (USA)

● 93-98 BESTECKE ALS STILLEBEN PHOTOGRA-PHIERT. DIESE SEITE V.L.N.R.: FREIE STUDIE EINES BESTECKS, DAS FÜR IKEA ENTWORFEN WURDE; HANDGEMACHTE PROTOTYPEN, EIN ENTWURF VON PULS DESIGN; BESTECK VON BSF; HANDGEFERTIGTE PROTOTYPEN VON GRIGAT + NEU DESIGN; EIN BESTECK VON BSF; FREIE STUDIE EINES IKEA-BESTECKS. DIE IKEA-BESTECKE WURDEN AUF EINER GLASSCHEIBE PHOTOGRAPHIERT. (GER)

▲ 92 NATURE MORTE – AUTOPROMOTION DES STUDIOS MOLKENTHIN À NEW YORK. (USA)

▲ 93-98 COUVERTS PHOTOGRAPHIÉS SOUS FORME DE NATURE MORTE. SUR CETTE PAGE DE GAUCHE À DROITE ET DE HAUT EN BAS: ÉTUDE LIBRE D'UN COUVERT CRÉÉ POUR IKEA; PROTOTYPES FAITS MAIN, CRÉATIONS DE PULS DESIGN; COUVERT DE BSF; PROTOTYPES FAITS MAIN DE GRIGAT + NEU DESIGN; COUVERT DE BSF; ÉTUDE LIBRE CRÉÉ POUR IKEA. LES COUVERTS POUR IKEA ONT ÉTÉ PHOTOGRAPHIÉS SUR UNE PLAQUE DE VERRE. (GER)

PHOTOGRAPHER:
JIM KRANTZ
CAMERA:
SINAR 4X5
FILM:
KODAK 64 DAYLIGHT
CLIENT:
INFORMATION
TECHNOLOGY
DESIGNER:
CARTER WEITZ
■ 99

PHOTOGRAPHER:
JIM KRANTZ
CAMERA:
SINAR 4X5
FILM:
KODAK 64 TUNGSTEN
CLIENT:
NEBRASKA PUBLIC
POWER DISTRICT
ART DIRECTOR:
CARTER WEITZ
● 100

PHOTOGRAPHER:
IRA GARBER
CAMERA:
SINAR 4X5
FILM:
FUJI RDP
CLIENT:
IRA GARBER
ART DIRECTOR:
IRA GARBER
DESIGNER:
SUZANNE DUNKL
▶■ 101

■ 99 THE ROPE IN THIS PHOTOGRAPH IS MEANT TO SERVE AS A METAPHOR TO IMPLY INTEGRATION AND FLEXIBILITY—THE QUALITIES OF A DATA PROCESSING COMPANY (WHICH COMMISSIONED THE PHOTOGRAPH). (USA)

■ 100 PHOTOGRAPH FROM A BOOK PUBLICIZING THE GOOD LIFE IN NEBRASKA. AMONG THE BENEFITS ONE CAN ENJOY IN MOVING TO THIS MID-WESTERN FARM STATE IS A WHOLESOME AND FAMILY-ORIENTED LIFESTYLE. (USA)

■ 101 EXAMPLE FROM A SERIES OF STILL LIFES OF ANTIQUE FISHING EQUIPMENT PHOTOGRAPHED IN A STUDIO. (USA)

● 99 DAS SEIL IN DIESER AUFNAHME DIENT ALS METHAPHER FÜR INTEGRATION UND FLEXIBILITÄT, DIE GRUNDBEGRIFFE EINES KONZEPTS FÜR DAS ERSCHEINUNGSBILD EINES RECHENZENTRUMS (AUFTRAGGEBER DIESER AUFNAHME). (USA)

● 100 AUFNAHME FÜR EIN BUCH, DAS DIE VORTEILE VON NEBRASKA ALS WOHNORT ANPREIST. SIE ZEIGT DEN LEBENSSTIL, DEN MAN ERWARTEN DARF, WENN MAN EIN SOLIDES, FAMILIENORIENTIERTES LEBEN FÜHRT. (USA)

● 101 BEISPIEL AUS EINER REIHE VON STILLEBEN ANTIKER ANGELGERÄTE, AUFGENOMMEN IN EINEM STUDIO. (USA)

▲ 99 LA CORDE REPRÉSENTÉE SYMBOLISE LES NOTIONS D'INTÉGRATION ET DE FLEXIBILITÉ QUI SONT À LA BASE DU CONCEPT D'IDENTITÉ COMMERCIALE D'UNE FIRME DE TRAITEMENT DE DONNÉES. (USA)

▲ 100 PHOTO RÉALISÉE POUR UN LIVRE QUI VANTE LES AVANTAGES DU NEBRASKA COMME LIEU D'HABITATION. L'IMAGE ILLUSTRE LE STYLE DE VIE QUE TOUTE FAMILLE SOLIDEMENT ÉTABLIE PEUT Y MENER. (USA)

▲ 101 EXEMPLE D'UNE SÉRIE DE NATURES MORTES REPRÉSENTANT D'ANCIENS MODÈLES DE CANNES À PÊCHE. PRISES EN STUDIO. (USA)

PHOTOGRAPHER:

JIM KRANTZ

CAMERA:

SINAR 4X5

FILM:

KODAK 64 DAYLIGHT

CLIENT:

UNION PACIFIC

RAILROAD

■ 102

■ 102 THE TRAIN SHOWN IN THIS PHOTOGRAPH FOR UNION PACIFIC RAILROAD IS AN ACTUAL PROTO-TYPE MODEL WEIGHING 80 LBS WITH A HEIGHT OF 4 FEET. (USA)

■ 103 BIRD OF PARADISE FLOWERS PHOTOGRAPHED ON A PIECE OF WEATHERED CORRUGATED METAL WITH MIXED SOURCE LIGHTING (COMBINATION OF HARD AND SOFT LIGHT). THIS SHOT IS USED FOR A SELF-PROMOTIONAL POSTER BY PHOTOGRAPHER KEN REID. (USA)

■ 104 THIS PHOTOGRAPH WAS TAKEN DURING THE COURSE OF AN ASSIGNMENT FOR THE SHERRY FEDERATION OF SPAIN. THE BRIEF HAD BEEN TO CAPTURE THE SPIRIT OF THE TOWN JEREZ, WHICH IS FAMOUS FOR ITS SHERRY. USED FOR SELF-PROMOTION BY THE PHOTOGRAPHER. (SPA)

● 102 DER ZUG IN DIESER AUFNAHME FÜR DIE UNION PACIFIC RAILROAD IST EIN ECHTER PROTO-TYP FÜR DIE PRODUKTION. DAS MODELL WIEGT 73 PFUND UND IST 1,20 M HOCH. (USA)

● 103 BLUMEN, DIE »PARADIESVÖGEL« GENANNT WERDEN, AUFGENOMMEN MIT EINER KOMBINATION VON HARTEM UND WEICHEM LICHT AUF EINEM VER-WITTERTEN STÜCK METALL. DIE AUFNAHME WURDE FÜR EIN EIGENWERBUNGSPLAKAT DES PHOTOGRA-PHEN KEN REID VERWENDET. (USA)

● 104 DIESES PHOTO ENTSTAND WÄHREND AUF-NAHMEN FÜR DEN VERBAND DER SHERRY-PRODU-ZENTEN SPANIENS. AUFGABE WAR ES, DIE ATMOS-PHÄRE DER FÜR IHREN SHERRY BEKANNTEN STADT JEREZ EINZUFANGEN. DER PHOTOGRAPH VERWEN-DET DIESE AUFNAHME ALS EIGENWERBUNG. (SPA)

▲ 102 LE TRAIN SUR CETTE PHOTO POUR LA COMPAGNIE DE CHEMINS DE FER UNION PACIFIC EST UN VÉRITABLE PROTOTYPE. LE MODÈLE PÈSE ENVIRON 33 KG ET MESURE 1,20 M. (USA)

▲ 103 CES FLEURS APPELÉES »OISEAUX DU PA-RADIS« ONT ÉTÉ PHOTOGRAPHIÉES SUR UN VIEUX MORCEAU DE TÔLE ONDULÉE EN COMBINANT ÉCLAIRAGE VIOLENT ET LUMIÈRE DOUCE. PUBLIÉE SOUS FORME D'AFFICHE, CETTE PHOTO SERT D'AUTOPROMOTION AU PHOTOGRAPHE. (USA)

▲ 104 CETTE PHOTO A ÉTÉ RÉALISÉE LORS DE PRISES DE VUES POUR L'ASSOCIATION DES PRO-DUCTEURS DE SHERRY D'ESPAGNE. IL S'AGISSAIT DE SAISIR L'ATMOSPHÈRE DE LA VILLE DE JEREZ, CÉLÈBRE POUR SON SHERRY. CETTE PHOTO SERT D'AUTOPROMOTION AU PHOTOGRAPHE. (SPA)

■ 105 THIS STILL LIFE OF A SILVER FLASK WAS SHOT WITH A TUNGSTEN LIGHT SOURCE IN THE STUDIO. IT WAS USED AS SELF-PROMOTION BY PHOTOGRAPHER ROBERT TARDIO. (USA)

■ 106 FROM A SERIES OF FOUR STILL LIFES FOR A DESIGNER FOR WHICH THE PHOTOGRAPHER WAS GIVEN CARTE BLANCHE. (USA)

■ 107 PART OF A STILL LIFE SERIES FOR SELF-PROMOTIONAL PURPOSES PHOTOGRAPHED WITH STUDIO FLASH LIGHTING. (USA)

■ 108 THIS STILL LIFE, CREATED FOR USE IN A PROMOTIONAL BROCHURE BY CONSOLIDATED PAPERS IN COMMEMORATION OF THE 50TH ANNIVERSARY OF THE NATIONAL BASEBALL HALL OF FAME AND MUSEUM, CONTAINS: A 1916 NATIONAL LEAGUE BASEBALL, MAX CAREY'S 1917 FIELDER'S GLOVE, A 1910 SCOREBOOK THAT BELONGED TO CASEY STENGEL, A CATCHER'S CHEST PROTECTOR (CIRCA 1900) AND A 1902 SEASON PASS FOR THE CINCINNATI REDS. (USA)

● 105 DIESES STILLEBEN MIT EINEM SILBERFLAKON WURDE MIT TUNGSTEN-LICHT IM STUDIO AUFGENOMMEN. DER PHOTOGRAPH ROBERT TARDIO VERWENDET ES ALS EIGENWERBUNG. (USA)

● 106 AUS EINER REIHE VON VIER STILLEBEN FÜR EIN DESIGN-STUDIO, DAS DEM PHOTOGRAPHEN VÖLLIG FREIE HAND LIESS. (USA)

● 107 DIESE STUDIOAUFNAHME GEHÖRT ZU EINER REIHE VON STILLEBEN, DIE DER PHOTOGRAPH ALS EIGENWERBUNG VERWENDET. (USA)

● 108 EIN BALL DER NATIONAL (BASEBALL) LEAGUE VON 1916, DER HANDSCHUH DES BERÜHMTEN BASEBALLSPIELERS MAX CAREY VON 1917, EIN SPIELPROTOKOLLBUCH VON 1910, DAS CASEY STENGEL GEHÖRTE, BRUSTSCHUTZ DES FÄNGERS (CA. 1900) UND EINE SAISONKARTE (1902) FÜR DIE CINCINNATI REDS. DIE AUFNAHME STAMMT AUS EINER BROSCHÜRE VON CONSOLIDATED PAPERS, DEREN THEMA DAS 50JÄHRIGE BESTEHEN DES NATIONAL BASEBALL MUSEUMS IN DEN USA IST. (USA)

▲ 105 CETTE NATURE MORTE AU FLACON D'ARGENT A ÉTÉ PRISE EN STUDIO AVEC UN ÉCLAIRAGE AU TUNGSTÉNE. LE PHOTOGRAPHE ROBERT TARDIO L'UTILISE POUR SON AUTOPROMOTION. (USA)

▲ 106 D'UNE SÉRIE DE QUATRE NATURES MORTES RÉALISÉES POUR UN STUDIO DE DESIGN QUI AVAIT DONNÉ CARTE BLANCHE AU PHOTOGRAPHE. (USA)

▲ 107 PHOTO PRISE EN STUDIO TIRÉE D'UNE SÉRIE DE NATURES MORTES QUE LE PHOTOGRAPHE EMPLOIE COMME AUTOPROMOTION. (USA)

▲ 108 UNE BALLE DE L'ÉQUIPE NATIONALE DE BASE-BALL DE 1916, LE GANT DU CÉLÉBRE JOUEUR MAX CAREY, DE 1917, UN LIVRE DE PROTOCOLE DE JEUX DE 1910 AYANT APPARTENU À CASEY STENGEL, LE CORSELET DE PROTECTION D'UN GARDIEN DE BUT (VERS 1900) ET UN ABONNEMENT POUR LA SAISON 1902 DES CINCINNATI REDS. CETTE PHOTO PROVIENT D'UNE BROCHURE DE CONSOLIDATED PAPERS SUR LE THÈME DU 50E ANNIVERSAIRE DU NATIONAL BASEBALL MUSEUM. (USA)

PHOTOGRAPHER:
ROBERT TARDIO
REPRESENTATIVE:
COLLEEN MCKAY
CAMERA:
SINAR P2 8X10/
NIKKOR 300MM
FILM:
KODAK 100 EKTACHROME 6122
DESIGNER:
ROBERT TARDIO/
ANITA CALERO
■ 105

PHOTOGRAPHER:
HANS NELEMAN
CAMERA:
SINAR
FILM:
EKTACHROME 8X10
CLIENT:
DESIGNTEX
ART DIRECTOR:
RICK BIEDEL
DESIGNER:
BONNELL DESIGN
■ 106

PHOTOGRAPHER:

SIGURDUR STEFAN

JONSSON

CAMERA:

CALUMET

FILM:

KODAK EKTACHROME

4X5 EPP 100

CLIENT:

SIGURDUR STEFAN

JONSSON

ART DIRECTOR:

SIGURDUR STEFAN

JONSSON

DESIGNER:

SIGURDUR STEFAN

JONSSON

■ 107

PHOTOGRAPHER:

TERRY HEFFERNAN

CAMERA:

SINAR 8X10

FILM:

KODAK EKTACHROME

100

CLIENT:

CONSOLIDATED

PAPERS, INC.

DESIGNER:

LESLEE AVCHEN/

LAURIE JACOBI

■ 108

BEST STILL LIFE

Photographer:

KLAUS FRAHM

Camera:

POLAROID 20X24

Film:

POLAPAN 52

Exposure:

F 98, 2 POPS, 12000 WS

Photo Editor:

KLAUS FRAHM

Client:

KLAUS FRAHM

Art Director:

KLAUS FRAHM

Designer:

KLAUS FRAHM

■ 109-111

■ 109-111 THE STILL LIFES WITH FLOWERS ABOVE RECEIVED THE "BEST OF CATEGORY AWARD" OF GRAPHIS PHOTO 91, MADE POSSIBLE BY THE PROFESSIONAL PHOTOGRAPHY DIVISION OF THE EASTMAN KODAK COMPANY. THE SERIES IS THE RESULT OF PERSONAL WORK DONE BY PHOTOGRAPHER KLAUS FRAHM. (GER)

● 109-111 DIE STILLEBEN MIT BLUMEN OBEN WURDEN MIT DEM «BEST OF CATEGORY» PREIS, VON DER PROFESSIONAL PHOTOGRAPHY DIVISION DER FIRMA EASTMAN KODAK FÜR GRAPHIS PHOTO 91 GESTIFTET, AUSGEZEICHNET. DER PHOTOGRAPH KLAUS FRAHM MACHTE DIESE SERIE WÄHREND EINES WORKSHOPS. (GER)

▲ 109-111 LES NATURES MORTES AVEC FLEURS FIGURANT CI-DESSUS ONT REÇU LE «BEST OF CATEGORY AWARD» DE GRAPHIS PHOTO 91, SPONSORISÉ PAR LA SECTION PHOTOGRAPHIC PROFESSIONNELLE DE EASTMAN KODAK. CETTE SÉRIE AVAIT ÉTÉ RÉALISÉE PAR LE PHOTOGRAPHE KLAUS FRAHM AU COURS D'UN WORKSHOP. (GER)

PHOTOGRAPHER:
CHARLES SHOTWELL
CAMERA:
SINAR
FILM:
POLAROID TYPE 59
CLIENT:
CHARLES SHOTWELL
ART DIRECTOR:
STEVE LISKA
DESIGNER:
ANNE SCHEDLER
■ 113

■ 113 AN UNUSUAL COMPOSITION WITH AN ALARM CLOCK AND A FLOWER VASE IN A POLAROID USED AS SELF-PROMOTION BY PHOTOGRAPHER CHARLES SHOTWELL. (USA)

■ 114 KATHRYN KLEINMAN'S INTERPRETATION OF A "WALL FLOWER" PHOTOGRAPHED FOR A BROCHURE WITH A FLORAL THEME USED TO DEMONSTRATE PAPER QUALITY. (USA)

■ 115 ENTITLED "KYOTO 1885," THE SUBJECT OF TEA SHOWN IN A TYPICAL FASHION. THIS PHOTO-GRAPH IS ONE FROM A SERIES ENTITLED "L'HEURE DU THÉ" AND WAS USED IN A SPECIAL PUBLICATION BY DAMANN TEA IMPORTERS. (FRA)

● 113 POLAROID-AUFNAHME VON EINER UNGEWÖHN-LICHEN KOMPOSITION VON WECKER UND BLUMEN-VASE, VON CHARLES SHOTWELL ALS EIGENWER-BUNG VERWENDET. (USA)

● 114 KATHRYN KLEINMANS VORSTELLUNG EINES «MAUERBLÜMCHENS». DIE AUFNAHME GEHÖRT ZU EINER DEM THEMA BLUMEN GEWIDMETEN BROSCHÜ-RE, DIE EINE PAPIERQUALITÄT VORSTELLT. (USA)

● 115 «KYOTO 1885» – DAS THEMA TEE ANHAND VON CLICHÉS DARGESTELLT. DIE AUFNAHME GE-HÖRT ZU EINER SERIE MIT DEM TITEL «L'HEURE DU THÉ», DIE VOM TEE-IMPORTEUR DAMANN FÜR EINE FIRMENPUBLIKATION VERWENDET WURDE. (FRA)

▲ 113 COMPOSITION INATTENDUE POUR CETTE NATURE MORTE AU VASE ET AU RÉVEIL RÉALISÉE SUR POLAROÏD ET SERVANT D'AUTOPROMOTION AU PHOTOGRAPHE. (USA)

▲ 114 LE «MUR FLEURI» IMAGINÉ PAR KATHRYN KLEINMAN. IL S'AGISSAIT D'UNE COMMANDE POUR UNE BROCHURE CONSACRÉE AUX FLEURS PRÉSEN-TANT UNE COLLECTION DE PAPIERS. (USA)

▲ 115 «KYOTO 1885» – LE THÈME DU THÉ AU TRA-VERS DES CLICHÉS TRADITIONNELS. LA PHOTO FAIT PARTIE DE LA SÉRIE «L'HEURE DU THÉ» ET ELLE A ÉTÉ UTILISÉE PAR L'IMPORTATEUR DE THÉS DE LUXE DAMANN POUR UNE BROCHURE. (FRA)

PHOTOGRAPHER:
KATHRYN KLEINMAN
CAMERA:
SINAR
FILM:
EKTACHROME PLUS
100
EXPOSURE:
F 22.5
CLIENT:
CONSOLIDATED
PAPER COMPANY
ART DIRECTOR:
MIRANDA MOSS/
YAMAMOTO MOSS
■ 114

PHOTOGRAPHER:
MICHEL DUBOIS
REPRESENTATIVE:
PAULE FRIEDLAND
CAMERA:
SINAR P 4X5
FILM:
T-MAX 100 ISO
PHOTO EDITOR:
EDITIONS LOUISE
CLIENT:
SOCIÉTÉ DAMANN
ART DIRECTOR:
MICHEL DUBOIS
DESIGNER:
MICHEL DUBOIS
■ 115

PHOTOGRAPHER:
YUTAKA KAWACHI
REPRESENTATIVE:
KENNEY & MEAD
CAMERA:
TOYO CAMERA 8X10/
210MM MACRO
FILM:
EKTACHROME 8X10
■ 116-118

■ 116-118 SERIES OF PERSONAL WORK USED BY YUTAKA KAWACHI FOR SELF-PROMOTIONAL PURPOSES. THE PHOTOGRAPH ON TOP SHOWS THE PHOTOGRAPHER AT THE AGE OF 10 WITH HIS FAMILY, THE COMPUR CAMERA IS FROM THE 1930S. THE VASE IN THE PHOTO IN THE MIDDLE IS BY LALIQUE; IT WAS FIRST SHOT IN BLACK-AND-WHITE, THEN THE PRINT WAS PHOTOGRAPHED IN COLOR WITH THE ROSE PETALS FALLING IN FRONT OF IT. THE STILL LIFE AT RIGHT SHOWS A LEATHER JACKET FROM A NEW YORK SHOP CALLED COCKPIT. THE GUN IS A 9 MM BERETTA. (USA)

● 116-118 EINE REIHE VON STILLEBEN, DIE DER NEW YORKER PHOTOGRAPH YUTAKA KAWACHI ALS EIGENWERBUNG VERWENDET. DAS PHOTO AUS DEM FAMILIENALBUM ZEIGT DEN PHOTOGRAPHEN IM ALTER VON 10 MIT SEINEN ELTERN, DIE COMPUR-KAMERA STAMMT AUS DEN 30ER JAHREN. DIE VASE AUF DEM MITTLEREN PHOTO IST VON LALIQUE; SIE WURDE ZUERST IN SCHWARZWEISS AUFGENOMMEN, DANN WURDE DER ABZUG FARBIG MIT FALLENDEN ROSENBLÄTTERN PHOTOGRAPHIERT. IM STILLEBEN RECHTS SIEHT MAN EINE LEDERJACKE AUS EINEM NEW YORKER LADEN UND EINE 9MM-BERETTA. (USA)

▲ 116-118 NATURES MORTES DE YUTAKA KAWACHI. L'APPAREIL PHOTO COMPUR DATE DES ANNÉES 1930 ET LA PHOTOGRAPHIE MONTRE KAWACHI À L'ÂGE DE 10 ANS, EN COMPAGNIE DE SES PARENTS. SUR LA PHOTO DU CENTRE, LE VASE EST UNE CRÉATION DE LALIQUE. IL AVAIT ÉTÉ D'ABORD PHOTOGRAPHIÉ EN NOIR ET BLANC; LES PÉTALES DE ROSES FURENT PRISES ULTÉRIEUREMENT EN COULEURS, DEVANT UNE ÉPREUVE DE LA PREMIÈRE PHOTO. CI-DESSUS, LA NATURE MORTE REPRÉSENTE OUTRE LA MONTRE UN BLOUSON ACHETÉ À NEW YORK ET UN PISTOLET BERETTA 9 MM. (USA)

PHOTOGRAPHER:
DOUGLAS BENEZRA
CAMERA:
SINAR F1
FILM:
EKTACHROME 64
CLIENT:
ACCENT EDITIONS/
PORTAL
PUBLICATIONS
ART DIRECTOR:
BETTE TRONO
■ 119

PHOTOGRAPHER:
DIDIER GAILLARD
CAMERA:
NIKON
CLIENT:
ART UNLIMITED
AMSTERDAM
◄■ 120-123

■ 119 STILL LIFE WITH ROSES AND WHITE TABLE CLOTH USED AS SELF-PROMOTION BY PHOTOGRAPHER DOUGLAS BENEZRA. (USA)

■ 120-123 PERSONAL WORK OF PHOTOGRAPHER DIDIER GAILLARD, AVAILABLE AS POSTCARDS PUBLISHED BY ART UNLIMITED, AMSTERDAM. (NLD)

● 119 STILLEBEN MIT ROSEN UND WEISSEM TISCHTUCH ALS EIGENWERBUNG DES PHOTOGRAPHEN DOUGLAS BENEZRA. (USA)

● 120-123 FREIE STUDIEN DES PHOTOGRAPHEN DIDIER GAILLARD. SIE SIND ALS POSTKARTEN BEI ART UNLIMITED, AMSTERDAM, ERHÄLTLICH. (NLD)

▲ 119 VASE DE ROSES SUR UNE NAPPE BLANCHE POUR CETTE NATURE MORTE – AUTOPROMOTION DU PHOTOGRAPHE DOUGLAS BENEZRA. (USA)

▲ 120-123 CES RECHERCHES PERSONNELLES ONT ÉTÉ ÉDITÉES EN CARTES POSTALES CHEZ ART UNLIMITED, À AMSTERDAM. (NLD)

PHOTOGRAPHER:
ROGER TURQUETI
CAMERA:
SINAR
CLIENT:
VOTRE BEAUTE
ART DIRECTOR:
PHILIPPE VAN DEN
PLAS
◄■ 124

PHOTOGRAPHER:
TERRY HEFFERNAN
CAMERA:
SINAR 8X10
FILM:
KODAK EKTACHROME
100
CLIENT:
THE AMERICAN
MUSEUM OF FLY
FISHING
■ 125

■ 124 THIS PHOTO SERVED AS AN ILLUSTRATION IN AN ARTICLE ON SHAMPOO IN THE FRENCH MAGAZINE *VOTRE BEAUTÉ*. (FRA)

● 124 DIESE AUFNAHME DIENTE ALS ILLUSTRATION EINES BEITRAGS ÜBER SHAMPOOS IN DER FRANZÖSISCHEN ZEITSCHRIFT *VOTRE BEAUTÉ*. (FRA)

▲ 124 CETTE PHOTOGRAPHIE A SERVI D'ILLUSTRATION POUR UN ARTICLE SUR LES SHAMPOOINGS PUBLIÉ DANS LE MAGAZINE *VOTRE BEAUTÉ*. (FRA)

■ 125 TURN OF THE CENTURY INDUSTRIALIST TURNED PHILANTHROPIST ANDREW CARNEGIE'S FLY-FISHING EQUIPMENT PHOTOGRAPHED BY TERRY HEFFERNAN AS PART OF A SERIES FOR THE AMERICAN MUSEUM OF FLY FISHING. (USA)

● 125 DIE ANGELAUSRÜSTUNG DES AMERIKANISCHEN GROSSINDUSTRIELLEN UND PHILANTROPEN ANDREW CARNEGIE, AUFGENOMMEN VON TERRY HEFFERNAN FÜR DAS AMERIKANISCHE MUSEUM FÜR FLIEGENFISCHEN. (USA)

▲ 125 L'ÉQUIPEMENT DE PÊCHE AYANT APPARTENU À L'INDUSTRIEL AMÉRICAIN ANDREW CARNEGIE, DEVENU PHILANTROPE, PHOTOGRAPHIÉ PAR TERRY HEFFERNAN POUR LE MUSÉE AMÉRICAIN DE LA PÊCHE À LA MOUCHE. (USA)

PHOTOGRAPHER:

EIICHIRO SAKATA

CAMERA:

TOYO VIEW 45G

FILM:

KODAK EPP 4X5

CLIENT:

NIPPON KODO CO.

LTD.

ART DIRECTOR:

NORINE LUKACZYK

DESIGNER:

NORINE LUKACZYK

■ 126, 127

PHOTOGRAPHER:

RINGO TANG

FILM:

KODAK T-MAX

ART DIRECTOR:

RINGO WONG

▶■ 128

■ 126, 127 THESE PHOTOGRAPHS WERE COMMIS-
SIONED FOR A CORPORATE BROCHURE OF A JAPA-
NESE COMPANY PRODUCING TRADITIONAL AND
MODERN INCENSE. (JPN)

■ 128 LILY REFLECTED IN A PIECE OF SLIGHTLY
CORRUGATED METAL, A PERSONAL WORK OF HONG
KONG BASED PHOTOGRAPHER RINGO TANG. (HKG)

● 126, 127 DIESE AUFNAHMEN WURDEN IN DER
FIRMENBROSCHÜRE EINES JAPANISCHEN HERSTEL-
LERS VON TRADITIONELLEN UND MODERNEN DUFT-
STOFFEN ABGEBILDET. (JPN)

● 128 EINE LILIE, REFLEKTIERT VON EINEM STÜCK
GEWELLTEN METALL – EINE FREIE STUDIE DES PHO-
TOGRAPHEN RINGO TANG AUS HONGKONG. (HKG)

▲ 126, 127 CES PHOTOS SONT TIRÉES DE LA
BROCHURE DESTINÉE AU GRAND PUBLIC D'UNE
FIRME JAPONAISE FABRIQUANT DE L'ENCENS
TRADITIONNEL ET MODERNE. (JPN)

▲ 128 UN LYS QUI SE REFLÉTE DANS UN MORCEAU
DE MÉTAL DÉFORMÉ – ÉTUDE PERSONNELLE D'UN
PHOTOGRAPHE DE HONKONG, RINGO TANG. (HKG)

FOOD

LEBENSMITTEL

CUISINE

■ 129 (PRECEDING SPREAD) THIS UNUSUAL VIEW OF ORANGES STILL ON THE BRANCHES OFFERS A STRIKING CONTRAST TO THE PHOTOGRAPH'S DELICATE COLOR COMPOSITION. (USA)

● 129 (VORHERGEHENDE SEITE) ORANGEN, MIT TEILEN DER ÄSTE AUFGENOMMEN, DIE EINEN EIGENARTIGEN KONTRAST ZU DER SENSIBLEN FARBKOMBINATION BILDEN. (USA)

▲ 129 (PAGE PRÉCÉDENTE) LES ORANGES AVEC LEUR TIGE FORMENT UN CONTRASTE ÉTRANGE AVEC LES AUTRES ÉLÉMENTS DE CETTE IMAGE AUX COULEURS EXTRÊMEMENT SUBTILES. (USA)

■ 130 UNPUBLISHED PHOTOGRAPH USED FOR SELF-PROMOTION AND FOR THE PHOTOGRAPHER'S PORTFOLIO. (USA)

● 130 UNVERÖFFENTLICHTE AUFNAHME, DIE ALS EIGENWERBUNG UND IM PORTFOLIO VON CAROL KAPLAN VERWENDET WIRD. (USA)

▲ 130 PHOTO INÉDITE UTILISÉE COMME AUTOPRO-MOTION ET FIGURANT DANS LE PORTFOLIO DE CAROL KAPLAN. (USA)

■ 131 EXAMPLE FROM A SERIES OF PHOTOGRAPHS COMMISSIONED TO FEATURE SPECIALTIES CREATED BY MEMBERS OF THE CLUB OF CHEFS FOR CATHAY PACIFIC AIRWAYS' INFLIGHT MENUS. "MALMÖ MARINATION" SYMBOLIZES THE DISHES CREATED BY WERNER VÖGELI, CHEF TO THE KING OF SWEDEN PHOTOGRAPHED BY JEREMY TAYLOR. (USA)

● 131 AUS EINER PHOTOREIHE, IN DER SPEZIALI-TÄTEN VORGESTELLT WERDEN, DIE MITGLIEDER EINES CLUBS VON SPITZENKÖCHEN FÜR DIE BORD-MENUS DER CATHAY PACIFIC AIRWAYS KREIERT HABEN. «MALMÖ MARINATION» SYMBOLISIERT DIE GERICHTE VON WERNER VÖGELI, DEM KOCH DES SCHWEDISCHEN KÖNIGSHAUSES. (USA)

▲ 131 D'UNE SÉRIE DE PHOTOS PRÉSENTANT LES SPÉCIALITÉS CRÉÉES PAR LES MEMBRES DU «CLUB DES CHEFS DES CHEFS» POUR LE MENU DE BORD DE LA COMPAGNIE AÉRIENNE CATHAY PACIFIC AIR-WAYS. LE POISSON «MARINÉ À LA MALMÖ» INTRO-DUIT LES PLATS DU CUISINIER DE LA MAISON ROYALE DE SUÉDE, WERNER VÖGELI. (USA)

■ 132 PHOTOGRAPH USED IN A FASHION FEATURE IN *VOGUE PARIS*. (FRA)

● 132 AUFNAHME AUS EINEM MODE-ARTIKEL IN *VOGUE PARIS*. (FRA)

▲ 132 PHOTO D'UN REPORTAGE DE MODE PUBLIÉ DANS *VOGUE PARIS*. (FRA)

PHOTOGRAPHER:
LAURIE RUBIN
REPRESENTATIVE:
RANDI FIAT & ASSOC.
FILM:
EKTACHROME 64
CLIENT:
CANTEEN CORP.
DESIGNER:
RANDEE ROBIN
◄■ 129

PHOTOGRAPHER:
CAROL KAPLAN
REPRESENTATIVE:
ROBIN FERNSELL
CAMERA:
NIKON
FILM:
AGFACHROME 1000 RS
CLIENT:
CAROL KAPLAN
STUDIOS
STYLIST:
JACQUELINE LEMIEUX
■ 130

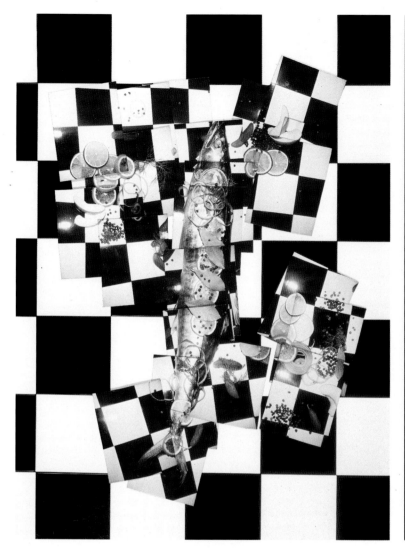

PHOTOGRAPHER:

JEREMY TAYLOR

CAMERA:

TOYO VIEW/

POLAROID SPECTRA

FILM:

POLAROID SPECTRA

FILM EPP 5X4

PHOTO EDITOR:

MARTY HALL

CLIENT:

CATHAY PACIFIC

AIRWAYS

ART DIRECTOR:

PETER COOK

DESIGNER:

LILIAN TANG

■ 131

PHOTOGRAPHER:

TIZIANO MAGNI

REPRESENTATIVE:

JULIAN MEIJER

ASSOCIATES

CLIENT:

VOGUE PARIS

ART DIRECTOR:

MARY SHANAHAN

■ 132

PHOTOGRAPHER:

LOUIS WALLACH

REPRESENTATIVE:

MARGE CASEY

ASSOCIATES

PHOTO EDITOR:

LOUIS WALLACH

CLIENT:

LOUIS WALLACH

PHOTOGRAPHY

ART DIRECTOR:

STANLEY CHURCH

DESIGNER:

STANLEY CHURCH

◀■ 133

PHOTOGRAPHER:

MARK WENDELL

HUTCHISON

REPRESENTATIVE:

CHARLES STROUPE

CAMERA:

SINAR F1 4X5/210MM

RODENSTOCK

FILM:

FUJICHROME 100/

KODAK 100

(2 VERSIONS)

EXPOSURE:

F 45/MULTIPLE

FLASH EXPOSURE

CLIENT:

LIGHT IMAGE, INC.

ART DIRECTOR:

MARK WENDELL

HUTCHISON

DESIGNER:

MARK WENDELL

HUTCHISON

■ 134

PHOTOGRAPHER:
TERRY HEFFERNAN
CAMERA:
SINAR 8X10
FILM:
KODAK EKTACHROME
100
CLIENT:
THE AMERICAN
MUSEUM OF FLY
FISHING
■ 135

PHOTOGRAPHER:
JAN OSWALD
CAMERA:
SINAR P 4X5
FILM:
KODAK EKTA-
CHROME 64
ART DIRECTOR:
JAN OSWALD
DESIGNER:
JAN OSWALD
■ 136, 137

■ 135 U.S. PRESIDENT (STEPHEN) GROVER CLEVE-LAND'S FLIES ON AN ATLANTIC SALMON. PHOTO-GRAPHED BY TERRY HEFFERNAN FOR A CALENDAR OF THE AMERICAN MUSEUM OF FLY FISHING IN MANCHESTER, VT. (USA)

■ 136, 137 THE BACKGROUND WAS PAINTED BY THE PHOTOGRAPHER AND LIT WITH STUDIO SPOTLIGHTS. THE PLATE IN THE PHOTOGRAPH AT RIGHT WAS MADE BY THE PHOTOGRAPHER. (USA)

● 135 DIE FLIEGEN VON U.S. PRÄSIDENT GROVER CLEVELAND AUF EINEM SALM AUS DEM ATLANTIK, AUFGENOMMEN VON TERRY HEFFERNAN FÜR EINEN KALENDER DES AMERIKANISCHEN MUSEUMS FÜR DAS FLIEGENFISCHEN IN MANCHESTER, VT. (USA)

● 136, 137 DER PHOTOGRAPH BEMALTE DEN HINTERGRUND UND BENUTZTE STUDIO-SPOTLICHT FÜR DIESE AUFNAHMEN. DEN TELLER IN DER ABBIL-DUNG RECHTS STELLTE ER SELBST HER. (USA)

▲ 135 LES MOUCHES DU PRÉSIDENT GROVER CLEVELAND SUR UN SAUMON DE L'ATLANTIQUE ONT ÉTÉ PHOTOGRAPHIÉES PAR TERRY HEFFERNAN POUR UN CALENDRIER DU MUSÉE DE LA PÊCHE À LA MOUCHE DE MANCHESTER. (USA)

▲ 136, 137 LE PHOTOGRAPHE A PEINT LE FOND ET IL A UTILISÉ LA LUMIÉRE DE SPOTS POUR CES PHOTOGRAPHIES DE STUDIO. IL A FABRIQUÉ LUI-MÊME L'ASSIETTE DE LA PHOTO DE DROITE. (USA)

PHOTOGRAPHER:
PETER MYERS
REPRESENTATIVE:
CAROLYN TRAYLER
PARTNERSHIP
CAMERA:
SINAR
FILM:
EKTACHROME 6117,
8X10
CLIENT:
TASTE MAGAZINE
ART DIRECTOR:
STEVE STAFFORD
■ 138

PHOTOGRAPHER:
HANS HANSEN
CAMERA:
SINAR 8X10
FILM:
KODAK EKTACHROME
EXPOSURE:
DOUBLE EXPOSURE,
STUDIO FLASH
CLIENT:
STERN
ART DIRECTOR:
WOLFGANG BEHNKEN
DESIGNER:
HANS HANSEN
STYLIST:
BARBARA KLOTH/
FRAUKE KOOPS
▶■ 139

■ 138 USING A COMBINATION OF PAINT TECHNIQUES AND PHOTOGRAPHY, THIS PICTURE FOR *TASTE MAGAZINE* WAS BASED ON A PAINTING BY PAUL CÉZANNE. (GBR)

■ 139 "HERRING AND VODKA ARE LIKE BROTHER AND SISTER" IS A RUSSIAN SAYING, AND POTATOES AND SALT BELONG TO THIS RUSSIAN DISH AS WELL. TODAY THIS SIMPLE FISH IS HARD TO FIND IN SOVIET FISHING GROUNDS AND HAS BECOME A RARE DELICACY. THE PHOTOGRAPH APPEARED IN *STERN* MAGAZINE'S JOURNAL "ESSEN UND TRINKEN" ("EATING AND DRINKING"). (GER)

● 138 DIESES IN *TASTE MAGAZINE* VERWENDETE BILD IST EINE KOMBINATION VON MALEREI UND PHOTOGRAPHIE UND BASIERT AUF EINEM BILD VON PAUL CÉZANNE. (GBR)

● 139 «HERING UND WODKA SIND WIE BRUDER UND SCHWESTER», SAGT EIN RUSSISCHES SPRICHWORT, UND AUCH KARTOFFELN UND SALZ GEHÖREN IN RUSSLAND DAZU. HEUTE IST DER EINFACHE FISCH IN DEN SOWJETISCHEN FANGGEWÄSSERN RAR UND ZU EINER DELIKATESSE GEWORDEN. DIESE AUFNAHME ERSCHIEN IM JOURNAL «ESSEN UND TRINKEN» DES *STERN*. (GER)

▲ 138 CETTE IMAGE PUBLIÉE DANS *TASTE MAGAZINE* COMBINE LES TECHNIQUES DE LA PEINTURE ET DE LA PHOTOGRAPHIE. ELLE EST INSPIRÉE D'UNE NATURE MORTE DE CÉZANNE. (GBR)

▲ 139 UN PROVERBE RUSSE DIT QUE «LE HARENG ET LA VODKA SONT COMME FRÈRE ET SŒUR». CE PLAT EST TOUJOURS ACCOMPAGNÉ DE POMMES DE TERRE ET DE SEL. AUJOURD'HUI, DEVENU RARE DANS LES EAUX SOVIÉTIQUES, CE POISSON EST UN METS DE CHOIX. CETTE PHOTOGRAPHIE EST PARUE DANS LES PAGES GASTRONOMIQUES DU MAGAZINE *STERN*. (GER)

PHOTOGRAPHER:

HANS HANSEN

CAMERA:

SINAR 4X5

FILM:

KODAK EKTACHROME

EXPOSURE:

STUDIO FLASH

CLIENT:

STERN

ART DIRECTOR:

WOLFGANG BEHNKEN

DESIGNER:

HANS HANSEN

STYLIST:

MARLIES
KLOSTERFELDE

■ 140-142

PHOTOGRAPHER:

JODY DOLE

REPRESENTATIVE:

DOUG BROWN

CAMERA:

NIKON F4

CLIENT:

HEUBLEIN, INC.

ART DIRECTOR:

BOB COLE

▶■ 143

■ 140-142 PHOTOGRAPHS USED AS FULL-PAGE INTRODUCTIONS TO RECIPES IN *STERN* MAGAZINE: AN OCEAN PERCH, A PUMPKIN, AND A SQUID. (GER)

■ 143 SMIRNOFF VODKA, RUSSIA'S FAVORITE VODKA BEFORE THE RUSSIAN REVOLUTION, IS "BACK IN THE USSR," NOW AS ITS LEADING IMPORTED VODKA. PHOTOGRAPH USED IN A CAMPAIGN FOR SMIRNOFF VODKA. (USA)

● 140-142 AUFNAHMEN ALS EINFÜHRUNGEN ZU REZEPTEN IM KÜCHENTEIL DES *STERN*: ROTBARBEN, EIN KÜRBIS UND EIN TINTENFISCH. (GER)

● 143 SMIRNOFF WODKA, RUSSLANDS BELIEBTESTER WODKA VOR DER OKTOBERREVOLUTION IST «BACK IN THE USSR», JETZT ALS DER FÜHRENDE IMPORTIERTE WODKA. AUFNAHME AUS EINER KAMPAGNE FÜR SMIRNOFF WODKA. (USA)

▲ 140-142 ROUGETS, CITROUILLE ET SEICHE REPRODUITS EN PLEINE PAGE DANS *STERN* POUR ILLUSTRER DES RECETTES DE CUISINE. (GER)

▲ 143 LA VODKA SMIRNOFF, LA VODKA PRÉFÉRÉE DES RUSSES AVANT LA RÉVOLUTION D'OCTOBRE EST «BACK IN THE USSR», OÙ ELLE EST LA PREMIÈRE MARQUE IMPORTÉE. PHOTO D'UNE CAMPAGNE PUBLICITAIRE. (USA)

PEOPLE

MENSCHEN

PERSONNES

PHOTOGRAPHER:
GREGORY HEISLER
CAMERA:
SINAR 8X10
PHOTO EDITOR:
TEMPLE SMITH
CLIENT:
ESQUIRE MAGAZINE
ART DIRECTOR:
RIP GEORGES
DESIGNER:
RIP GEORGES
◄■ 144

PHOTOGRAPHER:
AERNOUT OVERBEEKE
REPRESENTATIVE:
CHRISTA KLUBERT
CAMERA:
SINAR
PHOTO EDITOR:
HANS VAN
BLOMMESTEIN
CLIENT:
AVENUE MAGAZINE
ART DIRECTOR:
HANS VAN
BLOMMESTEIN
DESIGNER:
HANS VAN
BLOMMESTEIN
■ 145

PHOTOGRAPHER:
AERNOUT OVERBEEKE
REPRESENTATIVE:
CHRISTA KLUBERT
CAMERA:
SINAR
CLIENT:
AMSTERDAM BACH
SOLOISTS
ART DIRECTOR:
AERNOUT OVERBEEKE
DESIGNER:
AERNOUT OVERBEEKE
►■ 146

■ 144 (PRECEDING SPREAD) PORTRAIT OF GEENA DAVIS, FROM A COVER STORY FOR THE MEN'S MAGAZINE *ESQUIRE* ENTITLED "WOMEN WE LOVE," IN WHICH THE EDITORS TOOK AN AFFECTIONATE LOOK AT THEIR FAVORITE PERSONALITIES. (USA)

■ 145, 146 THE MOOD OF OLD DUTCH MASTER PAINTINGS IS PRESENT IN THIS PAIR OF PHOTO- GRAPHS, WHICH SHOW ARTIST JEROEN PRESSERS IN HIS STUDIO AND THE AMSTERDAM BACH SOLO- ISTS IN AN OLD CHURCH. THEY WERE PUBLISHED IN THE DUTCH MAGAZINE *AVENUE*. (NLD)

● 144 (VORHERGEHENDE SEITE) PORTRÄT DER FILMSCHAUSPIELERIN GEENA DAVIS. DIE AUFNAHME ENTSTAND FÜR EIN PROJEKT DER ZEITSCHRIFT *ESQUIRE* UNTER DEM TITEL «FRAUEN, DIE WIR LIEBEN». (USA)

● 145, 146 DIE STIMMUNG IN DIESEN AUFNAHMEN ERINNERT AN DIE WERKE ALTER HOLLÄNDISCHER MEISTER. SIE ZEIGEN DEN KÜNSTLER JEROEN PRESSERS IN SEINEM STUDIO UND DIE AMSTER- DAMER BACHSOLISTEN IN EINER ALTEN KIRCHE. DIE PHOTOS SIND IN *AVENUE* ERSCHIENEN. (NLD)

▲ 144 (PAGE PRÉCÉDENTE) PORTRAIT DE L'ACTRICE DE CINÉMA GEENA DAVIS. CETTE PHOTOGRAPHIE A ÉTÉ RÉALISÉE POUR UN PROJET DU MAGAZINE *ESQUIRE*, INTITULÉ «LES FEMMES QUE NOUS AIMONS». (USA)

▲ 145, 146 L'ATMOSPHÈRE DE CES PHOTOGRAPHIES ÉVOQUE LES INTÉRIEURS PEINTS PAR LES GRANDS MAÎTRES HOLLANDAIS. ON PEUT VOIR L'ARTISTE JEROEN PRESSERS DANS SON ATELIER ET LES SOLISTES DE BACH D'AMSTERDAM DANS UNE VIEILLE ÉGLISE. SÉRIE PUBLIÉE DANS *AVENUE*. (NLD)

PHOTOGRAPHER:
LILLIAN BIRNBAUM
CLIENT:
FRANKFURTER ALL-
GEMEINE MAGAZIN
ART DIRECTOR:
HANS-GEORG
POSPISCHIL
■ 147

PHOTOGRAPHER:
PATRICK
DEMARCHELIER
REPRESENTATIVE:
BRYAN BANTRY
CAMERA:
PENTAX 165
FILM:
KODAK 120, 64
PHOTO EDITOR:

ELISABETH BIONDI
CLIENT:
VANITY FAIR
MAGAZINE
ART DIRECTOR:
CHARLES
CHURCHWARD
DESIGNER:
MARINA SCHIANO
▶■ 148

■ 147 IT HAS BEEN SAID THAT WHILE VIRGINIA WOOLF HAD A GIFT FOR USING CLOTHING TO DESCRIBE A PERSON, GROUP OR LAYER OF SOCIETY IN HER WRITING, SHE HERSELF HATED BUYING CLOTHES. THE MODEL, WHO CLOSELY RESEMBLES THE AUTHOR, WEARS A DRESS TYPICAL OF THE STYLE OF MS. WOOLF'S ERA: GENEROUS YET RESTRAINED. THE PHOTOGRAPH APPEARED IN THE FRANKFURTER ALLGEMEINE MAGAZIN. (GER)

■ 148 A PORTRAIT OF FRENCH ACTRESS ISABELLE ADJANI WHICH WAS PUBLISHED IN VANITY FAIR MAGAZINE. (USA)

● 147 VON VIRGINIA WOOLF WIRD BEHAUPTET, DASS SIE EIN SICHERES GEFÜHL FÜR KLEIDUNG HATTE, WENN ES GALT, MENSCHEN ZU CHARAKTERI-SIEREN. SIE SELBST ABER HASSTE ES EINZUKAU-FEN. DAS MODELL, DAS DER SCHRIFTSTELLERIN GLEICHT, TRÄGT EIN KLEID, DAS AUCH VIRGINIA WOOLF GETRAGEN HABEN KÖNNTE: FREIZÜGIG UND ZUGEKNÖPFT ZUGLEICH. AUFNAHME AUS DEM FRANKFURTER ALLGEMEINE MAGAZIN. (GER)

● 148 EIN PORTRÄT DER FRANZÖSISCHEN SCHAU-SPIELERIN ISABELLE ADJANI, DAS IN DER ZEIT-SCHRIFT VANITY FAIR ERSCHIENEN IST. (USA)

▲ 147 ON DIT QUE VIRGINIA WOOLF AVAIT UN GOÛT TRÈS SÛR QUAND IL S'AGISSAIT DE CARACTÉRISER LE VÊTEMENT D'UNE PERSONNE OU D'UNE CLASSE SOCIALE. ELLE-MÊME DÉTESTAIT ALLER DANS LES MAGASINS. LE MODÈLE, QUI RESSEMBLE À L'ÉCRIVAIN, PORTE COMME ELLE UN VÊTEMENT AMPLE ET BOUTONNÉ, LAISSANT LE CORPS LIBRE. CETTE PHOTO A ÉTÉ RÉALISÉE POUR UN ARTICLE DU FRANKFURTER ALLGEMEINE MAGAZIN. (GER)

▲ 148 UN PORTRAIT DE L'ACTRICE FRANÇAISE ISABELLE ADJANI, PARU DANS LE MAGAZINE VANITY FAIR. (USA)

PHOTOGRAPHER:

GÜNTER

PFANNMÜLLER

REPRESENTATIVE:

STUDIO

PFANNMÜLLER

CAMERA:

HASSELBLAD

FILM:

KODAK T-MAX 100

PHOTO EDITOR:

PETER HESSLER

CLIENT:

BERTHOLD AG

ART DIRECTOR:

PETER HESSLER

■ 149-154

PHOTOGRAPHER:

JAMES B. WOOD

CAMERA:

NIKON F4

FILM:

KODAK TYPE B. 160

CLIENT:

JAMES B. WOOD

ART DIRECTOR:

JAMES B. WOOD

▶■ 155

■ 149-154 AN ADVERTISING CAMPAIGN PROMOTES THE IMAGE OF BERTHOLD TYPEFACES BY ASSOCI-ATING THE COMPANY WITH AN INTERNATIONAL ARRAY OF FAMOUS DESIGNERS. SHOWN HERE FROM LEFT TO RIGHT ARE: JOE DUFFY (DUFFY DESIGN GROUP), ANTON STANKOWSKI (GRAPHIC DESIGNER), PETER SCHMIDT (DESIGNER), MASSIMO VIGNELLI (VIGNELLI ASSOCIATES), KARL GERSTNER (THE FIRST G OF GGK), DR. FLORIAN LANGENSCHEIDT (LANGENSCHEIDT PUBLISHERS). (GER)

■ 155 PHOTOGRAPH TAKEN ON A STUDIO SET, USED FOR SELF-PROMOTIONAL PURPOSES. (USA)

● 149-154 PORTRÄTS BERÜHMTER LEUTE DER DESIGN- UND WERBEINDUSTRIE, DIE IN EINER IMAGE-KAMPAGNE FÜR BERTHOLD-SCHRIFTEN VER-WENDET WURDEN. VON LINKS NACH RECHTS: JOE DUFFY (DUFFY DESIGN GROUP), ANTON STANKOW-SKI (DESIGNER), PETER SCHMIDT (DESIGNER), MASSIMO VIGNELLI (ARCHITEKT UND DESIGNER, VIGNELLI ASSOCIATES), KARL GERSTNER (DAS ERSTE G VON GGK), DR. FLORIAN LANGENSCHEIDT (LANGENSCHEIDT VERLAG). (GER)

● 155 STUDIO-AUFNAHME, DIE DER PHOTOGRAPH ALS EIGENWERBUNG VERWENDET. (USA)

▲ 149-154 CES PORTRAITS DE CÉLÉBRITÉS DU MONDE DU DESIGN ET DE LA PUBLICITÉ ILLUS-TRAIENT UNE CAMPAGNE DE PRESTIGE POUR BER-THOLD, UNE ENTREPRISE SPÉCIALISÉE DANS LA TYPOGRAPHIE. DE GAUCHE À DROITE: JOE DUFFY (DUFFY DESIGN GROUP), ANTON STANKOWSKI (GRAPHISTE), PETER SCHMIDT (DESIGNER), MASSIMO VIGNELLI (VIGNELLI ASSOC.), KARL GERSTNER (LE PREMIER G DE GGK), DR. FLORIAN LANGENSCHEIDT (ÉDITEUR). (GER)

▲ 155 CETTE PHOTO, RÉALISÉE EN STUDIO, SERT D'AUTOPROMOTION AU PHOTOGRAPHE. (USA)

PHOTOGRAPHER:
SERGE COHEN
CLIENT:
FRANKFURTER ALL-
GEMEINE MAGAZIN
ART DIRECTOR:
HANS-GEORG
POSPISCHIL

■ 156

PHOTOGRAPHER:

WOLFGANG WESENER

CLIENT:

FRANKFURTER ALL-
GEMEINE MAGAZIN

ART DIRECTOR:

HANS-GEORG

POSPISCHIL

■ 157

■ 156 HEMINGWAY'S DOUBLE WITH A FISH, NOT QUITE THE SIZE OF THE ONES PAPA USED TO CATCH. PHOTOGRAPH USED IN AN ARTICLE ON THE LIFE OF HEMINGWAY IN THE *FRANKFURTER ALLGE-MEINE MAGAZIN.* (GER)

■ 157 A FEW LINES MAKE UP THE SELF-PORTRAIT OF AL HIRSCHFELD. THREE TO FOUR OF HIS WITTY ILLUSTRATIONS CONTINUE TO APPEAR EVERY WEEK IN *THE NEW YORK TIMES*—JUST AS THEY HAVE FOR THE PAST FIFTY YEARS. THIS PHOTOGRAPH APPEARED IN AN ARTICLE IN THE *FRANKFURTER ALLGEMEINE MAGAZIN.* (GER)

● 156 MIT SO KLEINEN FISCHEN WIE SEIN DOPPELGÄNGER IN DIESER AUFNAHME HÄTTE SICH PAPA HEMINGWAY KAUM ZUFRIEDENGEGEBEN. DIE AUFNAHME STAMMT AUS EINEM ARTIKEL IM *FRANK-FURTER ALLGEMEINE MAGAZIN.* (GER)

● 157 WENIGE LINIEN GENÜGEN DEM KARIKA-TURISTEN AL HIRSCHFELD FÜR SEIN SELBSTPOR-TRÄT. HEUTE WIE VOR EINEM HALBEN JAHRHUN-DERT BELIEFERT ER DIE *NEW YORK TIMES* MIT DREI, VIER ILLUSTRATIONEN PRO WOCHE. DIESE AUFNAHME ERSCHIEN IM *FRANKFURTER ALLGE-MEINE MAGAZIN.* (GER)

▲ 156 PÊCHEUR PASSIONNÉ, HEMINGWAY NE SE SERAIT JAMAIS CONTENTÉ D'UNE PRISE AUSSI MODESTE QUE CELLE-CI. LE SOSIE DE L'ÉCRIVAIN A ÉTÉ PHOTOGRAPHIÉ POUR UN ARTICLE PARU DANS LE *FRANKFURTER ALLGEMEINE MAGAZIN.* (GER)

▲ 157 QUELQUES TRAITS ONT SUFFI AU CARICA-TURISTE AL HIRSCHFELD POUR DESSINER CET AUTOPORTRAIT. VOILÀ PLUS D'UN DEMI-SIÈCLE QUE CE DERNIER FOURNIT 3 À 4 ILLUSTRATIONS PAR SEMAINE AU *NEW YORK TIMES.* CETTE PHOTO-GRAPHIE A ÉTÉ PUBLIÉE DANS LE *FRANKFURTER ALLGEMEINE MAGAZIN.* (GER)

PHOTOGRAPHER:
ROBERT PEDERSEN
CAMERA:
HASSELBLAD
FILM:
FUJICHROME
CLIENT:
CORPORATE
GRAPHICS INC.
ART DIRECTOR:
BENNETT ROBINSON
DESIGNER:
BENNETT ROBINSON
◀■ 158

PHOTOGRAPHER:
RICK RUSING
CAMERA:
HORSEMAN 4X5,
HASSELBLAD (MEN)
PHOTO EDITOR:
BARRY SHEPARD
CLIENT:
AUDI OF AMERICA,
INC.
ART DIRECTOR:
BARRY SHEPARD
DESIGNER:
KARIN BURKLEIN
ARNOLD
■ 159, 160

■ 158 A PORTRAIT OF ROBIN WIGHT AND PETER SCOTT, TAKEN TO ACCOMPANY THEIR CHAIRMAN'S STATEMENT IN THE WCRS GROUP'S ANNUAL REPORT FOR 1989. WHICH POINTS OUT THAT THE ADVERTISING AGENCY WAS ABLE TO LIVE UP TO ITS "OWN UNREASONABLE EXPECTATIONS OF ITSELF." (USA)

■ 159, 160 PHOTOGRAPHS FROM THE BROCHURE ADVERTISING THE 1990 AUDI V8 QUATTRO THE PHOTOGRAPHER'S ASSIGNMENT WAS TO BRING A MORE HUMAN ELEMENT TO THE COMPANY'S IMAGE, WHILE RETAINING A HIGH DEGREE OF STYLE. THE PHOTOGRAPHS OF THE CARS WERE MADE IN ARIZONA, THE PORTRAITS IN MUNICH. (USA)

● 158 PORTRÄT VON ROBIN WIGHT UND PETER SCOTT VON DER WERBEAGENTUR WCRS GROUP AUS DEM JAHRESBERICHT 1989. DARIN WIRD U.A. FESTGESTELLT, DASS ES DER AGENTUR GELUNGEN IST, «DIE EIGENEN UNREALISTISCHEN ERWARTUNGEN ZU ERFÜLLEN». (USA)

● 159, 160 IN EINER BROSCHÜRE FÜR AUDI V8 QUATTRO VERWENDETE AUFNAHMEN. DER AUFTRAG LAUTETE, DIE FIRMA MENSCHLICHER ERSCHEINEN ZU LASSEN UND GLEICHZEITIG STIL ZU ZEIGEN. DIE ALS HINTERGRUND VERWENDETEN AUFNAHMEN DER AUTOS ENTSTANDEN IN ARIZONA, DIE PORTRÄTS WURDEN IN MÜNCHEN GEMACHT. (USA)

▲ 158 CE PORTRAIT DE ROBIN WIGHT ET PETER SCOTT FIGURE DANS LE RAPPORT D'ACTIVITÉS 1989 DE L'AGENCE DE PUBLICITÉ WCRS. DANS CETTE BROCHURE, ON PEUT LIRE NOTAMMENT QUE CETTE ENTREPRISE A RÉUSSI À «RÉPONDRE AUX ESPOIRS LES PLUS INSENSÉS». (USA)

▲ 159, 160 CES PHOTOS ONT ÉTÉ PUBLIÉES DANS UNE BROCHURE SUR LA NOUVELLE AUDI V8 QUATTRO. L'OBJECTIF ÉTAIT DE METTRE EN RELIEF LE CÔTÉ HUMAIN DE L'ENTREPRISE, TOUT EN GARDANT UN CERTAIN STYLE. LES VOITURES DE L'ARRIÈRE-PLAN ONT ÉTÉ PHOTOGRAPHIÉES EN ARIZONA, LES PORTRAITS À MUNICH. (USA)

PHOTOGRAPHER:
MARC NORBERG
CAMERA:
HASSELBLAD
FILM:
KODAK X, 120 PLUS
CLIENT:
THE BLUES HEAVEN
FOUNDATION
ART DIRECTOR:
MARC NORBERG
■ 161, 162, 164, 165

PHOTOGRAPHER:
MARC NORBERG
CAMERA:
HASSELBLAD
FILM:
KODAK X, 120 PLUS
CLIENT:
MARC NORBERG
■ 163

■ 161-165 EXAMPLES FROM AN ONGOING SERIES OF PORTRAITS OF BLUES AND JAZZ MUSICIANS, A PERSONAL PROJECT BY THE PHOTOGRAPHER FOR THE BLUES HEAVEN ARCHIVES. SHOWN ARE (OPPOSITE, LEFT TO RIGHT): ROBERT JUNIOR LOCKWOOD, JOHNNY WINTER, COURTNEY PINE, B.B. KING, AND (THIS PAGE) LADY BIANCA. (USA)

● 161-165 BEISPIELE AUS EINER PORTRÄT-REIHE VON JAZZ- UND BLUES-MUSIKERN, DIE DER PHOTO-GRAPH AUF EIGENE RECHNUNG FÜR DAS «BLUES HEAVEN»-ARCHIV PHOTOGRAPHIERTE. GEGENÜBER VON LINKS NACH RECHTS: ROBERT JUNIOR LOCKWOOD, JOHNNY WINTER, COURTNEY PINE, B.B. KING UND (DIESE SEITE) LADY BIANCA. (USA)

▲ 161-165 EXEMPLES D'UNE SÉRIE DE PORTRAITS DE MUSICIENS DE JAZZ ET DE BLUES, QUE LE PHOTOGRAPHE A RÉALISÉE À SON PROPRE COMPTE POUR LES ARCHIVES DE LA FONDATION BLUES HEAVEN. PAGE CI-CONTRE, DE G. À D.: ROBERT JR. LOCKWOOD, JOHNNY WINTER, COURTNEY PINE, B.B. KING; SUR CETTE PAGE, LADY BIANCA. (USA)

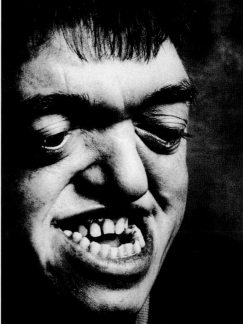

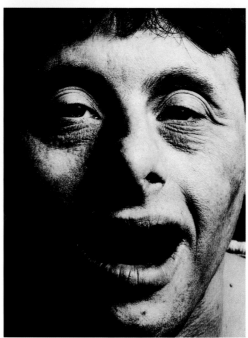

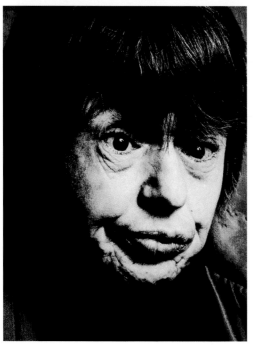

PHOTOGRAPHER:

JOHN CLARIDGE

CAMERA:

MAMIYA RZ

FILM:

KODAK TRI-X

CLIENT:

MACINTYRE

ART DIRECTOR:

KAREN BLINCOE

DESIGNER:

KAREN BLINCOE/

SIMON DRYLAND

◀■ 166-174

PHOTOGRAPHER:

NICK VEDROS

CAMERA:

HASSELBLAD, 2 1/4

FILM:

KODAK EKTACHROME

PN 100

EXPOSURE:

F 8.5, 1/125

CLIENT:

EASTMAN KODAK

ART DIRECTOR:

STEVE HALL

■ 175

■ 166-174 "PUTTING PEOPLE FIRST." THESE PORTRAITS OF PEOPLE WHO HAVE A MENTAL DISABILITY WERE SHOWN IN THE 1989 ANNUAL REVIEW OF THE MACINTYRE COMPANY DEDICATED TO HELPING CHILDREN AND ADULTS WITH SPECIAL NEEDS. (GBR)

■ 175 THIS COUPLE PROUDLY SHOWING A PORTRAIT FROM THEIR YOUNGER DAYS HAVE BEEN MARRIED OVER 60 YEARS. THE PHOTOGRAPH WAS SHOT BY NICK VEDROS AND USED IN AN EASTMAN KODAK CAMPAIGN: "A PROFESSIONAL PORTRAIT ISN'T EXPENSIVE. IT'S PRICELESS." (USA)

● 166-174 «MENSCHEN STEHEN AN ERSTER STELLE.» DIESE AUFNAHMEN VON MENSCHEN MIT HIRNSCHÄDEN WURDEN IM JAHRESBERICHT 1989 DER MACINTYRE COMPANY GEZEIGT, DIE SICH UM KINDER UND ERWACHSENE MIT SPEZIELLEN BE-DÜRFNISSEN KÜMMERT. (GBR)

● 175 STOLZ ZEIGEN DIE BEIDEN, DIE ÜBER 60 JAHRE MITEINANDER VERHEIRATET SIND, EIN POR-TRÄT AUS IHRER JUGEND. DIESE AUFNAHME STAMMT AUS EINER KAMPAGNE FÜR EASTMAN KODAK: «PROFESSIONELLE PORTRÄTS SIND NICHT TEUER, SIE SIND UNBEZAHLBAR.» (USA)

▲ 166-174 «LE PLUS IMPORTANT, C'EST L'ÊTRE HUMAIN.» CES PORTRAITS D'HANDICAPÉS MENTAUX ONT ÉTÉ PUBLIÉS DANS LE RAPPORT ANNUEL 1989 DE MACINTYRE COMPANY, UNE ASSOCIATION D'AIDE AUX ENFANTS ET ADULTES NÉCESSITANT DES SOINS SPÉCIAUX. (GBR)

▲ 175 CE COUPLE, MARIÉ DEPUIS PLUS DE 60 ANS, MONTRE AVEC FIERTÉ UN PORTRAIT PRIS AU TEMPS DE LEUR JEUNESSE. CETTE PHOTO PROVIENT D'UNE CAMPAGNE RÉALISÉE POUR EASTMAN KODAK: «LE PORTRAIT D'UN PROFESSIONNEL N'EST PAS CHER. IL EST SANS PRIX.» (USA)

PHOTOGRAPHER:

MICHAEL O'BRIEN

CAMERA:

HASSELBLAD

FILM:

FUJI RDP 120

PHOTO EDITOR:

DAVID FIELDS

CLIENT:

SPORTS ILLUSTRATED

DESIGN DIRECTOR:

STEVEN HOFFMAN

■ 176, 177

PHOTOGRAPHER:

MARC HAUSER

REPRESENTATIVE:

RANDI FIAT & ASSOC.,

CHICAGO/

ZARI INTERNATIONAL,

NEW YORK

CAMERA:

ARCA SWISS 4X5

REFLEX

FILM:

POLAROID 4X5

ART DIRECTOR:

MARC HAUSER

►■ 178

■ 176, 177 PORTRAITS FROM THE PAGES OF SPORTS ILLUSTRATED MAGAZINE. FORMER TENNIS CHAMPION CHRIS EVERT AND HER HUSBAND ANDY MILL WERE PHOTOGRAPHED AT THEIR NEW HOME IN ASPEN. THE PORTRAIT OF ARCHIE MOORE, A FORMER LIGHT HEAVYWEIGHT BOXING CHAMPION, ILLUSTRATED A CAREER RETROSPECTIVE ENTITLED "THE AGELESS WARRIOR." (USA)

■ 178 A POLAROID PORTRAIT SIMPLY ENTITLED "PAT" SERVES AS A SELF-PROMOTION PIECE FOR PHOTOGRAPHER MARC HAUSER. (USA)

● 176, 177 PORTRÄTS FÜR BEITRÄGE IN DER ZEITSCHRIFT SPORTS ILLUSTRATED. DIE AUFNAHME DES EHEMALIGEN TENNIS-STARS CHRIS EVERT MIT IHREM MANN ANDY MILL ENTSTAND AN IHREM NEUEN WOHNORT IN ASPEN, COLORADO. DER «KÄMPFER OHNE ALTER» – SO DER TITEL DIESER RETROSPEKTIVE – IST ARCHIE MOORE, EIN EHEMALIGER BOX CHAMPION IM MITTELGEWICHT. (USA)

● 178 «PAT». EIN POLAROID-PORTRÄT, DAS DER PHOTOGRAPH MARC HAUSER ALS EIGENWERBUNG VERWENDET. (USA)

▲ 176, 177 PORTRAITS ILLUSTRANT DES ARTICLES DU MAGAZINE SPORTS ILLUSTRATED. LA PHOTO DE L'EX-CHAMPIONNE DE TENNIS CHRIS EVERT AVEC SON MARI ANDY MILL A ÉTÉ PRISE À LEUR NOUVEAU DOMICILE D'ASPEN, DANS LE COLORADO. ARCHIE MOORE, SURNOMMÉ DANS CETTE RÉTROSPECTIVE «LE GUERRIER SANS ÂGE», EST UN ANCIEN CHAMPION DE BOXE POIDS MOYEN. (USA)

▲ 178 «PAT», UN PORTRAIT AU POLAROÏD, UTILISÉ COMME AUTOPROMOTION PAR LE PHOTOGRAPHE MARC HAUSER. (USA)

PHOTOGRAPHER:
MALCOLM KIRK
CLIENT:
SANDOZ AG
ART DIRECTOR:
NORBERT HEROLD/
RALPH
TAUBENBERGER
DESIGNER:
NORBERT HEROLD/
RALPH
TAUBENBERGER
■ 179-182

■ 179-182 PORTRAITS OF INHABITANTS OF PAPUA, NEW GUINEA, FROM LEFT TO RIGHT: ONE OF THE MELPA TRIBE (THE SINGLE STRIPED FEATHER COMES FROM THE PLUMAGE OF THE LONG-TAILED BUZZARD), A SAMO MAN FROM THE REGION OF THE NOMAD RIVER IN THE WEST PROVINCE (THE NOSEPEG IS MADE OF A CASSOWARY BONE), A HULI TRIBESMAN FROM THE SOUTHERN HIGHLAND PROVINCE (EVERDAY WIG MADE OF COLORED HUMAN HAIR), MENDI TRIBESMAN FROM THE SOUTHERN HIGHLAND PROVINCE (HIS HEAD-DRESS IS BORROWED FROM BIRD-CATCHERS). THE PHOTOGRAPHS ARE TAKEN FROM THE BOOK *PEOPLE AND MASKS* BY NEW YORK PHOTOGRAPHER MALCOLM KIRK, AND WERE ALSO USED FOR A SANDOZ CALENDAR. (USA)

● 179-182 MENSCHEN AUS PAPUA NEUGUINEA, VON LINKS NACH RECHTS: EIN ANGEHÖRIGER DES MELPA-STAMMES (DIE EINZELNE GESTREIFTE FEDER STAMMT AUS DEM GEFIEDER DES LANGSCHWÄNZIGEN BUSSARDS), EIN SAMO-MANN AUS DEM GEBIET DES NOMAD-RIVER IN DER WESTPROVINZ (DER NASENPFLOCK BESTEHT AUS EINEM KASUARKNOCHEN), EIN HULI-STAMMESANGEHÖRIGER AUS DER SÜDLICHEN HOCHLAND-PROVINZ (ALLTAGSPERÜCKE AUS GEFÄRBTEM MENSCHLICHEM HAAR), EIN MENDI-STAMMESANGEHÖRIGER AUS DER SÜDLICHEN HOCHLAND-PROVINZ (SEINEN KOPFSCHMUCK HAT ER VON VOGELFÄNGERN AUSGELIEHEN). DIE AUFNAHMEN STAMMEN AUS DEM BUCH »MENSCHEN UND MASKEN« UND WURDEN AUCH FÜR EINEN SANDOZ-KALENDER VERWENDET. (USA)

▲ 179-182 PAPOUS DE LA NOUVELLE-GUINÉE. DE GAUCHE À DROITE: UN MEMBRE DE LA TRIBU DES MELPA (LA GRANDE PLUME RAYÉE PROVIENT DU PLUMAGE D'UN BUSARD À LONGUE QUEUE); UN SAMO DE LA RÉGION DE LA NOMAD-RIVER, A L'OUEST DE L'ÎLE (L'ORNEMENT NASAL EST CONSTITUÉ D'UN OS DE CASOAR); UN INDIGÉNE DE LA TRIBU HULI, QUI VIT DANS LES MASSIFS MONTAGNEUX DE LA PROVINCE SUD (IL PORTE UNE PERRUQUE ORDINAIRE DE CHEVEUX TEINTS); UN MEMBRE DE LA TRIBU DES MENDI, QUI HABITE LUI AUSSI DANS LES MASSIFS MÉRIDIONAUX (IL A EMPRUNTÉ SA COIFFURE À UN OISELEUR). CES PHOTOGRAPHIES SONT TIRÉES DU LIVRE »DES HOMMES ET DES MASQUES« ET ONT ÉTÉ PUBLIÉES SOUS FORME DE CALENDRIER. (USA)

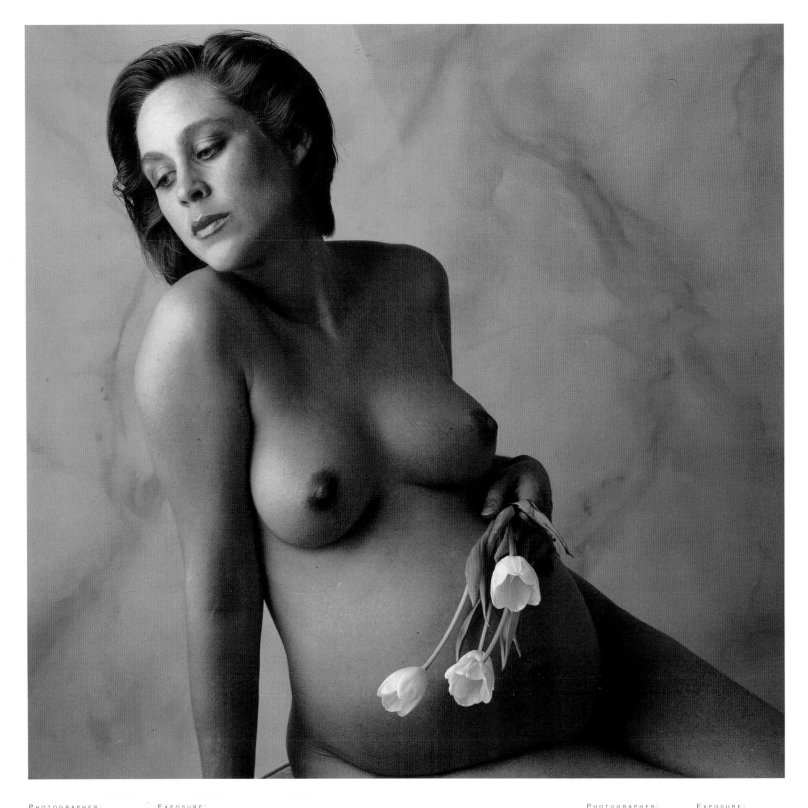

PHOTOGRAPHER:
LISA BOGDAN
CAMERA:
HASSELBLAD
FILM:
KODAK EKTACHROME
EPP 100+/120MM

EXPOSURE:
F 11.5, 1/60
CLIENT:
LISA BOGDAN
■ 183

PHOTOGRAPHER:
LISA BOGDAN
CAMERA:
NIKON F3
FILM:
KODACHROME
64/35MM

EXPOSURE:
F 8.5, 1/60
CLIENT:
TOWN & COUNTRY
ART DIRECTOR:
MELISSA TARDIFF
►■ 184

■ 183 *LORRAINE, PREGNANT NUDE STUDY NO. 2,* FROM A SERIES OF PHOTOGRAPHS ON THE FEMALE BODY DURING PREGNANCY. (USA)

■ 184 PORTRAIT OF AMALIA LACROZE DE FORTABAT, A PHILANTHROPIST RESIDING IN ARGENTINA. THIS PHOTOGRAPH WAS ASSIGNED BY *TOWN AND COUNTRY* MAGAZINE FOR AN ISSUE FOCUSING ON SPAIN. IT WAS SHOT AT THE GOLD MEDAL GALA, A BALL HELD AT THE PIERRE HOTEL IN NEW YORK, HOSTED BY THE SPANISH INSTITUTE. (USA)

● 183 *LORRAINE* – AKTSTUDIE. DIE AUFNAHME GEHÖRT ZU EINER SERIE ÜBER DEN WEIBLICHEN KÖRPER WÄHREND DER SCHWANGERSCHAFT. (USA)

● 184 PORTRÄT VON AMALIA LACROZE DE FORTABAT, EINER PHILANTHROPIN, DIE IN ARGENTINIEN LEBT. DIE AUFNAHME ENTSTAND IM AUFTRAG DER ZEITSCHRIFT *TOWN AND COUNTRY* FÜR EINE SPANIEN-AUSGABE ANLÄSSLICH EINER GALA IM NEW YORKER HOTEL PIERRE, VERANSTALTET VOM SPANISCHEN INSTITUT. (USA)

▲ 183 *LORRAINE* – ÉTUDE DE NU D'UNE SÉRIE DELISA BOGDAN SUR LES TRANSFORMATIONS DU CORPS DE LA FEMME DURANT LA GROSSESSE. (USA)

▲ 184 PORTRAIT D'AMALIA LACROZE DE FORTABAT, UNE PHILANTHROPE QUI VIT EN ARGENTINE. CETTE PHOTO A ÉTÉ RÉALISÉE POUR LE MAGAZINE *TOWN AND COUNTRY*, POUR ILLUSTRER UN NUMÉRO CONSACRÉ À L'ESPAGNE. ELLE A ÉTÉ PRISE À L'OCCASION D'UN GRAND GALA À L'HÔTEL PIERRE, ORGANISÉ PAR L'INSTITUT ESPAGNOL. (USA)

PHOTOGRAPHER:

MAX AGUILERA-
HELLWEG

REPRESENTATIVE:

ONYX ENTERPRISES

CAMERA:

FIELD CAMERA 4X5,
EBONY SV45

FILM:

POLAROID 55

PHOTO EDITOR:

ALISON MORLEY 185

D.J. STOUT 186-188

CLIENT:

*LOS ANGELES TIME
MAGAZINE* 185

TEXAS MONTHLY 186-188

ART DIRECTOR:

NANCY DUCKWORTH 185

D.J. STOUT 186-188

DESIGNER:

D.J. STOUT 186-188

◄■ 185-188

PHOTOGRAPHER:

DANNY TURNER

CAMERA:

ROLLEI 6006, 50MM

FILM:

FUJICHROME 100

PHOTO EDITOR:

D.J. STOUT

CLIENT:

TEXAS MONTHLY

ART DIRECTOR:

D.J. STOUT

DESIGNER:

D.J. STOUT

■ 189

■ 185-188 HISPANIC PHOTOGRAPHER MAX AGUI-LERA-HELLWEG TRAVELLED THE LENGTH OF THE TEXAS-MEXICO BORDER, POSING AS A STREET PHOTOGRAPHER WHILE IN SEARCH OF HIS ROOTS. THE RESULTS APPEARED IN *TEXAS MONTHLY* MAGAZINE. (USA)

■ 189 IN THIS PHOTOGRAPH, PART OF A *TEXAS MONTHLY* SERIES ON PORTRAIT PAITINGS AND THEIR SUBJECTS, SARAH LEA IS SHOWN WITH A PORTRAIT OF HERSELF, PAINTED BY HER HUSBAND, THE FAMOUS MURAL PAINTER, TOM LEA, IN 1947. (USA)

● 185-188 MAX AGUILERA-HELLWEG, EIN PHOTO-GRAPH SPANISCHER ABSTAMMUNG, REISTE ENT-LANG DER GRENZE ZWISCHEN TEXAS UND MEXIKO AUF DER SUCHE NACH SEINEN WURZELN. ER GING DABEI WIE EIN STRASSENPHOTOGRAPH VOR. DIE AUFNAHMEN ERSCHIENEN IN *TEXAS MONTHLY*. (USA)

● 189 FÜR EINEN PHOTO-ESSAY IN *TEXAS MONTHLY* ÜBER GEMALTE PORTRÄTS UND DIE DARGE-STELLTEN PERSONEN. SARAH LEA IST HIER MIT DEM PORTRÄT GEZEIGT, DAS IHR MANN, TOM LEA, EIN BERÜHMTER WANDMALER, 1947 MALTE. (USA)

▲ 185-188 MAX AGUILERA-HELLWEG, UN PHOTO-GRAPHE HISPANO-AMÉRICAIN, A ENTREPRIS UN VOYAGE LE LONG DE LA FRONTIÈRE ENTRE LE TEXAS ET LE MEXIQUE. À LA RECHERCHE DE SES RACINES. CES IMAGES ONT ÉTÉ PUBLIÉES DANS LE MAGAZINE *TEXAS MONTHLY*. (USA)

▲ 189 POUR UN ARTICLE DU *TEXAS MONTHLY* PRÉSENTANT DES PORTRAITS PEINTS ET LEURS MODÈLES. SARAH LEA POSE À CÔTÉ DU PORTRAIT QUE SON MARI. TOM LEA, CÉLÈBRE PEINTRE DE FRESQUES AMÉRICAIN, FIT D'ELLE EN 1947. (USA)

PHOTOGRAPHER:
DMITRI KASTERINE
CAMERA:
NIKON
FILM:
KODACHROME
CLIENT:
CHAMPION INTER-
NATIOANAL CORP.
ART DIRECTOR:
RICHARD HESS
DESIGNER:
RICHARD HESS
■ 190

PHOTOGRAPHER:
MARK HANAUER
REPRESENTATIVE:
ONYX ENTERPRISES
CAMERA:
SINAR 4X5, 210MM
FILM:
POLAROID 55
EXPOSURE:
F 5.6, 1/15
CLIENT:
ROBERT DOWNEY JR.
ART DIRECTOR:
MARK HANAUER
■ 191

PHOTOGRAPHER:
TOM HOOKE
CAMERA:
HASSELBLAD 2-3/4
FILM:
KODAK T-MAX 100
EXPOSURE:
F 11, 1/250
CLIENT:
WASHINGTON
EDUCATION ASSOC.
ART DIRECTOR:
PAUL MATTHAEUS
■ 192

PHOTOGRAPHER:
SUE BENNETT
CAMERA:
NIKON
FILM:
KODAK PANATOMIC X
CLIENT:
TREND MAGAZINE
ART DIRECTOR:
KITTY MCGEE
DESIGNER:
KITTY MCGEE
■ 193

PHOTOGRAPHER:

BETSY CAMERON

CAMERA:

NIKON F3, 105
MACRO

PHOTO EDITOR:

PAUL LIPTAK

CLIENT:

BRUCE MCGAW
GRAPHICS

■ 194

■ 190 PORTRAIT OF MARY ELIZABETH JOHNSON TAKEN IN ALVA, OKLAHOMA, FOR CHAMPION INTERNATIONAL CORPORATION. (USA)

■ 191 A PORTRAIT OF THE ACTOR ROBERT DOWNEY JR., USED AS SELF-PROMOTION BY MARK HANAUER IN *SELECT* MAGAZINE. (USA)

■ 192 THE ASSIGNMENT FROM THE WASHINGTON EDUCATION ASSOCIATION WAS TO DEPICT A NEGATIVE ROLE MODEL THAT STUDENTS MIGHT SEEK IN THE ABSENCE OF QUALITY EDUCATION. THE PHOTOGRAPH WAS USED FOR ADVERTISING. (USA)

■ 193 PORTRAIT OF RHYTHM AND BLUES SINGER FRANCINE REED TO ACCOMPANY AN ARTICLE IN *TRENDS MAGAZINE*. (USA)

■ 194 HAND-TINTED BLACK-AND-WHITE PHOTOGRAPH OF A LITTLE GIRL WEARING A HAT WITH DRY-PRESSED FLOWERS. (USA)

● 190 MARY ELIZABETH JOHNSON, AUFGENOMMEN IN ALVA, OKLAHOMA, FÜR DEN PAPIERHERSTELLER CHAMPION INTERNATIONAL. (USA)

● 191 EIN PORTRÄT DES SCHAUSPIELERS ROBERT DOWNEY JR., DAS DER PHOTOGRAPH ALS EIGENWERBUNG IN *SELECT* VERWENDETE. (USA)

● 192 DER AUFTRAG DER WASHINGTON EDUCATION ASSOCIATION LAUTETE, EINE NEGATIVE PERSON DARZUSTELLEN, DIE ZUM VORBILD FÜR SCHÜLER WERDEN KÖNNTE, DIE KEINE GUTE AUSBILDUNG BEKOMMEN. (USA)

● 193 PORTRÄT DER RHYTHM-AND-BLUES-SÄNGERIN FRANCINE REED FÜR EINEN ARTIKEL IN *TRENDS MAGAZINE*. (USA)

● 194 HANDKOLORIERTE SCHWARZWEISS-AUFNAHME EINES KLEINEN MÄDCHENS, GESCHMÜCKT MIT EINEM BLUMENHUT. (USA)

▲ 190 MARY ELIZABETH JOHNSON, PHOTOGRAPHIÉE À ALVA DANS L'OKLAHOMA, POUR LE FABRICANT DE PAPIER CHAMPION INTERNATIONAL. (USA)

▲ 191 PORTRAIT DE L'ACTEUR ROBERT DOWNEY JR. PARU DANS LE MAGAZINE *SELECT* ET UTILISÉ COMME AUTOPROMOTION. (USA)

▲ 192 LA WASHINGTON EDUCATION ASSOCIATION AVAIT DEMANDÉ AU PHOTOGRAPHE DE MONTRER UN PERSONNAGE NÉGATIF QUE DES ENFANTS AYANT REÇU UNE FORMATION INSUFFISANTE POURRAIENT IMITER. (USA)

▲ 193 PORTRAIT DE LA CHANTEUSE DE BLUES FRANCINE REED POUR UN ARTICLE PARU DANS *TRENDS MAGAZINE*. (USA)

▲ 194 PHOTO EN NOIR ET BLANC COLORÉE MAIN D'UNE PETITE FILLE PORTANT UN CHAPEAU ORNÉ DE FLEURS. (USA)

PHOTOGRAPHER:

STUART N. DEE

CAMERA:

CANON

CLIENT:

STUART N. DEE

ART DIRECTOR:

STUART N. DEE

■ 195

PHOTOGRAPHER:

YURI DOJC

REPRESENTATIVE:

VAN NETOFF

CAMERA:

NIKON

CLIENT:

YURI DOJC

▶■ 196

■ 195 PERSONAL WORK BY PHOTOGRAPHER STUART N. DEE. (CAN)

● 195 FREIE ARBEIT DES PHOTOGRAPHEN STUART N. DEE. (CAN)

▲ 195 ÉTUDE PERSONNELLE DU PHOTOGRAPHE STUART N. DEE. (CAN)

■ 196 THIS PHOTOGRAPH BELONGS TO A SERIES OF BLACK-AND-WHITE STUDIES BY JURI DOJC INTENDED FOR PUBLICATION IN BOOK FORM. (CAN)

● 196 DIESE AUFNAHME GEHÖRT ZU EINER SERIE VON SCHWARZWEISS-STUDIEN FÜR EIN BUCH DES PHOTOGRAPHEN JURI DOJC. (CAN)

▲ 196 D'UNE SÉRIE D'ÉTUDES EN NOIR ET BLANC DU PHOTOGRAPHE JURI DOJC QUI DEVRAIT ÊTRE PUBLIÉE SOUS FORME DE LIVRE. (CAN)

■ 197 FILM PRODUCER SHERRY LANSING WHO SEEMS TO BELONG IN FRONT RATHER THAN BEHIND THE CAMERA, WAS PHOTOGRAPHED IN THE POSE OF A STARLET FOR THE AMERICAN EXPRESS CARD-MEMBER CAMPAIGN FEATURING PORTRAITS OF FAMOUS PEOPLE. (USA)

■ 198 STRICTLY BY COINCIDENCE THE PHOTOGRA-PHER CAPTURED THIS SPONTANEOUS MOMENT OF PATRIOTIC FASHION ON THE FOURTH OF JULY. (USA)

■ 199 ON ASSIGNMENT FOR *NEW YORK TIMES SUNDAY MAGAZINE* THE PHOTOGRAPHER WAS GRANTED 20 MINUTES AND A VACANT OFFICE FOR THIS PORTRAIT OF ACTOR KEVIN COSTNER. COSTNER BECAME KNOWN AS ONE OF HOLLYWOOD'S GREAT RISK-TAKERS DURING 1989, WHEN HE PRODUCED, DIRECTED AND STARRED IN *DANCES WITH WOLVES*, A 3 1/2 HOUR FILM ON THE PLIGHT OF NATIVE AMERICANS IN THE LATE 1860S. (USA)

■ 200 THE ACTOR PETER WELLER AS ROBO COP, PORTRAYED FOR A FILM POSTER FOR ORION PIC-TURES, THE PHOTOGRAPHER CONVERTED HIS ORIG-INAL BLACK-AND-WHITE IMAGE TO COLOR USING A LARGE-FORMAT REGISTRATION SYSTEM. (USA)

● 197 DIE FILMPRODUZENTIN SHERRY LANSING, DIE EHER VOR ALS HINTER DIE KAMERA ZU GEHÖREN SCHEINT, WURDE IN DER POSE EINES STARLETS IM HINTERHOF DER PARAMOUNT STUDIOS AUFGENOM-MEN FÜR DIE AMERICAN EXPRESS-KAMPAGNE MIT PROMINENTEN KARTENINHABERN. (USA)

● 198 AUSGERECHNET AM 4. JULI, DEM NATIONAL-FEIERTAG DER USA, GELANG DEM PHOTOGRAPHEN DIESES TYPISCH AMERIKANISCHE PORTRÄT. (USA)

● 199 DIESES PORTRÄT DES SCHAUSPIELERS KEVIN COSTNER ENTSTAND FÜR DAS *NEW YORK TIMES SUNDAY MAGAZINE*. DER PHOTOGRAPH HATTE NUR 20 MINUTEN IN EINEM LEEREN BÜRO ZUR VERFÜ-GUNG. FÜR COSTNER WAR 1989 DAS JAHR, IN DEM ER ALLES AUF EINE KARTE SETZTE: ER WAR PRODU-ZENT, REGISSEUR UND DARSTELLER IN *DANCES WITH WOLVES*, EIN FILM, DER VOM KAMPF DER INDIANER ENDE 1860 HANDELT. (USA)

● 200 DER SCHAUSPIELER ROBERT WELLER ALS ROBOTER-POLIZIST, URSPRÜNGLICH FÜR EIN PLA-KAT DER ORION PICTURES AUFGENOMMEN. MIT HIL-FE EINES UMWANDLUNGSSYSTEMS WURDE AUS DER SCHWARZWEISS-AUFNAHME EIN FARBBILD. (USA)

▲ 197 LA PRODUCTRICE DE FILMS SHERRY LANSING PHOTOGRAPHIÉE DANS LA COUR DES STUDIOS DE LA PARAMOUNT DANS UNE POSE DE STARLETTE. D'UNE SÉRIE POUR UNE CAMPAGNE DE L'AMERICAN EXPRESS MONTRANT DES CÉLÉBRITÉS QUI POS-SÈDENT CETTE CARTE DE CRÉDIT. (USA)

▲ 198 CETTE PHOTO, PRISE LE 4 JUILLET, FÊTE NATIONALE AMÉRICAINE, SYMBOLISE AUX YEUX DU PHOTOGRAPHE LE PATRIOTISME. (USA)

▲ 199 CE PORTRAIT DE L'ACTEUR AMÉRICAIN KEVIN COSTNER A ÉTÉ RÉALISÉE POUR LE *NEW YORK TIMES SUNDAY MAGAZINE*. LE PHOTOGRAPHE NE DISPOSAIT QUE DE 20 MINUTES DANS UN BUREAU VIDE. EN 1989, COSTNER FUT À LA FOIS LE PRODUCTEUR, LE METTEUR EN SCÈNE ET L'ACTEUR DU FILM SUR LES INDIENS *DANCES WITH WOLVES*. IL A LUI-MÊME DU SANG CHEROKEE DANS LES VEINES. (USA)

▲ 200 LA PHOTO DE CE ROBOT-POLICIER (L'ACTEUR ROBERT WELLER) FUT D'ABORD PUBLIÉE SOUS FORME D'AFFICHE POUR ORION PICTURES. LE PHOTOGRAPHE A TRANSFORMÉ LA PHOTO NOIR ET BLANC EN UNE IMAGE COULEUR. (USA)

PHOTOGRAPHER:
ANNIE LEIBOVITZ
REPRESENTATIVE:
JIM MOFFATT
(ART + COMMERCE)
CLIENT:
AMERICAN EXPRESS

ART DIRECTOR:
PARRY MERKLEY/
RICK RABE
DESIGNER:
PARRY MERKLEY
■ 197

PHOTOGRAPHER:
GORDON BAER
CAMERA:
NIKON FM-2
FILM:
FUJICHROME
ART DIRECTOR:
GORDON BAER
■ 198

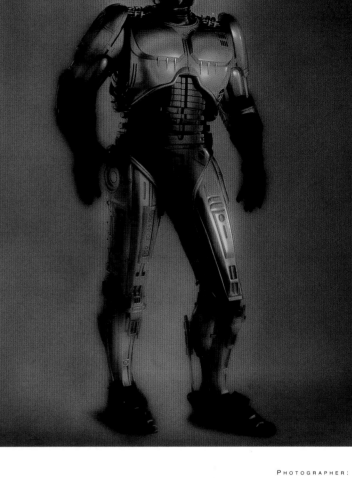

PHOTOGRAPHER:

BRIAN LANKER

REPRESENTATIVE:

KEN MANN

CAMERA:

HASSELBLAD

FILM:

FUJI 100

PHOTO EDITOR:

CATHY MANERI

CLIENT:

NEW YORK TIMES

SUNDAY MAGAZINE

■ 199

PHOTOGRAPHER:

WILLIAM HAWKES

REPRESENTATIVE:

FOX & SPENCER

CAMERA:

SINAR

FILM:

ORIGINAL T-MAX

100, 4X5/

CONVERTED ONTO

6117, 8X10

■ 200

PHOTOGRAPHER:
GIUSEPPE PINO
CAMERA:
HASSELBLAD 500
ELX
FILM:
KODAK EPP 120
EXPOSURE:
F 16, 1/125 AND
FLASH
PHOTO EDITOR:
GIUSEPPE PINO
CLIENT:
BENETTON SPA
ART DIRECTOR:
GIUSEPPE PINO
■ 201

PHOTOGRAPHER:
JIM GALANTE
REPRESENTATIVE:
RANDY COLE
CAMERA:
HASSELBLAD
■ 202

PHOTOGRAPHER:
NORITSUNE NOSE
CAMERA:
MAMIYA RZ 6X7,
180MM
FILM:
PLUS-X 120
EXPOSURE:
F 11, 1/125 A
STOROBE
SYNCHRONIZATION
▶■ 203

■ 201 LUCIANO BENETTON, POSING BEFORE A PAINTED CANVAS, IN A SWEATER THAT BEARS THE LABEL OF HIS OWN STORES. USED FOR PUBLIC RELATIONS PURPOSES FOR THE BENETTON CHAIN, (ITA)

■ 202 A PERSONAL STUDY BY PHOTOGRAPHER JIM GALANTE, THIS PHOTOGRAPH IS ACTUALLY A HAND-COLORED SILVER PRINT. (USA)

■ 203 IN THIS PERSONAL STUDY, THE PHOTOGRAPHER SHOWS THE CURRENT FASHION TREND OF MIXING OLD AND NEW, AND UNDER AND OUTER WEAR, AS THE MODEL COMBINES AN OLD-FASHIONED BUSTIER SET WITH VERY MODERN LEATHER PANTS. (JPN)

● 201 LUCIANO BENETTON IN EINEM PULLOVER VON BENETTON, AUFGENOMMEN VOR EINER GROSSEN, BEMALTEN LEINWAND. DAS PHOTO WIRD FÜR PUBLIC RELATIONS ZWECKE VERWENDET. (ITA)

● 202 EIN HANDKOLORIERTER SILBERDRUCK EINER SCHWARZWEISS-AUFNAHME DES PHOTOGRAPHEN JIM GALANTE. (USA)

● 203 IN DIESER PERSÖNLICHEN STUDIE EINER JAPANERIN KOMMENTIERT DER PHOTOGRAPH DEN GEGENWÄRTIGEN MODETREND, ALTES MIT NEUEM ZU KOMBINIEREN, EIN TREND, DER GLEICHZEITIG FÜR DIE KULTURELLE SITUATION JAPANS IN UNSEREM JAHRHUNDERT GÜLTIG IST. (JPN)

▲ 201 LUCIANO BENETTON EN PULL-OVER BENETTON, DEVANT UNE GRANDE TOILE PEINTE. CETTE PHOTO A ÉTÉ SÉLECTIONNÉE PAR LES SERVICES DE RELATIONS PUBLIQUES DE LA FIRME. (ITA)

▲ 202 TIRAGE AU GÉLATINO – BROMURE D'ARGENT POUR CETTE PHOTO NOIR ET BLANC COLORÉE MAIN DU PHOTOGRAPHE JIM GALANTE. (USA)

▲ 203 DANS CETTE ÉTUDE PERSONNELLE, LE PHOTOGRAPHE MONTRE UNE TENDANCE ACTUELLE DE LA MODE QUI CONSISTE À MÉLANGER L'ANCIEN ET LE MODERNE. LA JAPONAISE PORTE UN VIEUX MODÈLE DE BUSTIER QUI CONTRASTE AVEC LA MODERNITÉ DES PANTALONS EN CUIR. (ITA)

PHOTOGRAPHER:

HERB RITTS

REPRESENTATIVE:

VISAGES

PHOTO EDITOR:

LAURIE KRATOCHVIL

CLIENT:

ROLLING STONE

MAGAZINE

ART DIRECTOR:

FRED WOODWARD

■ 204

PHOTOGRAPHER:

HERB RITTS

REPRESENTATIVE:

VISAGES

CLIENT:

DISNEY STUDIOS

ART DIRECTOR:

HERB RITTS

▶■ 205

■ 204 PHOTOGRAPHER HERB RITTS STATES THAT HIS PHOTOGRAPHY HAS BEEN CALLED "UNGLAMOROUS GLAMOR." HERE WE SEE THE OFTEN-RECLUSIVE ACTOR WARREN BEATTY IN A RELAXED MOMENT, AS CAPTURED BY RITTS FOR THE PAGES OF *ROLLING STONE* MAGAZINE. (USA)

■ 205 MADONNA AS BREATHLESS MAHONEY AND WARREN BEATTY AS DICK TRACY, IN THE FILM OF THE SAME TITLE, ARE SHOWN SURROUNDED BY THEIR GANGSTER FOES IN THIS PUBLICITY PHOTOGRAPH TAKEN FOR DISNEY STUDIOS. IT LATER APPEARED IN *ROLLING STONE* MAGAZINE TO ACCOMPANY AN ARTICLE ON THE FILM. (USA)

● 204 GEMÄSS HERB RITTS HAT JEMAND SEINEN STIL ALS «UNGLAMOROUS GLAMOR» BEZEICHNET. DIESES SPEZIELLE PORTRÄT DES FILMSCHAU-SPIELERS WARREN BEATTY BEIM ENTSPANNEN ERSCHIEN IN EINEM ARTIKEL IN DER ZEITSCHRIFT *ROLLING STONE*. (USA)

● 205 MADONNA, ALS BREATHLESS MAHONEY, UND WARREN BEATTY, ALS DICK TRACY, IM GLEICH-NAMIGEN FILM, UMGEBEN VON GANGSTERN. DIE AUFNAHME ENTSTAND IM AUFTRAG DER DISNEY STUDIOS UND WURDE AUCH FÜR EINEN BEITRAG ÜBER DIESEN FILM IN DER ZEITSCHRIFT *ROLLING STONE* GEZEIGT. (USA)

▲ 204 SELON LES PROPRES TERMES DU PHOTO-GRAPHE HERB RITTS, ON A QUALIFIÉ SON STYLE DE «UNGLAMOROUS GLAMOR». CE PORTRAIT DE L'AC-TEUR DE FILM WARREN BEATTY EN TRAIN DE SE RELAXER A ÉTÉ PUBLIÉ DANS LE MAGAZINE *ROLLING STONE*. (USA)

▲ 205 MADONNA ET WARREN BEATTY, DANS LE RÔLE DE DICK TRACY, ENTOURÉS DES GANGSTERS DU FILM DU MÊME NOM. CETTE PHOTO A ÉTÉ RÉALISÉE POUR LES STUDIOS DISNEY POUR LE LANCEMENT DU FILM. ELLE A ÉTÉ ENSUITE PUBLIÉE DANS *ROLLING STONE* POUR ILLUSTRER UN ARTICLE SUR LE FILM. (USA)

PHOTOGRAPHER:
JEFFREY MUIR
HAMILTON
REPRESENTATIVE:
JEFFREY MUIR
HAMILTON
CAMERA:
SINAR 4X5
FILM:
POLAROID 55
PHOTO EDITOR:
KATHRYN POLK
CLIENT:
WOODS
LITHOGRAPHERS
ART DIRECTOR:
LISA HUMMEL
DESIGNER:
LISA HUMMEL
■ 206

■ 206 WOOD LITHOGRAPHERS ASSIGNED THIS PHOTOGRAPH AS PART OF A PROMOTIONAL CAMPAIGN, BUILT AROUND THE THEME OF "TOYS." (USA)

■ 207 THE SUBJECT OF THIS PORTRAIT HAD BEEN A COOK IN NEW ORLEANS. NOW HE IS UNEMPLOYED AND HOMELESS, LIVING ON THE STREETS OF KANSAS CITY. IN THIS PHOTOGRAPH, PART OF A SERIES OF PERSONAL WORK BY THE PHOTOGRAPHER, THE BEDSPRINGS SERVE AS A METAPHOR FOR THE IMPRISONMENT OF THE HOMELESS IN AMERICA. (USA)

■ 208 UNICEF COMMISSIONED PHOTOJOURNALIST STEPHENIE HOLLYMAN TO DOCUMENT THE EFFECTS OF APARTHEID ON CHILDREN LIVING IN THE COUNTRIES BORDERING SOUTH AFRICA FOR A BOOK ENTITLED *CHILDREN OF THE FRONT LINE*. THE PHOTOGRAPHER SPENT THREE MONTHS IN ANGOLA, MOZAMBIQUE, LESOTHO, NAMIBIA, ZIMBABWE, AND BOTSWANA. THE SUBJECT OF THIS PHOTOGRAPH IS A WOMAN LIVING IN LESOTHO, VERY NEAR THE SOUTH AFRICAN BORDER. (USA)

● 206 SPIELZEUG SOLLTE IN DIESER AUFNAHME FÜR EINE LITHOGRAPHENANSTALT EINE ROLLE SPIELEN. (USA)

● 207 DER MANN AUF DIESEM PHOTO WAR FRÜHER KOCH IN NEW ORLEANS UND IST HEUTE ARBEITSLOS ER LEBT ALS OBDACHLOSER IN DEN STRASSEN VON KANSAS CITY. DIESE AUFNAHME GEHÖRT ZU EINER SERIE VON FREIEN STUDIEN DES PHOTOGRAPHEN. DIE SPRUNGFEDERN AUF DEM BILD DIENEN IHM ALS METAPHER FÜR DIE GEFÄNGNISÄHNLICHE SITUATION DER OBDACHLOSEN. (USA)

● 208 DIE UNICEF BEAUFTRAGTE DIE PHOTOJOURNALISTIN STEPHENIE HOLLYMAN, DIE AUSWIRKUNGEN DER APARTHEID AUF DIE KINDER IN DEN ANGRENZENDEN LÄNDERN SÜDAFRIKAS FÜR EIN BUCH MIT DEM TITEL *CHILDREN OF THE FRONT LINE* ZU DOKUMENTIEREN. DREI MONATE LANG REISTE SIE DURCH ANGOLA, MOZAMBIQUE, LESOTHO, NAMIBIA, ZIMBABWE UND BOTSWANA. DIE FRAU AUF DEM PHOTO LEBT NAHE DER GRENZE ZWISCHEN LESOTHO UND SÜDAFRIKA. (USA)

▲ 206 INTERPRÉTATION PERSONNELLE SUR LE THÈME DES JOUETS, RÉALISÉE POUR UN IMPRIMEUR-LITHOGRAPHE. (USA)

▲ 207 PORTRAIT D'UN CUISINIER AU CHÔMAGE ET SANS-ABRI DE LA NOUVELLE-ORLÉANS QUE LE PHOTOGRAPHE A RENCONTRÉ DANS LES RUES DE KANSAS CITY. CETTE PHOTO FAIT PARTIE D'UNE SÉRIE D'ÉTUDES PERSONNELLES. LES RESSORTS DU MATELAS SONT POUR LE PHOTOGRAPHE UNE MÉTAPHORE DE LA SITUATION SANS ISSUE DONT CET HOMME EST PRISONNIER. (USA)

▲ 208 L'UNICEF AVAIT DEMANDÉ À STEPHENIE HOLLYMAN, PHOTOREPORTER AMÉRICAINE, DE DOCUMENTER LES EFFETS DE L'APARTHEID SUR LES ENFANTS DANS LES PAYS BORDANT L'AFRIQUE DU SUD POUR UN LIVRE INTITULÉ *CHILDREN OF THE FRONT LINE*. PENDANT TROIS MOIS, ELLE A VOYAGÉ EN ANGOLA, AU MOZAMBIQUE, AU LESOTHO, EN NAMIBIE, AU ZIMBABWE ET AU BOTSWANA. LA FEMME SUR CETTE PHOTO VIT AU LESOTHO, PRÈS DE LA FRONTIÈRE SUD-AFRICAINE. (USA)

PHOTOGRAPHER:
NICK VEDROS
CAMERA:
SINAR BRON 4X5
FILM:
KODAK EKTACHROME
EPP 100 PLUS
CLIENT:
VEDROS &
ASSOCIATES
ART DIRECTOR:
NICK VEDROS
■ 207

PHOTOGRAPHER:
STEPHENIE
HOLLYMAN
CAMERA:
NIKON F3
FILM:
KODACHROME 64
PHOTO EDITOR:
PETER DAVID
CLIENT:
UNICEF
■ 208

PHOTOGRAPHER:
MARC HAUSER
REPRESENTATIVE:
RANDI FIAT &
ASSOC., CHICAGO/
ZARI INTERNA-
TIONAL, NEW YORK
CAMERA:
HASSELBLAD
FILM:
KODAK EKTACHROME
CLIENT:
JOHN BUTSCH &
ASSOCIATES 209

ARISTA RECORDS 210
CONNOISSEUR 211
PSYCHOLOGY TODAY
212
ART DIRECTOR:
GARY ALFREDSON/
LYNN DANGEL 209
MARC HAUSER 210
KAREN SILVERSTEIN 211
LESTER GOODMAN 212
DESIGNER:
GARY ALFREDSON/
LYNN DANGEL 209
■ 209-212

PHOTOGRAPHER:
JAN SAUDEK
REPRESENTATIVE:
ART UNLIMITED
CAMERA:
FLEXAREL
FILM:
FOMA 6X6
PHOTO EDITOR:
JAN SAUDEK
ART DIRECTOR:
JAN SAUDEK
DESIGNER:
JAN SAUDEK
▶■ 213

■ 209-212 PORTAITS BY MARC HAUSER FOR A VARIETY OF ASSIGNMENTS. FROM LEFT TO RIGHT: THE PHOTO OF THE YOUNG WOMAN WAS USED FOR SELF-PROMOTION IN *CREATIVE ACCESS*; POP SINGER PATTI SMITH WAS PHOTOGRAPHED FOR ARISTA RECORDS; THE PORTRAIT OF INFLUENTIAL CHICAGO ART CRITIC DENNIS ADRIAN WAS TAKEN FOR *CONNOISSEUR* MAGAZINE; AND BEN FELDMAN WHO HAS SOLD NEARLY A BILLION DOLLAR'S WORTH OF LIFE INSURANCE, WAS PHOTOGRAPHED FOR *PSYCHOLOGY TODAY*. (USA)

■ 213 THIS PHOTOGRAPH, UNTITLED, IS ONE FROM A SERIES TAKEN BY JAN SAUDEK IN PRAGUE. (CSR)

● 209-212 PORTRÄTS DES PHOTOGRAPHEN MARC HAUSER, V.L.N.R.: DIE JUNGE FRAU IN BLAUER SEIDE PHOTOGRAPHIERTE ER FÜR EIGENWER-BUNGSZWECKE IN DER ZEITSCHRIFT *CREATIVE ACCESS*; POP-SÄNGERIN PATTI SMITH FÜR ARISTA RECORDS; DAS PORTRÄT DES EINFLUSSREICHEN KUNSTKRITIKERS DENNIS ADRIAN AUS CHICAGO WURDE FÜR *CONNOISSEUR* AUFGENOMMEN. BEN FELDMAN, EINEN ÄUSSERST ERFOLGREICHEN VER-SICHERUNGSVERTRETER, PHOTOGRAPHIERTE ER FÜR DIE ZEITSCHRIFT *PSYCHOLOGY TODAY*. (USA)

● 213 DIESE SZENE (OHNE TITEL) PHOTOGRAPHIER-TE JAN SAUDEK BEI EINEM BESUCH IN PRAG. (CSR)

▲ 209-212 PORTRAITS DU PHOTOGRAPHE MARC HAUSER. DE G. À DR. ET DE HAUT EN BAS: PHOTO UTILISÉE COMME AUTOPROMOTION DANS LE MAGA-ZINE *CREATIVE ACCESS*; LA CHANTEUSE PATTI SMITH PHOTOGRAPHIÉE POUR LES DISQUES ARISTA; LE PORTRAIT DE DENNIS ADRIAN, UN CRITIQUE D'ART DE CHICAGO A ÉTÉ RÉALISÉ À SON DOMICILE POUR LE MAGAZINE *CONNOISSEUR*; BEN FELDMAN, UN AGENT D'ASSURANCE PROSPÈRE, DANS SON BUREAU, POUR UN ARTICLE PARU DANS LE MAGA-ZINE *PSYCHOLOGY TODAY*. (USA)

▲ 213 SANS TITRE. JAN SAUDEK A PHOTOGRAPHIÉ CETTE SCÈNE LORS D'UNE VISITE À PRAGUE. (CSR)

BEST PEOPLE

PHOTOGRAPHER:

BRIAN LANKER

REPRESENTATIVE:

KEN MANN

CAMERA:

HASSELBLAD

FILM:

T-MAX 100

PHOTO EDITOR:

BRIAN LANKER

CLIENT:

STEWART, TABORI &

CHANG, INC.

■ 214-216

PHOTOGRAPHER:

JAMES SALZANO

REPRESENTATIVE:

MARTY BOGHOSIAN

CAMERA:

HASSELBLAD

FILM:

FUJICHROME RDP 120

EXPOSURE:

F 8, 1/15

CLIENT:

ADVERTISING

AGE/CREATIVITY 217

GREY

ENTERTAINMENT 218

ART DIRECTOR:

JAMES SALZANO

▶■ 217, 218

■ 214-216 FROM A SERIES FEATURING PORTRAITS OF PROMINENT BLACK WOMEN: SEPTIMA CLARK, ONE OF THE HEROES OF THE CIVIL RIGHTS MOVEMENT; MS. CORETTA SCOTT KING, PRESIDENT AND CHIEF EXECUTIVE OF THE KING CENTER FOR NONVIOLENT SOCIAL CHANGE; AND EVA JESSYE, CHORAL DIRECTOR FOR THE FIRST BROADWAY PRODUCTION OF PORGY AND BESS. THIS PHOTOGRAPH HAS RECEIVED THE BEST IN CATEGORY, PEOPLE, AWARD FOR THE GRAPHIS PHOTO 91 COMPETITION, SPONSORED BY EASTMAN KODAK. (USA)

■ 217, 218 BRITISH PHOTOGRAPHER/DIRECTOR DAVID BAILEY AND AMERICAN ENTERTAINMENT LEGEND GEORGE BURNS. THE PHOTO SESSION TOOK PLACE IN A BACKSTAGE DRESSING ROOM; WHILE MR. BURNS SANG SOME SONGS, THE PHOTOGRAPHER QUICKLY SHOT FOUR ROLLS OF FILM. (USA)

● 214-216 SCHWARZE FRAUEN, DIE FÜR DIE ENTWICKLUNG DER USA EINE GROSSE ROLLE SPIELTEN: SEPTIMA CLARK, EINE DER VERTRETERINNEN DER BÜRGERRECHTSBEWEGUNG, CORETTA SCOTT KING, DIREKTORIN UND LEITERIN DES KING-ZENTRUMS FÜR GEWALTLOSE SOZIALE VERÄNDERUNGEN UND EVA JESSYE, CHORLEITERIN DER ERSTEN BROADWAY-PRODUKTION VON PORGY UND BESS. DIESE AUFNAHME WURDE MIT DEM «BEST OF CATEGORY AWARD» FÜR DIE KATEGORIE MENSCHEN VON GRAPHIS PHOTO 91 AUSGEZEICHNET. (USA)

● 217, 218 DER BRITISCHE PHOTOGRAPH/REGISSEUR DAVID BAILEY UND DER AMERIKANISCHE KOMIKERS GEORGE BURNS, DER HEUTE 95 JAHRE ALT IST. DEM PHOTOGRAPHEN WURDEN NUR WENIGE MINUTEN GEWÄHRT. DAS PORTRÄT IST DAS ERGEBNIS VON VIER ROLLEN FILM. (USA)

▲ 214-216 D'UN PROJET PERSONNEL QUI MONTRE LES FEMMES DE COULEUR AYANT JOUÉ UN RÔLE IMPORTANT AUX USA: SEPTIMA CLARK, REPRÉSENTANTE DU MOUVEMENT DES DROITS CIVIQUES; CORETTA SCOTT KIN, DIRECTRICE DU KING CENTER, QUI S'ENGAGE POUR DES TRANSFORMATIONS SOCIALES SANS VIOLENCE; LA DIRECTRICE DES CHŒURS DE LA PREMIÈRE PRODUCTION DE PORGY AND BESS À BROADWAY, EVA JESSYE. CE DERNIER PORTRAIT A REÇU LE «BEST OF CATEGORY AWARD/ PEOPLE» DU CONCOURS GRAPHIS PHOTO 91. (USA)

▲ 217, 218 LE PHOTOGRAPHE ET METTEUR EN SCÈNE ANGLAIS DAVID BAILEY ET LE COMIQUE AMÉRICAIN GEORGE BURNS DANS SA LOGE. POUR CETTE DERNIÈRE PHOTO, UNE COMMANDE DE GREY ENTERTAINMENT, LE PHOTOGRAPHE NE DISPOSAIT QUE DE QUELQUES MINUTES: IL PRIS 4 FILMS. (USA)

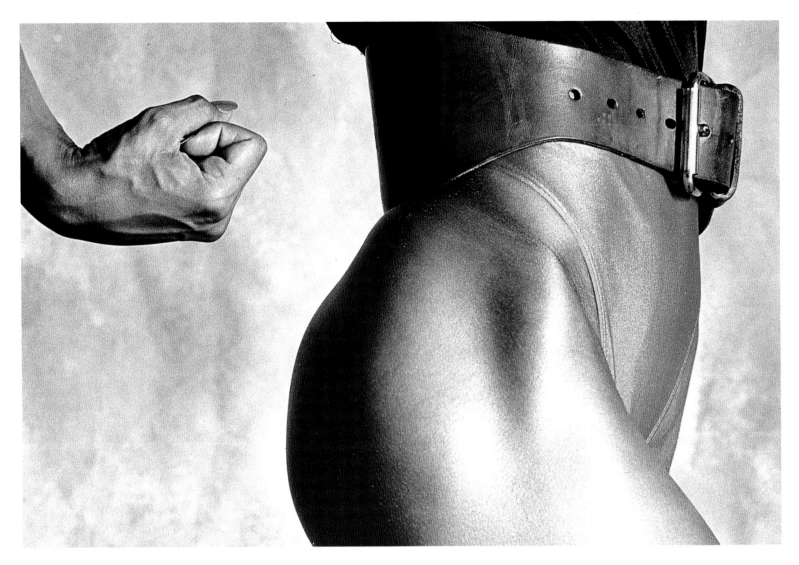

PHOTOGRAPHER:
JOHN RUNNING
CAMERA:
NIKON F3
FILM:
KODAK TRI-X
CLIENT:
RUMRILL-HOYT
ART DIRECTOR:
STEVE HALL
■ 219

PHOTOGRAPHER:
JOHN RUNNING
CAMERA:
NIKON F3
FILM:
ILFORD HP5 PLU
CLIENT:
BENNETT-RIINNI
GALLERY
DESIGNER:
JOHN RUNNING
▶■ 220, 221

■ 219 ONE OF A SERIES OF PHOTOS USED TO ADVERTISE KODAK BLACK-AND-WHITE FILM AND PRINTING PAPER. THE ASSIGNMENT WAS TO EMPHASIZE THE "STRENGTH OF BLACK AND WHITE." (USA)

■ 220, 221 THESE TWO PHOTOS "TRAIN HARD" AND "TRAIN CLEAN" ARE PART OF AN ONGOING SERIES OF POSTERS OF WOMEN BODY-BUILDERS. THE PHOTOGRAPHER'S AIM WAS TO GIVE EXPRESSION TO THE SENSUALITY OF STRENGTH. (USA)

● 219 AUS EINER REIHE VON AUFNAHMEN ALS WERBUNG FÜR SCHWARZWEISS-FILME VON KODAK. DER AUFTRAG WAR, DIE «STÄRKE VON SCHWARZWEISS» ZUM AUSDRUCK ZU BRINGEN. (USA)

● 220, 221 DIESE BEIDEN PHOTOS – «TRAINIERE HART», «TRAINIERE SAUBER» – GEHÖREN ZU EINER PLAKATREIHE ÜBER FRAUEN, DIE BODY-BUILDING BETREIBEN. ES GING UM DIE VISUALISIERUNG VON «SINNLICHKEIT DER STÄRKE». (USA)

▲ 219 PHOTO D'UNE SÉRIE UTILISÉE POUR LA PUBLICITÉ DES FILMS KODAK NOIR ET BLANC. LE PHOTOGRAPHE DEVAIT ICI SOULIGNER «LA FORCE DU NOIR ET BLANC». (USA)

▲ 220, 221 CES DEUX PHOTOS PRISES À L'ENTRAÎNEMENT FONT PARTIE D'UNE SÉRIE D'AFFICHES SUR LES FEMMES QUI PRATIQUENT LE CULTURISME. LE PHOTOGRAPHE A CHERCHÉ À RENDRE «LA SENSUALITÉ DE LA FORCE». (USA)

PHOTOGRAPHER:
MARC NORBERG
CLIENT:
BOYS AND GIRLS
CLUBS OF CHICAGO
DESIGNER:
GREG SAMATA/
PAT SAMATA
■ 222

PHOTOGRAPHER:
KEITH CARTER
CAMERA:
HASSELBLAD, 80MM
FILM:
ILFORD FP4
EXPOSURE:
F 8, 1/125
PHOTO EDITOR:
D.J. STOUT
CLIENT:
TEXAS MONTHLY
ART DIRECTOR:
D.J. STOUT
DESIGNER:
D.J. STOUT
■ 223

PHOTOGRAPHER:

RUSS SCHLEIPMAN

CAMERA:

NIKON F3

FILM:

KODACHROME 64

EXPOSURE:

F 5.6, 1/250

CLIENT:

ROCKRESORTS

ART DIRECTOR:

RICHARD BRUZZI

DESIGNER:

MOLLY NELSON

■ 224

■ 222 FUTURE LIFESAVERS—A PORTRAIT OF THE TWINS LISA AND LAUREN DILORETTO ILLUSTRATE THE ANNUAL REPORT OF THE BOYS AND GIRLS CLUBS OF CHICAGO. (USA)

■ 223 THIS PHOTO WAS MADE AT A SMALL NON-DENOMINATIONAL CHURCH ON LITTLE COW CREEK, NEWTON COUNTY IN TEXAS. ORIGINALLY A PERSONAL PROJECT, IT WAS PUBLISHED BY *TEXAS MONTHLY* AS "THE SOUL OF EAST TEXAS." (USA)

■ 224 AN ARIZONA RESORT HOTEL ASSIGNED PHOTOGRAPHER RUSS SCHLEINMAN TO DEPICT ACTIVITIES AVAILABLE FOR GUESTS. THIS IMAGE REFERS TO BACK COUNTRY TOURS WITH AN INDIAN GUIDE. (USA)

● 222 ZUKÜNFTIGE LEBENSRETTERINNEN – EIN PORTRÄT DER ZWILLINGE LISA UND LAUREN DILO-RETTO ALS ILLUSTRATION EINES JAHRESBERICHTES DER BOYS AND GIRLS CLUBS VON CHICAGO. (USA)

● 223 DIESE AUFNAHME ENTSTAND IN EINER NICHT KONFESSIONSGEBUNDENEN KLEINEN KIRCHE IN LITTLE COW CREEK, TEXAS. SIE WURDE IN *TEXAS MONTHLY* UNTER DEM TITEL «DIE SEELE DES OSTENS VON TEXAS» VERÖFFENTLICHT. (USA)

● 224 EIN FERIENHOTEL IN ARIZONA BEAUFTRAGTE DEN PHOTOGRAPHEN, DIE FREIZEITMÖGLICHKEITEN FÜR DIE GÄSTE ZU DOKUMENTIEREN. DIESE AUF-NAHME BEZIEHT SICH AUF AUSFLÜGE INS HINTER-LAND MIT EINEM INDIANISCHEN FÜHRER. (USA)

▲ 222 UNE NOUVELLE GÉNÉRATION DE SAUVE-TEURS: PORTRAIT DES JUMELLES LISA ET LAUREN DILORETTO ILLUSTRANT UN RAPPORT ANNUEL DES BOYS AND GIRLS CLUBS DE CHICAGO. (USA)

▲ 223 CETTE PHOTO A ÉTÉ RÉALISÉE DANS UNE PETITE ÉGLISE DE LITTLE COW CREEK, AU TEXAS, QUI N'EST RATTACHÉE À AUCUNE CONFESSION. ELLE A ÉTÉ PUBLIÉE DANS LE *TEXAS MONTHLY* SOUS LE TITRE «L'ÂME DE L'EST DU TEXAS». (USA)

▲ 224 UN HÔTEL DE VACANCES EN ARIZONA DEMAN-DA AU PHOTOGRAPHE DE DOCUMENTER TOUTES LES DISTRACTIONS QUI S'OFFRENT AUX CLIENTS. CETTE PHOTO A TRAIT AUX EXCURSIONS DANS L'ARRIÈRE-PAYS EN COMPAGNIE D'UN GUIDE INDIEN. (USA)

PHOTOGRAPHER:
ROBERT VAN DER
HILST
CLIENT:
MARIE CLAIRE
■ 225

PHOTOGRAPHER:
HERB RITTS
REPRESENTATIVE:
VISAGES
▶■ 226

■ 225 THE CONTRASTING LIFESTLYE OF TWO GENERATIONS WERE CAPTURED IN THE UNDERGROUND STATION AT ALEXANDERPLATZ IN EAST BERLIN PRIOR TO THE REUNIFICATION OF GERMANY. THE PHOTOGRAPH APPEARED IN THE FRENCH MAGAZINE MARIE CLAIRE. (FRA)

■ 226 DJIMON WITH OCTOPUS, FROM THE COLLECTION OF HERB RITTS PHOTOGRAPHS ENTITLED MEN/WOMEN. EROTICISM IS A CONSTANT PRESENCE IN RITT'S PHOTOGRAPHY, WHETHER THE PURPOSE IS CELEBRITY REPORTAGE, FASHION, OR HIS OWN PERSONAL WORK. THIS PHOTOGRAPH, EXHIBITING A MORE ANDROGYNOUS SENSUALITY, WAS ACTUALLY TAKEN ON THE ROOF OF HIS HOLLYWOOD HOME. (USA)

● 225 DER KONTRAST ZWISCHEN GENERATIONEN UND LEBENSAUFFASSUNGEN, DOKUMENTIERT MIT EINEM PHOTO, DAS VOR DER WIEDERVEREINIGUNG IN DER U.BAHNSTATION ALEXANDER-PLATZ IM EHEMALIGEN OSTBERLIN ENTSTAND. ES ERSCHIEN IN DER ZEITSCHRIFT MARIE CLAIRE. (FRA)

● 226 »DJIMON MIT TINTENFISCH«, EINE AUFNAHME AUS HERB RITTS PHOTOBAND MEN/WOMEN. EROTIK SPIELT IN SEINEN PHOTOGRAPHIEN EINE GROSSE ROLLE, OB ES SICH UM AUFNAHMEN VON BERÜHMTHEITEN, UM MODEPHOTOS ODER UM FREIE ARBEITEN HANDELT. DIESE AUFNAHME, EHER EIN ZWITTER, WAS DIE EROTIK ANGEHT, MACHTE HERB RITTS AUF DEM DACH SEINES HAUSES IN HOLLYWOOD. (USA)

▲ 225 CETTE PHOTO, PRISE AVANT LA RÉUNIFICATION DE BERLIN DANS LA STATION DE MÉTRO D'ALEXANDERPLATZ À BERLIN-EST, MONTRE DE MANIÈRE SAISISSANTE LE CONTRASTE ENTRE DEUX GÉNÉRATIONS ET DEUX MODES DE VIE. ELLE A ÉTÉ PUBLIÉE DANS MARIE CLAIRE. (FRA)

▲ 226 »DJIMON ET LA POULPE«, UNE PHOTOGRAPHIE TIRÉE DU LIVRE DE HERB RITTS MEN/ WOMEN. L'ÉROTISME JOUE UN RÔLE ESSENTIEL CHEZ RITTS, QU'IL S'AGISSE DE PORTRAITS DE STARS, DE PHOTOS DE MODE OU D'ÉTUDES PERSONNELLES. CETTE IMAGE D'UNE EXTRÊME SENSUALITÉ PRÉSENTE UN CARACTÈRE ANDROGYNE. ELLE A ÉTÉ PRISE SUR LE TOIT DE LA MAISON DU PHOTOGRAPHE. (USA)

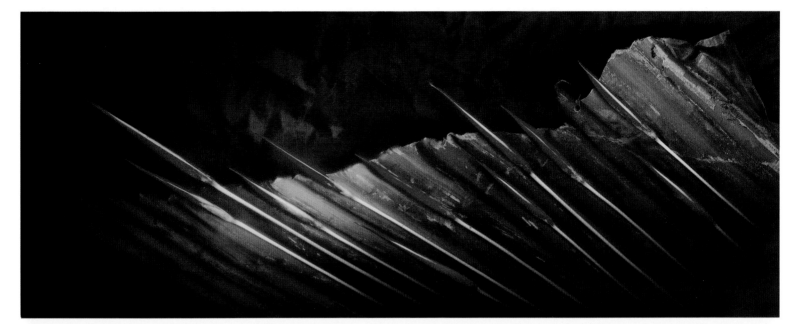

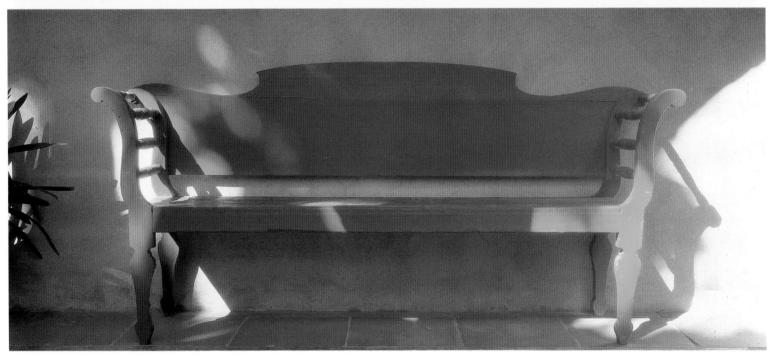

PHOTOGRAPHER:

KEN REID

CAMERA:

FATIF 8X10

FILM:

KODAK 64 EKTA-

CHROME DAYLIGHT

CLIENT:

KEN REID

DESIGNER:

BETSY REID

▲
▲■ 103

PHOTOGRAPHER:

HARRY DE ZITTER

CAMERA:

LINHOF

TECHNORAMA 6X12

FILM:

KODAK EPR 120

EXPOSURE:

F 11, 1/15

CLIENT:

SHERRY FEDERA-

TION OF SPAIN

ART DIRECTOR:

GERT VAN ZANTEN

■ 104

PRODUCTS

SACHAUFNAHMEN

PRODUITS

■ 227 (PRECEDING SPREAD) THIS PHOTOGRAPH WAS TAKEN ON A FAIR. UNFORTUNATELY, THE PHOTOGRAPHER IS UNKNOWN. (SPA)

■ 228 PHOTOGRAPH OF A NEW MODEL OF OMEGA WATCH FOR *L'UOMO VOGUE*. (ITA)

■ 229 PHOTO USED IN AN ADVERTISEMENT FOR HANDBAGS. THE CLIENT WANTED TO EMPHASIZE THE HIGH QUALITY OF HIS PRODUCTS WITHIN THE FRAMEWORK OF A PROVOCATIVE IMAGE. THREE MULTIPLE EXPOSURES WERE USED. (USA)

■ 230 THIS PHOTOGRAPH FOR THE ITALIAN TRADE COMMISSION HAD TO IMPLY BOTH A CONTEMPORARY FEELING AND A CONNECTION TO THE ARTISTIC MASTERS OF ITALIAN RENAISSANCE. FIVE MULTIPLE EXPOSURES ACROSS ONE SHEET OF 8X10 FILM WERE USED. (USA)

● 227 (VORHERGEHENDE SEITE) DIESE AUFNAHME ENTSTAND WÄHREND EINER MESSE. LEIDER IST DER NAME DES PHOTOGRAPHEN NICHT BEKANNT. (SPA)

● 228 AUFNAHME EINES NEUEN UHRENMMODELLS DER MARKE OMEGA FÜR *L'UOMO VOGUE*. (ITA)

● 229 AUFNAHME FÜR EINE HANDTASCHENANZEIGE. DER HERSTELLER WOLLTE DIE EXKLUSIVITÄT SEINER PRODUKTE HERVORHEBEN UND GLEICHZEITIG EINE GANZ SPEZIELLE PRÄSENTATION DER HANDTASCHE. (USA)

● 230 SOWOHL DIE ZEITGENÖSSISCHE QUALITÄT DES SCHMUCKS ALS AUCH DIE GROSSE KÜNSTLERISCHE TRADITION DER ITALIENISCHEN RENAISSANCE SOLLTEN IN DIESER AUFNAHME ZUM AUSDRUCK KOMMEN. (USA)

▲ 227 (PAGE PRÉCÉDENTE) CETTE PHOTOGRAPHIE A ÉTÉ PRISE AU COURS D'UNE FOIRE. LE NOM DU PHOTOGRAPHE EST MALHEUREUSEMENT INCONNU. (SPA)

▲ 228 PHOTOGRAPHIE D'UN NOUVEAU MODÈLE DE MONTRE OMEGA, PARUE DANS *L'UOMO VOGUE*. (ITA)

▲ 229 SAC PHOTOGRAPHIÉ POUR UNE PUBLICITÉ PLEINE PAGE PARUE DANS LES MAGAZINES *TOWN AND COUNTRY* ET *NEW YORK*. LE CLIENT DÉSIRAIT METTRE L'ACCENT SUR LA QUALITÉ DE CE PRODUIT HAUT DE GAMME D'UNE MANIÉRE ORIGINALE. (USA)

▲ 230 RÉALISÉE POUR LA CHAMBRE DE COMMERCE ITALIENNE, CETTE PHOTOGRAPHIE ÉVOQUE LA TRADITION ARTISTIQUE DE LA RENAISSANCE ITALIENNE, À LAQUELLE VIENT S'AJOUTER LA QUALITÉ TECHNIQUE CONTEMPORAINE..(USA)

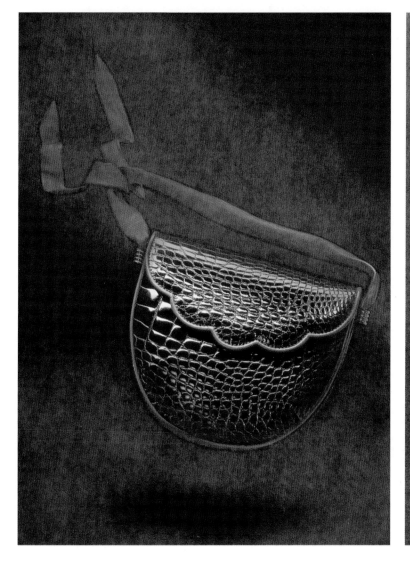

PHOTOGRAPHER:
STEFANO BIANCHI
CAMERA:
SINAR F2 10X12
FILM:
KODAK VPL 10X12
CLIENT:
L'UOMO VOGUE
◀■ 228

PHOTOGRAPHER:
DAVID HOLT
CAMERA:
SINAR P2 8X10
FILM:
EKTACHROME 100
EXPOSURE:
3 MULTIPLE
EXPOSURES
CLIENT:
MARK CROSS
ART DIRECTOR:
CHRISTINE COFFIN
AMATO
■ 229

PHOTOGRAPHER:
DAVID HOLT
CAMERA:
SINAR P2 8X10
FILM:
EKTACHROME 100
8X10
EXPOSURE:
5 MULTIPLE
EXPOSURES
CLIENT:
ITALIAN TRADE
COMMISSION
ART DIRECTOR:
BRUCE MALIN
■ 230

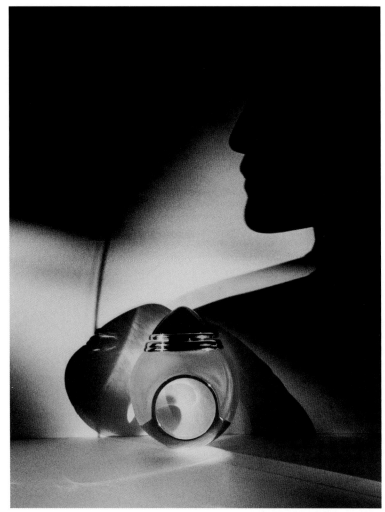

PHOTOGRAPHER:
MARC LE MENÉ
CLIENT:
BOUCHERON
ART DIRECTOR:
ALEXIS STROUKOFF
(PROMOTION *VOGUE*
PARIS)
■ 231

PHOTOGRAPHER:
MARC LE MENÉ
CLIENT:
AZZARO
ART DIRECTOR:
ALEXIS STROUKOFF
(PROMOTION *VOGUE*
PARIS)
● 232

PHOTOGRAPHER:
STEVE SHARP
REPRESENTATIVE:
CHERRY ARNOLD
CAMERA:
HASSELBLAD/SINAR
8X10P
FILM:
EKTACHROME 100
POLAROID 809
CLIENT:
STEVE SHARP
ART DIRECTOR:
STEVE SHARP
▶■ 233

■ 231, 232 THESE PHOTOGRAPHS ARE PART OF A SPECIAL *VOGUE PARIS* PROMOTION FOR BOUCHE-RON JEWELERS AND AZZARO EAU DE PARFUM. TYPICAL OF PHOTOGRAPHER MARC LE MENÉ'S STYLE IS THEIR PLAY OF SILHOUETTES AND SHADOWS, WHICH EVOKE A MYSTERIOUS AND EROTIC ATMOSPHERE. (FRA)

■ 233 THE ORIGINAL IMAGE FOR THIS PHOTOGRAPH WAS TAKEN WITH A 2¼ FILM. A 11X14 CIBACHROME WAS MADE AND THEN COPIED ON 8X10 POLAROID TRANSFER FILM. THE TRANSFER AND THE ORIGINAL TRANSPARENCY WERE SCANNED INTO A DIGITAL "PAINTBOX" SYSTEM. THE SUNGLASSES WERE REPRODUCED DIRECTLY FROM THE TRANSPARENCY TO BRING OUT THE CONTRAST OF THEIR TEXTURE AND COLOR. (USA)

● 231, 232 DIESE AUFNAHMEN SIND TEIL DER SPE-ZIELLEN PROMOTION *VOGUE PARIS* FÜR DEN JUWE-LIER BOUCHERON UND EIN EAU DE TOILETTE VON AZZARO. TYPISCH FÜR DEN PHOTOGRAPHEN MARC LE MENÉ IST DAS SPIEL MIT SILHOUETTEN UND SCHATTEN, MIT DEM ER EINE EROTISCHE, GEHEIM-NISVOLLE STIMMUNG ERZEUGT. (FRA)

● 233 FÜR DIESES BILD MACHTE DER PHOTOGRAPH EIN DIAPOSITIV. DANN WURDE EIN 11X14 CIBA-CHROME ANGEFERTIGT UND AUF EINEN 8X10 POLA-ROID-TRANSFER-FILM ÜBERTRAGEN; DER TRANSFER UND DAS ORIGINALDIA WURDEN IN EIN PAINTBOX-DIGITALSYSTEM EINGELESEN. DIE SONNENBRILLE WURDE DIREKT VOM DIA REPRODUZIERT, UM DEN GEWÜNSCHTEN KONTRAST ZU DER TEXTUR UND FARBE ZU ERREICHEN. (USA)

▲ 231, 232 IMAGES PROMOTIONNELLES POUR LE GRAND JOAILLIER BOUCHERON ET POUR UNE EAU DE PARFUM DE LORIS AZZARO, PUBLIÉES DANS *VOGUE PARIS*. LE JEU DES SILHOUETTES ET DES OMBRES EST TYPIQUE DU STYLE DU PHOTOGRAPHE, MARC LE MENÉ, QUI, ICI, SUSCITE UNE ATMOS-PHÈRE MYSTÉRIEUSE ET ÉROTIQUE. (FRA)

▲ 233 POUR RÉALISER CETTE IMAGE AUTOPROMO-TIONNELLE, LE PHOTOGRAPHE PRIT D'ABORD UNE DIAPOSITIVE, PUIS IL FIT UN CIBACHROME 11X14 AVANT D'OPÉRER UN TRANSFERT SUR POLAROÏD; LE RÉSULTAT FUT PASSÉ AU SCANNER (SYSTEME DIGITAL «PAINTBOX»). LES LUNETTES DE SOLEIL ÉTANT REPRODUITES DIRECTEMENT À PARTIR DE LA DIAPOSITIVE, AFIN DE MARQUER UN CONTRASTE SAISISSANT DE TEXTURE ET DE COULEUR. (USA)

PHOTOGRAPHER:
GILLES BENSIMON
REPRESENTATIVE:
YASUKO AUSTIN
CAMERA:
NIKON
FILM:
FUJI RFP
PUBLICATION DIRECTOR:

RÉGIS PAGNIEZ
CLIENT:
ELLE MAGAZINE
ART DIRECTOR:
OLIVIA BADRUTT-
GIRON
DESIGNER:
FANNY PAGNIEZ
◀■ 234

PHOTOGRAPHER:
HORST STASNY
CAMERA:
SINAR 13X18/4X5
EXPOSURE:
STUDIOFLASH
PHOTO EDITOR:
HANS PETER
HÖTZMANNSEDER

CLIENT:
HAGAN SKIFABRIK
ART DIRECTOR:
HANS PETER
HÖTZMANNSEDER
DESIGNER:
HANS PETER
HÖTZMANNSEDER
■ 235, 236

■ 234 AN ARRAY OF TRENDY SNEAKERS PRESENTED IN A FULL-PAGE PHOTOGRAPH ACCOMPANYING A STREET STYLE FASHION FEATURE ENTITLED "GETTING THE RAP" IN *ELLE* MAGAZINE. (USA)

■ 235, 236 TWO PHOTOGRAPHS FROM A CATALOG PROMOTING THE FASHIONABLE AND DECORATIVE DESIGN OF SKI EQUIPMENT FROM HAGAN. A SPECIAL CONTRAST WAS ADDED TO THE PIECE BY THE PHOTOMONTAGE OF COLOR PHOTOGRAPHS OF THE PRODUCTS AND BLACK-AND-WHITE IMAGES OF THE MODELS. (AUT)

● 234 DIESE KOMPOSITION MIT MODISCHEN TURN-SCHUHEN, DIE IM ZEICHEN DES RAP-TANZES VOLL IM TREND LIEGEN, WURDE IN EINEM MODEBEITRAG IN DER ZEITSCHRIFT *ELLE* VERWENDET. (USA)

● 235, 236 AUS DEM KATALOG DER HAGAN-SKI-FABRIK, DEREN WERBUNG AUF MODE UND DEM DE-KOR DER SKIS AUFBAUT. DER SPEZIELLE KONTRAST WURDE MIT HILFE EINER PHOTOMONTAGE DER FARBDIAS VON DEN PRODUKTEN UND DER ZUM TEIL IM LABOR VERFREMDETEN SCHWARZWEISS-AUFNAH-MEN DER MODELLE ERREICHT. (AUT)

▲ 234 CETTE PHOTO PRÉSENTANT DES MODÈLES DE CHAUSSURES POUR DANSER LE RAP A ÉTÉ PUBLIÉE DANS *ELLE* MAGAZINE POUR ILLUSTRER UN ARTICLE INTITULÉ «COMMENT SAISIR LE RAP». (USA)

▲ 235, 236 DEUX EXEMPLES FIGURANT DANS LE CATALOGUE D'UN FABRICANT DE SKIS. L'ACCENT EST MIS SUR LE STYLISME TRÈS MODE ET LA DÉCORATION DES SKIS HAGAN. L'EFFET DE CONTRASTE ENTRE LA PHOTO COULEUR DES SKIS ET LA FIGURE EN NOIR ET BLANC A ÉTÉ OBTENU GRÂCE À UN PHOTOMONTAGE. (AUT)

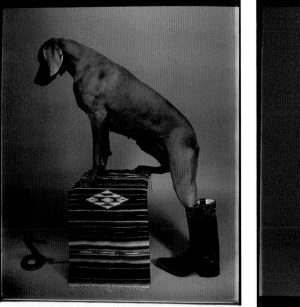

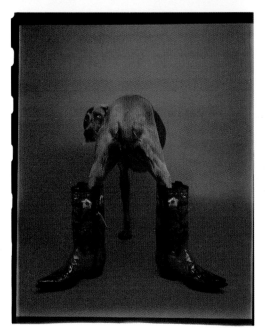

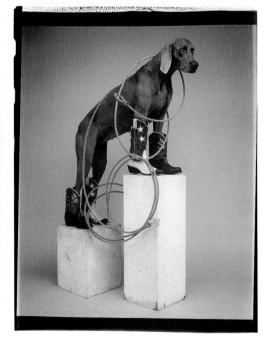

PHOTOGRAPHER:

WILLIAM WEGMAN

CAMERA:

POLAROID 20X24

FILM:

POLAROID

PHOTO EDITOR:

D.J. STOUT

CLIENT:

TEXAS MONTHLY

ART DIRECTOR:

D.J. STOUT

DESIGNER:

D.J.STOUT

■ 237-243

■ 237-243 PHOTOGRAPHER WILLIAM WEGMAN HAD HIS FAMOUS DOG, FAY RAY, POSE FOR A FEATURE ON TEXAS COWBOY BOOTS IN *TEXAS MONTHLY*. HE USED THE 20"X24" POLAROID CAMERA LOCATED AT THE POLAROID STUDIOS IN NEW YORK TO CREATE THE IMAGES. (USA)

● 237-243 DER PHOTOGRAPH WILLIAM WEGMAN LIESS SEINEN HUND, FAY RAY, ALS MODELL FÜR EINEN ARTIKEL ÜBER COWBOY-STIEFEL IN *TEXAS MONTHLY* POSIEREN. ER ARBEITETE MIT DER 20"X24" POLAROID-KAMERA IM NEW YORKER POLA-ROID STUDIO. (USA)

▲ 237-243 LE PHOTOGRAPHE WILLIAM WEGMAN A FAIT POSER SON CHIEN, FAY RAY, POUR UN ARTICLE SUR LES BOTTES DE COW-BOY PARU DANS LE *TEXAS MONTHLY*. CETTE SÉRIE DE PHOTOS A ÉTÉ PRISE DANS LES STUDIOS POLAROÏD DE NEW YORK, AVEC L'APPAREIL POLAROÏD 20"X24". (USA)

■ 244 THE MONOCHROMIC PART OF THIS PHOTO-GRAPH WAS ORIGINALLY DONE FOR AVON PRODUCTS. SUZANNE BUCKLER RESHOT IT BY USING A NEW TECHNIQUE THAT ADDS TEXTURE AND MOVEMENT, AND THEN ADDED THE SNEAKER. USED FOR SELF-PROMOTIONAL PURPOSES. (USA)

■ 245 TAKEN ON ASSIGNMENT FOR A *LEARS* MAGAZINE FEATURE, THIS PHOTOGRAPH. WAS NOT PUBLISHED. (USA)

■ 246 PHOTOGRAPHER GUIDO ROSENMANN IS SHOWN PEERING THROUGH AN OLD STEREO CAMERA THAT CREATED THE ILLUSION OF A THREE-DIMENSIONAL IMAGE. THIS PORTRAIT SERVES AS SELF-PROMOTION. (USA)

● 244 DIESE AUFNAHME WAR URSPRÜNGLICH EIN AUFTRAG VON AVON. FÜR EIGENWERBUNGSZWECKE MACHTE SUZANNE BUCKLER EINE ZWEITE AUF-NAHME DAVON MIT EINER SPEZIELLEN TECHNIK, DIE MEHR TEXTUR HERAUSHOLT, UND FÜGTE DEN TURN-SCHUH HINZU. (USA)

● 245 DIESE AUFNAHME ENTSTAND FÜR EINEN ARTIKEL IN DER ZEITSCHRIFT *LEARS*, WURDE ABER NICHT VERWENDET. (USA)

● 246 DER PHOTOGRAPH GUIDO ROSENMANN SCHAUT HIER DURCH EINE ALTE STEREO-KAMERA, DIE PLASTISCH WIRKENDE BILDER ERZEUGTE. DER PHOTOGRAPH STEVE HATHAWAY BENUTZT DIE AUFNAHME ALS EIGENWERBUNG. (USA)

▲ 244 POUR CETTE PHOTO AUTOPROMOTIONNELLE SUZANNE BUCKLER A RÉUTILISÉ UNE IMAGE MONO-CHROME CRÉÉE POUR UNE CAMPAGNE DES PRODUITS AVON, Y SUPERPOSANT UNE TEXTURE GRÂCE À UN PROCÉDÉ TECHNIQUE PERSONNEL ET AJOUTANT LA CHAUSSURE DE SPORTS. (USA)

▲ 245 CETTE PHOTO FUT RÉALISÉE POUR ILLUS-TRER UN ARTICLE DE *LEARS* MAGAZINE. ELLE N'A PAS ÉTÉ PUBLIÉE. (USA)

▲ 246 LE PHOTOGRAPHE GUIDO ROSENMANN REGARDE AU TRAVERS D'UNE VIEILLE CAMÉRA STÉRÉO, UN APPAREIL DE PHOTOGRAPHIE EN RELIEF. CE PORTRAIT SERT D'AUTOPROMOTION À STEVE HATHAWAY. (USA)

PHOTOGRAPHER:
SUSANNE BUCKLER
REPRESENTATIVE:
MOSS & MEIXLER
CAMERA:
SINAR 8X10
FILM:
KODAK 6122 8X10
CLIENT:
AVON PRODUCTS
■ 244

PHOTOGRAPHER:
JODY DOLE
REPRESENTATIVE:
DOUG BROWN
CAMERA:
NIKON F4
CLIENT:
LEARS MAGAZINE
■ 245

PHOTOGRAPHER:
STEVE HATHAWAY
REPRESENTATIVE:
LYDIA CARRIERE
CAMERA:
SINAR P
FILM:
EKTACHROME 100
EXPOSURE:
2 SEPARATE
EXPOSURES
►■ 246

PHOTOGRAPHER:
HERMANN-JOSEF
BAUS
CAMERA:
HASSELBLAD
FILM:
FUJI SUPER HG 400/
KODAK GPF 160
CLIENT:
ZANDERS
FEINPAPIERE AG
■ 247-249

■ 247-249 THREE PHOTOGRAPHS SHOWING DETAILS OF A NEW ART PAPER COATING MACHINE FOR PAPERS MADE BY ZANDERS. IT ALLOWS TO PRODUCE A HIGH QUALITY GLOSSY PAPER, AND WAS INTRODUCED IN A PUBLICATION ADDRESSED TO CUSTOMERS AND SHAREHOLDERS. (GER)

● 247-249 DREI DETAILAUFNAHMEN EINER NEUEN KUNSTDRUCK-STREICHMASCHINE DER FIRMA ZANDERS FEINPAPIERE. DIESE MASCHINE DIENT ZUR VERBESSERUNG DER OBERFLÄCHENEIGENSCHAFTEN DES PAPIERS UND WURDE KUNDEN UND AKTIONÄREN VORGESTELLT. (GER)

▲ 247-249 TROIS PHOTOS DE DETAIL DE LA NOUVELLE COUCHEUSE DE LA FABRIQUE DE PAPIERS FINS ZANDERS. CETTE MACHINE PERMET DE PRODUIRE UN PAPIER COUCHÉ BRILLANT QUI FAIT RESSORTIR TOUTE 'LA FINESSE DE L'IMPRESSION. (GER)

PHOTOGRAPHER:

PAUL IB HENRIKSEN

REPRESENTATIVE:

PAUL IB HENRIKSEN

CAMERA:

SINAR 4X5

FILM:

EKTACHROME 6105,

100

EXPOSURE:

FLASH

CLIENT:

BANG & OLUFSEN

ART DIRECTOR:

JOHN BOYE

DESIGNER:

JOHN BOYE

■ 250-256

■ 250-256 PHOTOGRAPHS FROM A BROCHURE FOR BANG & OLUFSEN, PRESENTING THE LATEST HIFI-APPLIANCES, TV SETS, COMPACT DISC PLAYERS, VIDEO SETS, REMOTE CONTROLS, AMPLIFIERS AND LOUDSPEAKERS. ALTHOUGH ALL OF THE PRODUCTS WERE PHOTOGRAPHED IN THE STUDIO, IN THE PHOTOGRAPH SHOWN ABOVE, THE SMALL DETAIL IMAGES WERE ADDED IN THE LAB, INCLUDING THE SHADOWS WHICH GIVE THE ILLUSION THAT THE PRODUCTS ARE LEANING AGAINST THE WALL. (DEN)

● 250-256 AUFNAHMEN AUS EINER BROSCHÜRE FÜR BANG & OLUFSEN, IN DER DIE NEUESTEN HIFI-GERÄTE, FERNSEHAPPARATE, COMPACT-DISC-SPIELER, VIDEOGERÄTE, FERNSTEUERUNGEN, VERSTÄRKER UND LAUTSPRECHER VORGESTELLT WERDEN. ALLE AUFNAHMEN WURDEN IM STUDIO GEMACHT. BEI DEM PHOTO OBEN WURDEN DIE KLEINEN DETAILAUFNAHMEN IM LABOR HINEIN-MONTIERT. DURCH DIE SCHATTEN SIEHT ES AUS, ALS SEIEN SIE GEGEN DIE WAND GELEHNT. (DEN)

▲ 250-256 PHOTOS TIRÉES D'UNE BROCHURE DE BANG & OLUFSEN PRÉSENTANT LES DERNIÈRES NOUVEAUTÉS DE MATÉRIEL HAUTE-FIDÉLITÉ: TÉLÉVISIONS, LECTEURS DE DISQUES COMPACT, MAGNÉTOSCOPES, TÉLÉCOMMANDE, CHAÎNES HI-FI ET ENCEINTES STÉRÉO. ELLES ONT TOUTES ÉTÉ RÉALISÉES EN STUDIO. DANS L'IMAGE CI-DESSUS QUELQUES PHOTOS DE DÉTAIL ONT ÉTÉ AJOUTÉES. GRÂCE À D'HABILES EFFETS D'OMBRE PORTÉE, ELLES ONT L'AIR POSÉES CONTRE LE MUR. (DEN)

PHOTOGRAPHER:
BERNHARD ANGERER
CAMERA:
SINAR 4X5
CLIENT:
ÖSPAG/LAUFEN
ART DIRECTOR:
FRANZ MERLICEK/
JÜRGEN MICK
DESIGNER:
JÜRGEN MICK
■ 257

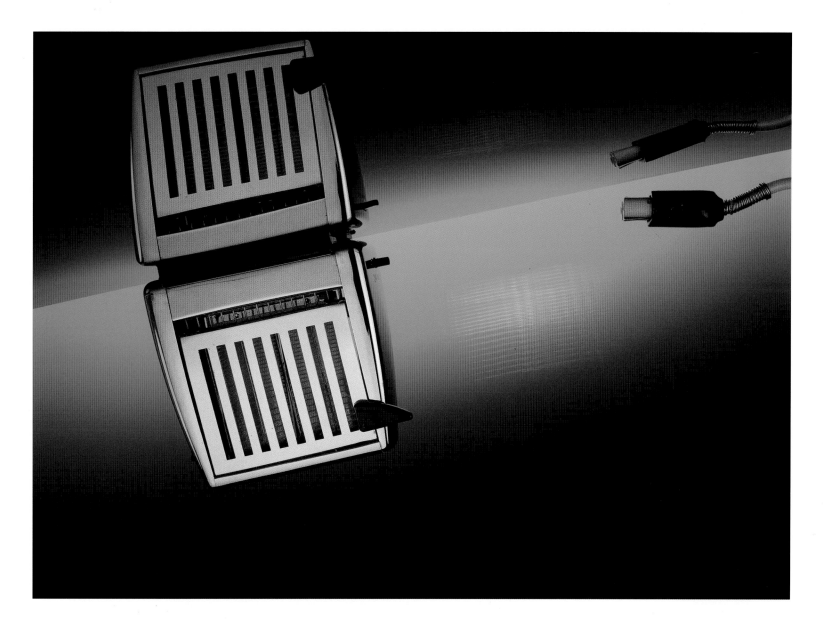

PHOTOGRAPHER:
BERND SCHOLZEN
CAMERA:
SINAR 9X12
FILM:
PLANFILM
■ 258

■ 257 THIS STUDIO PHOTOGRAPH WAS DONE FOR A CATALOG PRESENTING SANITARY INSTALLATIONS DESIGNED BY F.A. PORSCHE FOR LAUFEN. THE IDEA WAS TO SHOW THAT GOOD DESIGN FOLLOWS FUNCTION AND THAT IT WORKS IN THE SMALLEST SPACE. (AUT)

■ 258 FOUR DIFFERENT EXPOSURES WERE COMBINED TO CREATE THIS PHOTOGRAPH OF A TOASTER IN OPERATION: ONE, THE TOASTER ALONE SET AGAINST A BLACK BACKGROUND; TWO, A SEPARATE PHOTOGRAPH OF THE WIRES WITHIN THE TOASTER; THREE, THE INSERTION OF THE WIRES BETWEEN THE TOASTER AND THE ELECTRICAL PLUG; AND FOUR, THE BACKGROUND. (GER)

● 257 DIESE STUDIOAUFNAHME GEHÖRT ZU EINEM KATALOG DER FIRMA LAUFEN, IN DEM BADEZIMMEREINRICHTUNGEN DES DESIGNERS F.A. PORSCHE VORGESTELLT WERDEN. DER HERSTELLER WOLLTE BEWEISEN, DASS GUTES DESIGN KEINE FRAGE DER QUADRATMETER IST. (AUT)

● 258 DIESE AUFNAHME DES «RUNNING TOASTER» BESTEHT AUS VIER EINZELBELICHTUNGEN: ZUERST WURDE DER TOASTER AUSGELEUCHTET UND MIT SCHWARZEM HINTERGRUND PHOTOGRAPHIERT, 2. DIE GLÜHFÄDEN IM TOASTER NACHBELEUCHTET; 3. DIE EINBELICHTUNG DER GLÜHFÄDEN ZWISCHEN TOASTER UND STECKER UND 4. DIE DURCHLEUCHTUNG DES HINTERGRUNDS. (GER)

▲ 257 CETTE PHOTO PRISE EN STUDIO EST TIRÉE D'UN CATALOGUE QUI PRÉSENTE LES NOUVELLES INSTALLATIONS SANITAIRES CRÉÉES PAR LE DESIGNER F.A. PORSCHE POUR LAUFEN. L'IMAGE VISUALISE «LES NOUVELLES PERSPECTIVES DANS LES SALLES DE BAINS». (AUT)

▲ 258 POUR CETTE PHOTO D'UN TOASTER, LE FILM A ÉTÉ EXPOSÉ À QUATRE REPRISES, NOTAMMENT POUR RENDRE LE FOND ET LES FILAMENTS À INCANDESCENCE: LE TOASTER A D'ABORD ÉTÉ PRIS SEUL CONTRE LE FOND NOIR, LES FILAMENTS À INCANDESCENCE ONT ÉTÉ PHOTOGRAPHIÉS SÉPARÉMENT, PUIS ENTRE LE TOASTER ET LA PRISE, LE FOND EN DERNIER. (GER)

PHOTOGRAPHER:

NIKOLAY ZUREK

CAMERA:

NIKON F3

FILM:

PLUS-X

CLIENT:

GATX LEASING

CORP.

ART DIRECTOR:

NIKOLAY ZUREK

DESIGNER:

BILL CAHAN

◄■ 259

PHOTOGRAPHER:

RENÉ STAUD

CAMERA:

SINAR 8X10

FILM:

KODAK THUNGSTEN

200/100

CLIENT:

SÜDWEST VERLAG

260, 263

PORSCHE 261, 262

ART DIRECTOR:

RENÉ STAUD

■ 260-263

■ 259 PART OF A BOEING 747 PHOTOGRAPHED BY NIKOLAY ZUREK AT LOS ANGELES INTERNATIONAL AIRPORT FOR THE ANNUAL REPORT OF THE GATX LEASING CORP. (USA)

■ 260-263 PHOTOGRAPHS FROM A SERIES ORIGINALLY COMMISSIONED BY THE PUBLISHER SÜDWEST, USED FOR SELF-PROMOTION. F.L.T.R.: SIDE VIEW OF A FERRARI F 40 (A MULTIPLE EXPOSURE COMBINING SHOTS OF THE CAR AND BACKGROUND); A PORSCHE SPEEDSTER ON WATER REFLECTING THE GROUND; A MONTAGE OF TWO SINGLE SHOTS OF A PORSCHE 911 AND 928; AND A FERRARI F 40 PHOTOGRAPHED IN THE STUDIO ON A MIRRORED SURFACE. A MIXTURE OF FLASH AND ARTIFICIAL LIGHT CREATES THE EFFECT IN THE LATTER. (GER)

● 259 DETAIL EINER BOEING 747, AUFGENOMMEN AUF DEM INTERNATIONALEN FLUGHAFEN VON LOS ANGELES FÜR DEN JAHRESBERICHT DER GATX LEASING CORP. (USA)

● 260-263 AUFNAHMEN AUS EINER SERIE FÜR DEN SÜDWEST-VERLAG, DIE DER PHOTOGRAPH RENÉ STAUD ALS EIGENWERBUNG BENUTZT. VON LINKS NACH RECHTS: SEITENANSICHT EINES FERRARI F 40; PORSCHE SPEEDSTER, IM STUDIO AUF WASSER-SPIEGELFLÄCHE IM GEGENLICHT AUFGENOMMEN; MONTAGE AUS ZWEI EINZELSTUDIOAUFNAHMEN DES PORSCHE 911/928; FERRARI F40, AUF SPIEGEL-FLÄCHE ÜBER WASSERBECKEN AUFGENOMMEN, MIT BLITZ UND KUNSTLICHT, UM DEN SPEZIELLEN EFFEKT DER UNSCHÄRFE ZU ERREICHEN. (GER)

▲ 259 DÉTAIL D'UN BOEING 747 DE L'AÉROPORT DE LOS ANGELES PHOTOGRAPHIÉ EN NOIR ET BLANC POUR ILLUSTRER LE RAPPORT ANNUEL 1989 DE GATX LEASING CORP.. (USA)

▲ 260-263 CES PHOTOS RÉALISÉES POUR LES ÉDITIONS SÜDWEST À MUNICH ET PUBLIÉES SOUS FORME D'AFFICHETTES SERVENT D'AUTOPROMOTION AU PHOTOGRAPHE RENÉ STAUD. DE G. À D.: PROFIL D'UNE FERRARI F40; LA PORSCHE SPEED-STER PHOTOGRAPHIÉE EN STUDIO EN CONTRE-JOUR, SUR UN MIROIR D'EAU; PHOTOMONTAGE RÉUNISSANT DEUX MODÉLES DE PORSCHE 911 ET 928, PRIS EN STUDIO SÉPARÉMENT;LA FERRARI F40 PHOTOGRAPHIÉE EN STUDIO SUR UN MIROIR D'EAU, AVEC FLASH ET LUMIERE ARTIFICIELLE. (GER)

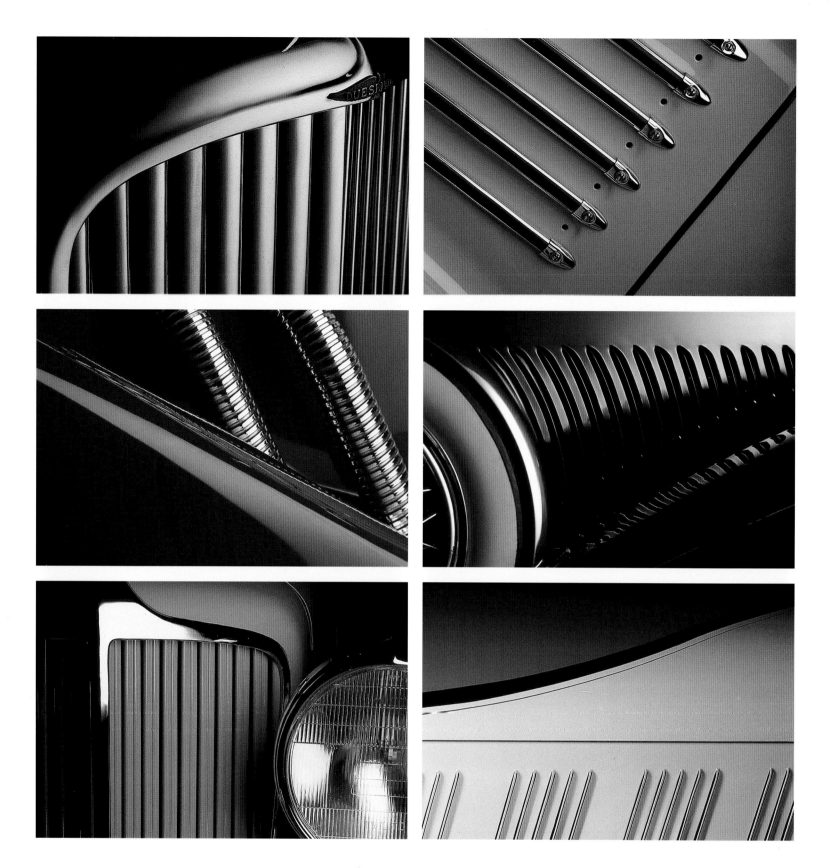

PHOTOGRAPHER:

MICHAEL FURMAN

REPRESENTATIVE:

ELAINE SOREL

CAMERA:

NIKON F3

FILM:

KODACHROME 25

CLIENT:

MICHAEL FURMAN

PHOTOGRAPHER,

LTD.

ART DIRECTOR:

MICHAEL GUNSELMAN

■ 264-270

■ 264-270 EXAMPLES OF A SERIES OF PHOTO-GRAPHS SHOWING DETAILS OF OLD CARS FOR A SELF-PROMOTION CALENDAR OF MICHEAL FURMAN. THEY WERE TAKEN AT THE AUBURN-CORD-DUESEN-BERG MUSEUM IN AUBURN, INDIANA. LIGHTING AND CAMERA POSITION WERE ALL HAND-HELD, AS THE CARS COULD NOT BE REMOVED FROM THEIR DIS-PLAY SETTING. OPPOSITE FROM LEFT TO RIGHT: 1931 DUESENBERG CONVERTIBLE SEDAN; 1931 CORD CABRIOLET; 1936 AUBURN PHAETON; 1931 DUESENBERG VICTORIA; 1931 CORD CABRIOLET; 1925 AUBURN MODEL 8.88 ROADSTER; (THIS PAGE) 1931 CORD CABRIOLET. (USA)

● 264-270 BEISPIELE DER DETAILAUFNAHMEN VON ALTEN AUTOS AUS EINEM EIGENWERBUNGSKALEN-DER FÜR MICHAEL FURMAN. ALLE AUFNAHMEN WUR-DEN IM AUBURN-CORD-DUESENBERG-MUSEUM IN AUBURN, INDIANA, GEMACHT. DA DIE AUTOS NICHT BEWEGT WERDEN DURFTEN, MUSSTEN BELEUCH-TUNG UND KAMERA IN DER HAND GEHALTEN WERDEN. GEGENÜBER VON LINKS NACH RECHTS: DUESENBERG SEDAN VON 1931 MIT FALTDACH; CORD CABRIOLET, 1931; AUBURN PHAETON, 1936; DUESENBERG VICTORIA, 1931; CORD CABRIOLET, 1931; AUBURN MODELL 8.88 ROADSTER, 1925; (DIESE SEITE) CORD CABRIOLET, 1931. (USA)

▲ 264-270 DÉTAILS DE CARROSSERIES DE VIEILLES VOITURES ILLUSTRANT LE CALENDRIER AUTOPRO-MOTIONNEL DU PHOTOGRAPHE MICHAEL FURMAN. TOUTES LES PHOTOS ONT ÉTÉ RÉALISÉES DANS LE AUBURN-CORD-DUESENBERG MUSEUM À AUBURN, DANS L'INDIANA. LES VOITURES NE POUVANT ÊTRE DÉPLACÉES, IL A FALLU TENIR LES LAMPES À LA MAIN ET UTILISER L'APPAREIL PHOTO SANS L'AIDE D'UN PIED. 264: DUESENBERG SEDAN DÉCAPOTABLE DE 1931; 265, 268 ET 270: LE CABRIOLET CORD DE 1931; 266: LA AUBERN PHAETON DE 1936; 267: LA DUESENBERG VICTORIA DE 1931; 269: LA AUBURN 8.88 ROADSTER. (USA)

PHOTOGRAPHER:

MARIO CARRIERI

CAMERA:

LINHOF 5X7 (13X18)

CLIENT:

KNOLL

INTERNATIONAL

ART DIRECTOR:

MARIO CARRIERI

DESIGNER:

RICHARD MEIER

■ 271, 272

■ 271, 272 PHOTOGRAPHS OF CHAIRS DESIGNED BY THE ARCHITECT RICHARD MEIER FOR THE KNOLL ART EDITION SERIES. (GER)

■ 273 THIS IMAGE IS PART OF AN ON-GOING SERIES OF DOUBLE-SPREAD ADS FOR NEVAMAR CORPORATION WHICH SELLS DECORATIVE LAMINATES. THE PRODUCT LINE ADVERTISED HERE IS CALLED "CONTOURS" AND THE IDEA WAS TO USE A SNAKE TO EMPHASIZE THE MATERIAL'S ABILITY TO CONFORM TO CURVED SURFACES. IT IS A NON-POISONOUS GREEN ROUGH 27-INCH SNAKE FROM CALIFORNIA WHICH WAS SUSPENDED THROUGH TWO LOOPS OF MONOFILAMENT LINE SECURED ABOVE THE SET. PEGS IN THE BACK OF THE TALL CYLINDER SUPPORTED THE SNAKE'S COILED END. THE SNAKE WAS COAXED INTO POSITION BY RUBBING IT LIKE MOLDING PUTTY. IT TOOK FOUR DAYS TO CATCH IT IN THE RIGHT ONDULATION. (USA)

■ 274 THE NEW MITSUBISHI COLT WAS PHOTOGRAPHED OUTSIDE ON A CLOUDY SUMMER EVENING. IN ORDER TO OBTAIN THE IMPRESSION OF SPEED, THE PHOTOGRAPHER MOUNTED HIS CAMERA ON A MOBILE FOOT AS IS USED FOR MOVIE CAMERAS. THE PHOTO IS USED FOR A PROMOTIONAL POSTER SPEAKING OF "TOMORROW'S MEMORIES." (JPN)

● 271, 272 ZWEI AUFNAHMEN VON STÜHLEN DES ARCHITEKTEN RICHARD MEIER FÜR DIE KNOLL ART EDITION. (GER)

● 273 DIESE AUFNAHME GEHÖRT ZU EINER ANZEIGENKAMPAGNE FÜR NEVAMAR KUNSTSTOFFBESCHICHTUNGEN. HIER WIRD DIE LINIE «CONTOURS» VORGESTELLT. DAS MATERIAL ZEICHNET SICH DURCH BESONDERE GESCHMEIDIGKEIT AUS, UND DIE SCHLANGE SOLLTE DIESE EIGENSCHAFT UNTERSTREICHEN. ES IST EINE UNGIFTIGE, CA. 80CM LANGE, GRÜNE SCHLANGE AUS KALIFORNIEN, UND SIE HÄNGT AN ZWEI PLASTIKFÄDEN. AN DER RÜCKSEITE DES GROSSEN ZYLINDERS IST IHR AUFGEROLLTES ENDE MIT STIFTEN BEFESTIGT. SCHLIESSLICH WURDE SIE WIE EINE MODELLIERMASSE BEARBEITET, UM DIE GEWÜNSCHTE POSITION ZU ERHALTEN. ES DAUERTE VIER TAGE, BIS DIE STELLUNG PERFEKT WAR. (USA)

● 274 DER NEUE MITSUBISHI COLT WURDE AN EINEM BEWÖLKTEN SOMMERABEND DRAUSSEN PHOTOGRAPHIERT. UM DEN EINDRUCK VON GESCHWINDIGKEIT ZU ERREICHEN, BEFESTIGTE DER PHOTOGRAPH DIE KAMERA WIE BEI FILMAUFNAHMEN AUF EINEM FAHRBAREN FUSS. DER SLOGAN: «ERINNERUNGEN VON MORGEN». (JPN)

▲ 271, 272 DES CHAISES CRÉÉES PAR LE DESIGNER RICHARD MEIER POUR «ART EDITION», DU FABRICANT DE MEUBLES KNOLL INTERNATIONAL. (GER)

▲ 273 CETTE IMAGE INTITULÉE «SERPENT» FAIT PARTIE D'UNE SÉRIE DE PUBLICITÉS DOUBLE PAGE CRÉÉES POUR NEVAMAR CORP., UNE FIRME QUI VEND DES ACIERS LAMINÉS DÉCORATIFS. CHACUNE PRÉSENTE UNE COMPOSITION QUI ILLUSTRE LES CARACTÉRISTIQUES DES PRODUITS DE L'ENTREPRISE, ICI LA LIGNE «CONTOURS». LE PHOTOGRAPHE A ESSAYÉ DE SOULIGNER L'ADAPTABILITÉ DE CE MATÉRIAU AUX SURFACES COURBES. LE SERPENT VERT NON-VENIMEUX D'ENVIRON 80 CM A ÉTÉ SPÉCIALEMENT EXPÉDIÉ DE CALIFORNIE AU STUDIO DU PHOTOGRAPHE, DANS L'OHIO. IL ÉTAIT SUSPENDU À DEUX FILS DE NYLON TENDUS AU-DESSUS DU DÉCOR. IL A FALLU 4 JOURS POUR OBTENIR L'ONDULATION SOUHAITÉE. (USA)

▲ 274 LA NOUVELLE MITSUBISHI CORD A ÉTÉ PHOTOGRAPHIÉE PAR UNE SOIRÉE D'ÉTÉ NUAGEUSE. L'EFFET DE VITESSE A ÉTÉ OBTENU GRÂCE À UN TRAVELLING, L'APPAREIL PHOTO ÉTANT FIXÉ SUR UN PIED MOBILE UTILISÉ POUR LES PRISES DE VUES CINÉMATOGRAPHIQUES. LA PHOTO SUGGÈRE «LA MÉMOIRE DE DEMAIN». (JPN)

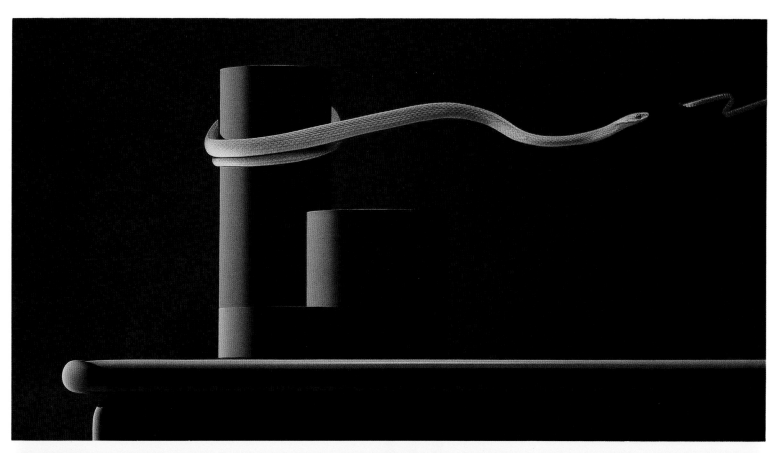

PHOTOGRAPHER:
FRED BENDER
CAMERA:
SINAR P2 4X5
FILM:
KODAK 4X5
EKTACHROME 100
PLUS
EXPOSURE:
F 32

CLIENT:
NEVAMAR
CORPORATION
ART DIRECTOR:
BOB BENDER/
DOUG FISHER/
EVA CASSIDY
RHODE/
WILLIAM WALKER
▲
▲■ 273

PHOTOGRAPHER:
YASUO MIZUNO
CAMERA:
NIKON F3,
105MM, 2.5
FILM:
KODACHROME 64
CLIENT:
MITSUBISHI MOTORS
CORPORATION
ART DIRECTOR:
TAKAYUKI ITOH
DESIGNER:
MIWAKO EBISAWA
■ 274

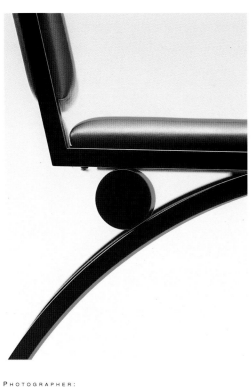

PHOTOGRAPHER:
LEE CRUM
CLIENT:
LACKAWANNA
LEATHER COMPANY
ART DIRECTOR:
DAN LENNON
DESIGNER:
DAN LENNON
▶■ 278

PHOTOGRAPHER:
NOBUO ASAYAMA
CAMERA:
TOYO VIEW 4X5G
FILM:
KODAK EKTACHROME
PHOTO EDITOR:
TOYOMU
SHIMODAIRA
CLIENT:
KOKUYO CO. LTD.
ART DIRECTOR:
NOBUO ASAYAMA
DESIGNER:
FUMIHIKO OKUYAMA
■ 275-277

■ 275-277 THESE PHOTOGRAPHS, FROM A BRO-CHURE FOR THE KOKUYO CO., LTD., EMPHASIZE THE PURITY OF FORM OF THIS DESIGNER FURNITURE BY FOCUSING ON THE DETAILS OF THE LINE. (JPN)

● 275-277 DIESE DETAILAUFNAHMEN FÜR EINE BROSCHÜRE DER FIRMA KOKUYO UNTERSTREICHEN DIE STRENGE, SCHLICHTE FORM DER DESIGNER-MÖBEL, DIE DIESE FIRMA ANBIETET. (JPN)

▲ 275-277 CES TROIS PHOTOS RÉALISÉES POUR UNE BROCHURE DE KOKUYO CO LTD. METTENT EN RELIEF LA PURETÉ DE LA LIGNE DES MEUBLES DE DESIGN VENDUS PAR CETTE FIRME. (JPN)

■ 278 PHOTOGRAPH FROM A CALENDAR FOR THE LACKAWANNA LEATHER COMPANY. (USA)

● 278 AUS EINEM KALENDER FÜR DIE LEDERFIRMA LACKAWANNA LEATHER COMPANY. (USA)

▲ 278 PHOTO FIGURANT DANS LE CALENDRIER D'UNE ENTREPRISE SPÉCIALISÉE DANS LE CUIR. (USA)

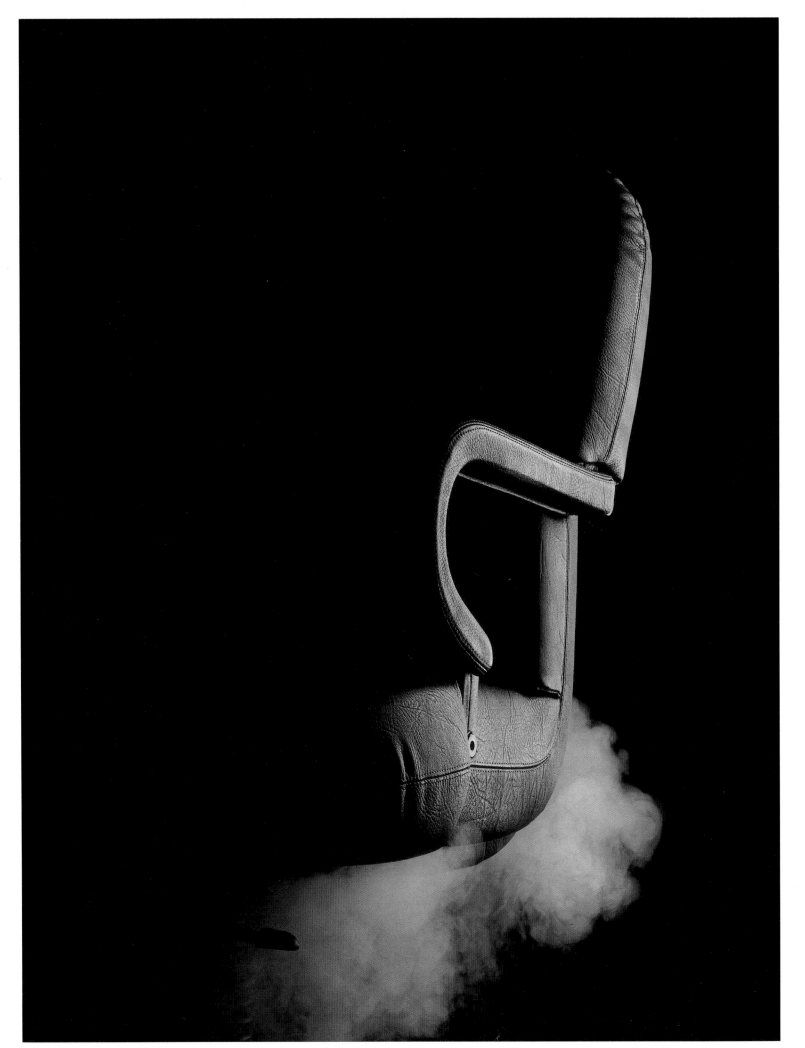

■ 279 A FURTHER EXAMPLE FROM THE KNOLL EDITION SERIES. THE CHAIR HAS BEEN DESIGNED BY AXEL WALDECKER. (GER)

■ 280 THE "EMBRYO" CHAIR DESIGNED BY MARC NEWSON IN 1988 FOR DE DE CE, A LEADING DESIGN COMPANY BASED IN SYDNEY. THE CHAIR IS EXHIBITED IN THE POWERHOUSE MUSEUM FOR APPLIED ARTS AND SCIENCES IN SYDNEY. (AUS)

■ 281 THIS IMAGE WAS SHOWN WITHIN THE FRAME OF AN EXHIBITION CALLED "EXPERIMENTATIONS" AT THE POWERHOUSE MUSEUM OF SYDNEY. THE PHOTOGRAPH IS MEANT TO DEMONSTRATE ELECTRICAL ENERGY. (AUS)

● 279 AUFNAHME FÜR DIE KNOLL ART EDITION, BEI DER VERSCHIEDENE PHOTOGRAPHEN MÖBEL AUF IHRE ART INTERPRETIEREN. (GER)

● 280 DER «EMBRYO»-STUHL, VON MARC NEWSON 1988 FÜR DE DE CE, EINE DESIGN-FIRMA IN SYDNEY, ENTWORFEN. DER STUHL IST IM POWERHOUSE MUSEUM, EINEM MUSEUM FÜR ANGEWANDTE KUNST UND WISSENSCHAFT, AUSGESTELLT. (AUS)

● 281 DIESES BILD WURDE IM RAHMEN EINER AUSSTELLUNG MIT DEM TITEL «EXPERIMENTATIONS» IM POWERHOUSE MUSEUM VON SYDNEY AUSGESTELLT. DIE PHOTOGRAPHIE SOLL ELEKTRISCHE ENERGIE DARSTELLEN. (AUS)

▲ 279 RECHERCHE PHOTOGRAPHIQUE POUR «KNOLL ART EDITION»: LES PHOTOGRAPHES PEUVENT Y INTERPRÉTER LIBREMENT LES MEUBLES. (GER)

▲ 280 LA CHAISE «EMBRYO» CRÉÉE PAR MARC NEWSON EN 1988 ET PRODUITE PAR DE DE CE, PRINCIPALE FIRME DE DESIGN DE SIDNEY, EST EXPOSÉE AU POWERHOUSE MUSEUM, MUSÉE DES ARTS APPLIQUÉS ET DES SCIENCES DE SIDNEY. (AUS)

▲ 281 CETTE IMAGE A ÉTÉ EXPOSÉE DANS LE CADRE D'UNE EXPOSITION INTITULÉE «EXPÉRIMENTATIONS», PRÉSENTÉE AU POWERHOUSE MUSEUM DE SIDNEY. LA PHOTO ÉVOQUE L'ÉNERGIE ÉLECTRIQUE. (AUS)

PHOTOGRAPHER:
AXEL WALDECKER
REPRESENTATIVE:
CAMERA UNO
CAMERA:
HORSEMAN 8X10
FILM:
KODAK EPP 100
CLIENT:
KNOLL
INTERNATIONAL
ART DIRECTOR:
WOLF KAISER

◄■ 279

PHOTOGRAPHER:
PENELOPE CLAY
CAMERA:
SINAR P
FILM:
KODAK EPR 5X4
CLIENT:
POWERHOUSE
MUSEUM
ART DIRECTOR:
PENELOPE CLAY
DESIGNER:
MARC NEWSON

■ 280

PHOTOGRAPHER:
ANDREW FROLOWS
CAMERA:
SINAR P
FILM:
KODAK EPN 5X4
CLIENT:
POWERHOUSE
MUSEUM
ART DIRECTOR:
ANDREW FROLOWS
DESIGNER:
ALISON WARD

■ 281

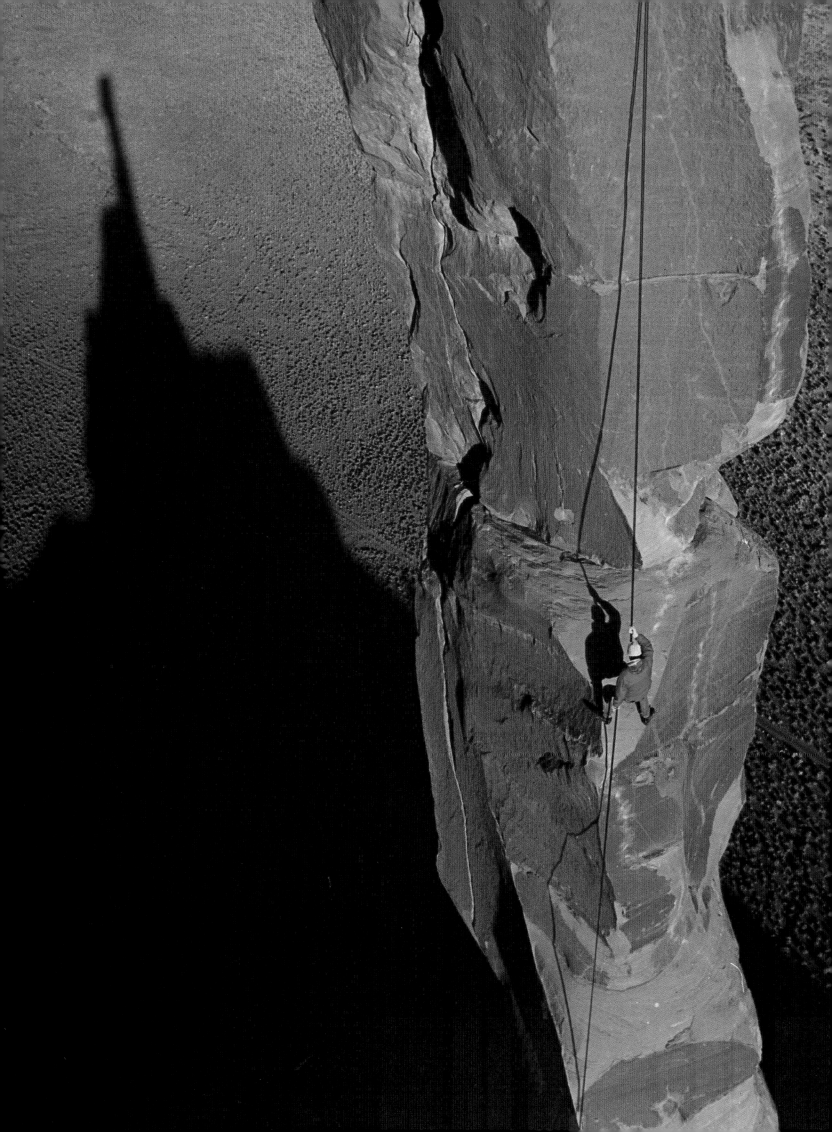

OUTDOOR

AUSSENAUFNAHMEN

EXTÉRIEURS

PHOTOGRAPHER:
STEPHEN WILKES
CAMERA:
LEICA 28MM
FILM:
EKTAR 25
EXPOSURE:
F 4, 1/500
CLIENT:
KODAK
ART DIRECTOR:
FRANK PERRY
◀■ 282

PHOTOGRAPHER:
BRUNO J. ZEHNDER
CAMERA:
NIKON
FILM:
KODACHROME PKR 64
EXPOSURE:
1/250
PHOTO EDITOR:
BRUNO J. ZEHNDER
CLIENT:
ZOOM MAGAZINE
ART DIRECTOR:
JACQUES CLAYSSEN
DESIGNER:
JOEL LAROCHE
■ 283

PHOTOGRAPHER:

DENNIS MANARCHY

CAMERA:

SWISS ARC

CLIENT:

MITSUBISHI

ART DIRECTOR:

RICK BOYKO

■ 284

■ 282 (PRECEDING SPREAD) THIS PHOTOGRAPH OF THE "TOTEM POLE", ONE OF THE NATURAL WONDERS OF COLORADO'S MONUMENT VALLEY, WAS TAKEN FROM A HELICOPTER BY A PRODUCTION CREW THAT INCLUDED A TEAM OF PROFESSIONAL STUNT MEN. THE CLIMBER IS RAPPELLING FROM A HEIGHT OF 600 FEET. (USA)

■ 283 ICEBERG AND BIRD IN THE ANTARCTIC. THE SUN WAS LOW. PHOTOGRAPHER BRUNO J. ZEHNDER WAITED IN A SMALL BOAT FOR THE LITTLE BIRD TO FLY INTO THE EXACT SPOT OF LIGHT ON THE TOP OF THE ICEBERG. AN UNSTABLE BOAT ADDED ADVENTURISM TO THE ENTERPRISE. (USA)

■ 284 PHOTOGRAPH USED FOR A POSTER ADVERTISING LARGE-SCREEN TV SETS MADE BY MITSUBISHI. THE HEADLINE POINTS OUT THE ATTRACTION OF THE PRODUCT GIVEN THE RISE IN HOME-VIDEO RENTALS. (USA)

● 282 (VORHERGEHENDE SEITE) DIESE AUFNAHME DES TOTEM POLE, EINES NATURWUNDERS IM MONUMENT VALLEY, COLORADO, WURDE VON EINEM HUBSCHRAUBER AUS GEMACHT. DIE HERSTELLUNG BEDINGTE EIN TEAM PROFESSIONELLER STUNT- MÄNNER. DER KLETTERER SEILTE SICH ÜBER EINE DISTANZ VON 183 METER AB. (USA)

● 283 EISBERG UND VOGEL IN DER ANTARKTIS. DIE SONNE STAND NIEDRIG AM HORIZONT, UND DER PHOTOGRAPH WARTETE IN EINEM WINZIGEN BOOT, BIS DER KLEINE VOGEL GENAU IM LICHT DER SPITZE DES EISBERGS WAR. BEI DER AUFNAHME WÄRE DAS BOOT BEINAHE GEKENTERT. (USA)

● 284 DIESE AUFNAHME WURDE ALS PLAKAT- WERBUNG FÜR FERNSEHAPPARATE VON MITSUBISHI VERWENDET. DER SLOGAN: »EINEN FILM SIEHT MAN SICH AM BESTEN AUF EINER GROSSEN LEINWAND (BILDSCHIRM) AN«. (USA)

▲ 282 (PAGE PRÉCÉDENTE) CETTE PHOTO DU TOTEM POLE, PIC ROCHEUX QUI S'ÉLÈVE DANS LA MONUMENT VALLEY AU COLORADO, A ÉTÉ PRISE D'UN HÉLICOPTÈRE. POUR LA RÉALISER, IL A FALLU MOBILISER TOUTE UNE ÉQUIPE D'ACROBATES PROFESSIONNELS. L'ALPINISTE DESCEND EN RAPPEL SUR 183 MÈTRES. (USA)

▲ 283 ICEBERG ET OISEAU DANS L'ANTARCTIQUE. LE PHOTOGRAPHE, INSTALLÉ SUR UNE PETITE BARQUE, A DÛ ATTENDRE QUE L'OISEAU SOIT JUSTE DANS LA LUMIÈRE. L'INSTABILITÉ DE L'EMBARCA- TION RENDIT CETTE OPÉRATION FORT PÉRILLEUSE. LA PHOTO A ÉTÉ PUBLIÉE DANS ZOOM. (USA)

▲ 284 D'UNE CAMPAGNE DE PUBLICITÉ POUR LES TÉLÉVISEURS MITSUBISHI. CETTE PHOTO D'UN CINÉMA A ÉTÉ REPRODUITE SOUS FORME D'AFFICHE: «LE MEILLEUR MOYEN DE REGARDER UN FILM A TOUJOURS ÉTÉ LE GRAND ÉCRAN.» (USA)

PHOTOGRAPHER:
HUBERT CROISILLE
REPRESENTATIVE:
ERNOULT FEATURES
CAMERA:
NIKON
PHOTO EDITOR:
FRANÇOIS BLA
CLIENT:
NITRO
■ 285

PHOTOGRAPHER:
ALBERT WATSON
CAMERA:
HASSELBLAD
CLIENT:
BYBLOS
ART DIRECTOR:
NANDO MIGLIO
■ 286, 287

■ 285 THIS SOMEWHAT IRONIC PHOTOGRAPH OF A BIG AMERICAN CAR IN FRONT OF A CATTLE BARN WAS TAKEN IN TEXAS. IT WAS PUBLISHED IN THE MAGAZINE *NEWLOOK*. (FRA)

■ 286, 287 VIEWS OF THE HAMPTONS ON LONG ISLAND, WHERE WELL-TO-DO NEW YORKERS HAVE THEIR SUMMER HOUSES. THE PHOTOGRAPHS WERE USED IN A CATALOG FOR THE BYBLOS FALL/WINTER FASHIONS. (ITA)

● 285 DIESES RECHT IRONISCHE BILD EINES GROSSEN AMERIKANISCHEN AUTOS VOR EINEM VIEHSTALL ENTSTAND IN TEXAS. ES WURDE IN DER ZEITSCHRIFT *NEWLOOK* GEZEIGT. (FRA)

● 286, 287 DER STRAND VON HAMPTON AUF LONG ISLAND, WO WOHLHABENDE NEW YORKER IHRE SOMMERHÄUSER HABEN, WAR AUFNAHMEORT FÜR DEN BYBLOS-MODEKATALOG MIT DER HERBST/WINTERMODE. (ITA)

▲ 285 CETTE PHOTO ASSEZ IRONIQUE D'UNE GROSSE VOITURE AMÉRICAINE DEVANT UN HANGAR À BESTIAUX A ÉTÉ PRISE AU TEXAS. ELLE A ÉTÉ PUBLIÉE DANS *NEWLOOK*. (FRA)

▲ 286, 287 CES DEUX PHOTOGRAPHIES POUR LE CATALOGUE DE MODE AUTOMNE/HIVER DE BYBLOS ONT ÉTÉ RÉALISÉES SUR LES PLAGES DE LONG ISLAND, LIEU DE VILLÉGIATURE DES NEW-YORKAIS FORTUNÉS. (ITA)

PHOTOGRAPHER:

ALFRED SEILAND

CAMERA:

WISTA 453F

FILM:

KODAK VERICOLOR

II/L

PHOTO EDITOR:

ALFRED SEILAND

ART DIRECTOR:

ALFRED SEILAND

DESIGNER:

ALFRED SEILAND

■ 288, 289

■ 288, 289 THESE PHOTOGRAPHS WERE TAKEN BY ALFRED SEILAND DURING EXTENSIVE TRAVELLING THROUGH THE UNITED STATES AND THEY WERE PUBLISHED IN A BOOK ENTITLED *EAST COAST/ WEST COAST*. THE ONE OPPOSITE WAS TAKEN IN A VILLAGE CALLED TRURO IN MASSACHUSETTS, THE ONE ON THIS PAGE SHOWS THE PROMENADE OF CORONADO, CALIFORNIA. (USA)

● 288, 289 DER ÖSTERREICHISCHE PHOTOGRAPH ALFRED SEILAND MACHTE DIESE AUFNAHMEN BEI AUSGEDEHNTEN REISEN DURCH DIE USA. SIE WURDEN IN EINEM BUCH MIT DEM TITEL *EAST COAST/ WEST COAST* VERÖFFENTLICHT. DIE AUFNAHME GEGENÜBER ENTSTAND IN EINEM DORF IN MASSACHUSETTS, DIE PROMENADE AUF DIESER SEITE GEHÖRT ZU CORONADO IN KALIFORNIEN. (USA)

▲ 288, 289 CES DEUX PHOTOGRAPHIES EN COULEURS DU PHOTOGRAPHE AUTRICHIEN ALFRED SEILAND, PRISES AU COURS DE SES VOYAGES AUX USA, ONT ÉTÉ PUBLIÉES DANS UN LIVRE INTITULÉ «CÔTE EST/ CÔTE OUEST». LA PHOTO CI-CONTRE A ÉTÉ PRISE DANS UN VILLAGE DU MASSACHUSETTS; SUR CETTE PAGE, ON DÉCOUVRE LA PROMENADE DE CORONADO EN CALIFORNIE. (USA)

PHOTOGRAPHER:

JIM QUAILE/

TONY GAYE

(G/Q STUDIOS LTD.)

REPRESENTATIVE:

HILLARY SKEANS

CAMERA:

SINAR P 8X10

FILM:

EKTACHROME 64

CLIENT:

G/Q STUDIOS

ART DIRECTOR:

JIM QUAILE

DESIGNER:

JOE PERRONE

■ 290

PHOTOGRAPHER:

CHRISTIAN FÉVRIER

CAMERA:

CANON T.90/

ZOOM 80-200 FO

FILM:

POLARIZING FILTER

EXPOSURE:

1/250

CLIENT:

AMERICAN PHOTO

ART DIRECTOR:

MARK GARTLAND

DESIGNER:

PATRICIA

MARROQUIN

▶■ 291

■ 290 WHAT APPEAR TO BE MUD-COVERED STONES IN THIS PHOTOGRAPH ARE ACTUALLY MUSHROOMS, PAINTED AND SUBMERGED IN WATER. THEY ARE PART OF A SERIES OF SELF-PROMOTION PIECES FEATURING PAINTED FRUITS AND BACKGROUNDS AS THE SUBJECT MATTER. (USA)

■ 291 ERIC TABARLY'S YACHT "CÔTE D'OR" IS SHOWN CLOSE TO AN ENOURMOUS ICEBERG NOT FAR FROM THE COAST OF NEWFOUNDLAND DURING THE TRANSATLANTIC RACE LORIENT/ST. PIERRE-ET-MIQUELON/LORIENT. PHOTOGRAPHER CHRISTIAN FÉVRIER CAPTURED THIS IMAGE WHILE SITTING IN A SMALL FISHING BOAT THAT WAS LEAKING VERY BADLY AND CAME CLOSE TO SINKING ON THE WAY BACK TO SHORE. LUCKILY, FÉVRIER IS A SAILOR OF THIRTY YEARS' EXPERIENCE. (FRA)

● 290 WAS AUF DIESEM PHOTO WIE SCHLAMM-BEDECKTE STEINE AUSSIEHT, SIND IN WIRKLICH-KEIT PILZE, DIE BEMALT UND IN EINE FLÜSSIGKEIT GETAUCHT WURDEN. DIE AUFNAHME GEHÖRT ZU EINER EIGENWERBUNGSREIHE DES PHOTOGRAPHEN-TEAMS JIM QUAILE UND TONY GAYE. (USA)

● 291 DIE HOCHSEEJACHT «CÔTE D'OR» VON ERIC TABARLY VOR EINEM RIESIGEN EISBERG IN DER NÄHE VON NEUFUNDLAND WÄHREND EINER TRANS-ATLANTIK-REGATTA VON LORIENT/ST. PIERRE-ET-MIQUELON/LORIENT. DIE AUFNAHME WURDE VON EINEM KLEINEN FISCHERBOOT AUS GEMACHT, DAS LECK WAR UND BEI DER RÜCKKEHR BEINAHE SANK. DER PHOTOGRAPH CHRISTIAN FÉVRIER SEGELT SELBST SEIT 30 JAHREN, UND ER SCHREIBT FÜR VIELE JACHT-MAGAZINE. (FRA)

▲ 290 CES «GALETS» RECOUVERTS DE BOUE SONT EN RÉALITÉ DES CHAMPIGNONS QUI ONT ÉTÉ PEINTS ET IMMERGÉS DANS L'EAU. LA PHOTO FAIT PARTIE D'UNE SÉRIE METTANT EN SCENE DES FRUITS ET LÉGUMES PEINTS DANS DES DÉCORS ARTIFICIELS. (USA)

▲ 291 LE MAXI-YACHT D'ÉRIC TABARLY, «CÔTE D'OR» PRÈS D'UN ÉNORME ICEBERG NON LOIN DE TERRE-NEUVE. CETTE PHOTO A ÉTÉ RÉALISÉE LORS DE LA COURSE TRANSATLANTIQUE LORIENT/ST-PIERRE-ET-MIQUELON/LORIENT EN 1987, À PARTIR D'UN PETIT BATEAU DE PÊCHE QUI PRENAIT L'EAU ET QUI FAILLIT COULER AU RETOUR. LE PHOTOGRAPHE PRATIQUE LA VOILE DEPUIS 30 ANS ET COLLABORE À DE NOMBREUX MAGAZINES DE YACHTING. (FRA)

PHOTOGRAPHER:
GEOFFREY
CLIFFORD
REPRESENTATIVE:
MARGE CASEY
CAMERA:
NIKON F3
FILM:
FUJICHROME PRO-
FESSIONAL RFP 50
EXPOSURE:
F 4, 1/500 WITH
POLARIZER

PHOTO EDITOR:
GEOFFREY
CLIFFORD
CLIENT:
TURTLE HOLIDAYS
ART DIRECTOR:
CRAIG DICKEN/
DEBORAH KAISER
▲◄■ 292

PHOTOGRAPHER:
GEOFFREY
CLIFFORD
REPRESENTATIVE:
MARGE CASEY
CAMERA:
NIKON F3
FILM:
KODACHROME
PROFESSIONAL 200

EXPOSURE:
F 2, 1/500
PHOTO EDITOR:
JOHN GARRE
CLIENT:
GENERAL ELECTRIC
ART DIRECTOR:
JOHN GARRE
◄■ 293

PHOTOGRAPHER:
PAUL MCGUIRK
CAMERA:
NAGAOKA
SEISAKUSHO 4X5
CLIENT:
MCGUIRK/
HELICON PRESS
DESIGNER:
ELIZABETH HELLING
■ 294

■ 292 AN AERIAL VIEW OF TURTLE ISLAND (YASAWA CHAIN OF THE FIJI ISLANDS) TAKEN FOR A TRAVEL BROCHURE ON "TURTLE HOLIDAYS," AND SHOWING THE ONLY TYPE OF TRANSPORTATION AVAILABLE. THE PHOTO WAS TAKEN AT MID-DAY WHEN THE WATER IS VERY BLUE AND THE TIDE IS HIGH. (USA)

■ 293 THIS PHOTOGRAPH WAS TAKEN ON LOCATION AT HUNTER ARMY AIRFIELD, SAVANNAH, GEORGIA. THE ASSIGNMENT FOR GENERAL ELECTRIC AIRCRAFT ENGINE DIVISION WAS TO FOCUS ON THE RELIABILITY OF THE T34GE ENGINE FOR THE SIKORSKY BLACK HAWK HELICOPTER. (USA)

■ 294 A PERSONAL STUDY OF A BOAT BY PAUL MCGUIRK, WORKING EARLY IN THE MORNING ON THE SHORES OF CAPE COD, MASSACHUSETTS. (USA)

● 292 EINE LUFTAUFNAHME VON «TURTLE ISLAND» (YASAWA-GRUPPE DER FIJI-INSELN). DIE AUFNAHME WAR FÜR «TURTLE HOLIDAYS» BESTIMMT UND ZEIGT, WIE MAN DIE INSEL ERREICHT. DAS PHOTO ENTSTAND MITTAGS, ALS DER WASSERSTAND HOCH UND DAS WASSER TIEFBLAU WAR. (USA)

● 293 ORT DIESER AUFNAHME WAR DAS HUNTER-MILITÄRFLUGFELD IN SAVANNAH, GEORGIA. DIE FLUGZEUGMOTOREN-ABTEILUNG VON GENERAL ELECTRIC WOLLTE DIE VERLÄSSLICHKEIT DER MOTOREN FÜR DIE SIKORSKY BLACK HAWK-HUBSCHRAUBER DEMONSTRIEREN. (USA)

● 294 FREIE STUDIE VON PAUL MCGUIRK. ER PHOTOGRAPHIERTE DAS BOOT FRÜH AM MORGEN AM STRAND VON CAPE COD, MASSACHUSETTS. (USA)

▲ 292 VUE AÉRIENNE DE TURTLE ISLAND (DANS L'ARCHIPEL DES FIDJI) POUR TURTLE HOLIDAYS. MONTRANT LE MOYEN DE TRANSPORT UTILISÉ POUR Y ACCÉDER. LA PHOTO A ÉTÉ PRISE À LA MI-JOURNÉE AFIN D'ATTEINDRE UN DEGRÉ MAXIMUM DE SATURATION DES COULEURS. (USA)

▲ 293 RÉALISÉE POUR GENERAL ELECTRIC, CETTE PHOTO A ÉTÉ PRISE À SAVANNAH, EN GÉORGIE, SUR LE TERRAIN D'ENTRAÎNEMENT AÉRIEN DE L'ARMÉE AMÉRICAINE. IL S'AGISSAIT DE MONTRER LA FIABILITÉ DU MOTEUR T34 GE DE L'HÉLICOPTÈRE SIKORSKY BLACK HAWK. (USA)

▲ 294 ÉTUDE PERSONNELLE DU PHOTOGRAPHE PAUL MCGUIRK. LA BARQUE A ÉTÉ PRISE TÔT LE MATIN SUR LA PLAGE DE CAPE COD, MASS. (USA)

BEST OUTDOOR

PHOTOGRAPHER:

JOHN ISAAC

CAMERA:

MAXXUM 9000

FILM:

KODACHROME 200

PHOTO EDITOR:

RICHARD V. BRYANT

CLIENT:

MINOLTA CAMERA

CO. LTD.

ART DIRECTOR:

FRED O. BECHLEN

■ 295

PHOTOGRAPHER:

ALFRED SEILAND

CAMERA:

WISTA 45SP

FILM:

KODAK VERICOLOR

II/L, 4X5

EXPOSURE:

F 45, 1/8

CLIENT:

*FRANKFURTER ALL-
GEMEINE MAGAZIN*

ART DIRECTOR:

HANS-GEORG

POSPISCHIL

▶■ 296

■ 295 THIS DRAMATIC SCENE, WHICH HAS THE LOOK AND FEEL OF A PAINTING WAS PHOTOGRAPHED DURING THE TRADITIONAL "FANTASIA" FETE OF MOROCCO. JOHN ISAAC, WHO CALLS THIS HIS FAVORITE PHOTOGRAPH, WAITED FOR THE RIGHT MOMENT AND ANGLE AS THE SUN WAS SETTING. THIS PHOTOGRAPH HAS RECEIVED THE BEST IN CATEGORY, OUTDOOR, AWARD FOR THE GRAPHIS PHOTO 91 COMPETITION, SPONSORED BY EASTMAN KODAK. (USA)

■ 296 A MOTEL IN RENO, NEVADA, PHOTOGRAPHED IN THE MID-DAY SUN FOR AN ARTICLE IN *FRANKFURTER ALLGEMEINE MAGAZINE* ON ROADSIDE MOTELS AND THE UNIQUELY AMERICAN LOVE OF FAST CARS AND THE OPEN ROAD. (GER)

● 295 DIESE DRAMATISCHE SZENE, DIE WIE EIN GEMÄLDE WIRKT, WURDE BEIM TRADITIONNELLEN MAROKKANISCHEN «FANTASIA»-FEST VON JOHN ISAAC FESTGEHALTEN. JOHN ISAAC MACHTE DIE AUFNAHME BEI SONNENUNTERGANG, IM RICHTIGEN MOMENT, IM RICHTIGEN WINKEL. DIESE AUFNAHME WURDE MIT DEM «BEST OF CATEGORY AWARD» FÜR DIE KATEGORIE AUSSENAUFNAHMEN VON GRAPHIS PHOTO 91 AUSGEZEICHNET. (USA)

● 296 EIN MOTEL IN RENO, NEVADA, IM MITTAGS-LICHT AUFGENOMMEN. DAS PHOTO GEHÖRT ZU EINEM ARTIKEL IM *FRANKFURTER ALLGEMEINE MAGAZIN* ÜBER MOTELS, DIE FÜR DIE AMERIKANER DER INBEGRIFF DES MOBILEN LEBENS SIND, (GER)

▲ 295 LA CHARGE DES CAVALIERS LORS D'UNE «FANTASIA», FÊTE MAROCAINE TRADITIONNELLE, ÉVOQUE CERTAINES PEINTURES DE BATAILLES. LE PHOTOGRAPHE, JOHN ISAAC CONSIDÈRE CETTE PHOTO COMME L'UNE DE SES PRÉFÉRÉES. IL L'A RÉALISÉE AU COUCHER DU SOLEIL. CETTE PHOTO A REÇU LE «BEST OF CATEGORY AWARD/OUTDOOR» DU CONCOURS GRAPHIS PHOTO 91 SPONSORISÉ PAR EASTMAN KODAK. (USA)

▲ 296 UN MOTEL À RENO DANS LE NEVADA, PRIS EN PLEIN MIDI. CETTE PHOTO ILLUSTRAIT UN ARTICLE DU *FRANKFURTER ALLGEMEINE MAGAZIN* CONSACRÉ AUX AUTOROUTES AMÉRICAINES ET AUX MOTELS, SYMBOLES DE LA MOBILITÉ. (GER)

PHOTOGRAPHER:

HARRY DE ZITTER

CAMERA:

LINHOF

TECHNORAMA 6X12

FILM:

KODAK EPR 120

EXPOSURE:

F 11, 1/125

CLIENT:

THE NEW ENGLAND

LIFE INSURANCE CO.

ART DIRECTOR:

TOM SIMONS

■ 297

PHOTOGRAPHER:

KEVIN HUTCHISON

CAMERA:

NIKON F3

FILM:

KODAK T-MAX 100

EXPOSURE:

F 11, 1/250

PHOTO EDITOR:

KEVIN HUTCHISON

CLIENT:

INDIANA

UNIVERSITY

ART DIRECTOR:

RICK FARIS

DESIGNER:

RICK FARIS

■ 298

PHOTOGRAPHER:
NADAV KANDER
REPRESENTATIVE:
DAVID BURNHAM,
UNITED KINGDOM/
STOCKLAND
MARTEL, USA/
VERONIQUE PERES
DOMERGUE, FRANCE
CAMERA:
6X17
■ 299

PHOTOGRAPHER:
DAVID MAISEL
REPRESENTATIVE:
ARLENE JOHNSON
CAMERA:
FUJI 617
FILM:
FUJI 50D
DESIGNER:
VIGNELLI
ASSOCIATES
■ 300

■ 297 WITH THIS PHOTOGRAPH TAKEN ON NAN-TUCKET ISLAND, PHOTOGRAPHER HARRY DE ZITTER CAPTURED THE SPIRIT OF NEW ENGLAND. FROM A SERIES OF POSTERS PROMOTING THE *TRAVELS WITH HARRY* EXHIBITION SPONSORED BY THE NEW ENGLAND LIFE INSURANCE COMPANY. (USA)

■ 298 LATE AFTERNOON LIGHT ADDS A SPECIAL FEELING TO THIS PHOTOGRAPH OF THE VIEW ACROSS A SMALL BAY. CATTAILS SWAY IN THE BACKGROUND OF THIS IMAGE FOCUSING ON TRENDS IN RECREATION FOR THE INDIANA UNIVERSITY PRESS. (USA)

■ 299 THIS PANORAMIC PHOTOGRAPH WAS TAKEN IN MOROCCO BY NADAV KANDER AND USED FOR THE PHOTOGRAPHER'S SELF-PROMOTION. (GBR)

■ 300 A STORM OFF THE CALIFORNIA COAST AT POINT REYES, PART OF A SELF-PROMOTION BROCHURE FOR PHOTOGRAPHER DAVID MAISEL FEATURING PANORAMIC VIEWS OF THE AMERICAN LANDSCAPE. (USA)

● 297 MIT DIESER AUF NATUCKET ISLAND ENTSTAN-DENEN AUFNAHME GELANG ES HARRY DE ZITTER, DIE TYPISCHE STIMMUNG DER LANDSCHAFT EINZUFANGEN. SIE GEHÖRT ZU EINER PLAKATREIHE DER NEW ENGLAND LIFE INSURANCE CO. FÜR DIE AUSSTELLUNG «TRAVEL WITH HARRY». (USA)

● 298 DIE NACHMITTAGSSONNE ERMÖGLICHTE DEN GEWÜNSCHTEN KONTRAST FÜR DIESE AUFNAHME EINER KLEINEN BUCHT, DEREN SCHILF SICH ALS IDEALER HINTERGRUND BOT. ES GING UM DIE DAR-STELLUNG VON FREIZEITMÖGLICHKEITEN IN EINER PUBLIKATION DER INDIANA UNIVERSITY. (USA)

● 299 DIESE PANORAMA-AUFNAHME ENTSTAND IN MAROKKO UND WIRD VON NADAV KANDER FÜR EIGENWERBUNGSZWECKE VERWENDET. (GBR)

● 300 EIN STURM VOR DER KÜSTE VON POINT REYES, KALIFORNIEN. DIE AUFNAHME GEHÖRT ZU EINER EIGENWERBUNGSBROSCHÜRE VON DAVID MAISEL MIT PANORAMA-AUFNAHMEN AMERIKANI-SCHER LANDSCHAFTEN. (USA)

▲ 297 LE PHOTOGRAPHE A SU SAISIR L'ATMOS-PHÈRE CARACTÉRISTIQUE DES PAYSAGES DE LA NOUVELLE-ANGLETERRE. CET EXEMPLE EST TIRÉ D'UNE SÉRIE DE PHOTOS RÉALISÉES POUR UNE COMPAGNIE D'ASSURANCES DE BOSTON ET ÉDITÉES SOUS FORME D'AFFICHES. (USA)

▲ 298 CETTE PHOTO EN NOIR ET BLANC, RÉALISÉE POUR UNE PUBLICATION DE L'INDIANA UNIVERSITY, MONTRE L'UNE DES ACTIVITÉS DE LOISIRS LES PLUS EN VOGUE AUJOURD'HUI. LE PÊCHEUR A ÉTÉ PHOTOGRAPHIÉ SUR UN ARRIÈRE-PLAN DE ROSEAUX EN FIN D'APRÉS-MIDI. (USA)

▲ 299 CETTE PHOTOGRAPHIE PANORAMIQUE AUTO-PROMOTIONNELLE DE NADAV KANDER A ÉTÉ PRISE AU MAROC. (GBR)

▲ 300 L'ORAGE SUR LA CÔTE À POINT REYES EN CALIFORNIE. PHOTO POUR LA BROCHURE DU PHO-TOGRAPHE DAVID MAISEL INTITULÉE «HORIZONS». ELLE RASSEMBLE UNE COLLECTION DE PHOTOS PANORAMIQUES DE PAYSAGES AMÉRICAINS. (USA)

PHOTOGRAPHER:
GEIR JORDAHL
CLIENT:
PORTAL
PUBLICATIONS LTD.
ART DIRECTOR:
SUZANNE
MCGOLDRICK/
ANDRÉ SALA
DESIGNER:
SANDEE YEE
▲
◄■ 301

PHOTOGRAPHER:
STEPHENIE
HOLLYMAN
CAMERA:
NIKON F3
PHOTO EDITOR:
PETER DAVID
CLIENT:
UNICEF
ART DIRECTOR:
PETER DAVID
◄■ 302

PHOTOGRAPHER:
JAY MAISEL
REPRESENTATIVE:
EMILY VICKERS
CAMERA:
NIKON F3
CLIENT:
ROYAL VIKING LINE
ART DIRECTOR:
RICH SILVERSTEIN
■ 303

■ 301 THIS PHOTOGRAPH WAS PUBLISHED AS A POSTER PROMOTING TOURISM TO WAIKIKI BEACH ON THE ISLAND OF HAWAII. (USA)

■ 302 THE KALAHARI DESERT OF BOTSWANA, PHOTOGRAPHED BY STEPHENIE HOLLYMAN. WHILE ON ASSIGNMENT FOR UNICEF, SHE WAS IN A PLANE CARRYING THE "FLYING DOCTORS" EMPLOYED BY UNICEF WHEN SHE CAPTURED THIS SPECTACULAR VIEW. (USA)

■ 303 TAKEN ON ASSIGNMENT IN THE CARIBBEAN, THIS PHOTOGRAPH APPEARED AS A PROMOTION FOR THE CRUISES OF THE ROYAL VIKING LINES. (USA)

● 301 DIESE AUFNAHME WURDE FÜR EIN TOURISTIKPLAKAT VERWENDET, DAS FÜR DIE WAIKIKI BEACH VON HAWAII WIRBT. (USA)

● 302 DIE KALAHARI-WÜSTE VON BOTSWANA. AUFGENOMMEN VON STEPHENIE HOLLYMAN WÄHREND SIE FÜR UNICEF IM SÜDLICHEN AFRIKA PHOTOGRAPHIERTE. SIE BEFAND SICH IM FLUGZEUG DER VON DER UNICEF ENTSANDTEN «FLIEGENDEN ÄRZTE», ALS SIE DIE AUFNAHME MACHTE. (USA)

● 303 DIESE AUFNAHME ENTSTAND IN DER KARIBIK FÜR EINE KREUZFAHRTENWERBUNG DER ROYAL VIKING LINES. (USA)

▲ 301 PHOTO UTILISÉE SUR UNE AFFICHE DE PROMOTION TOURISTIQUE POUR WAIKIKI BEACH, UNE STATION BALNÉAIRE D'HAWAII. (USA)

▲ 302 LE DÉSERT DE KALAHARI EN AFRIQUE MÉRIDIONALE. CETTE PHOTO A ÉTÉ PRISE AU BOTSWANA POUR LE COMPTE DE L'UNICEF. LA PHOTOGRAPHE AVAIT ÉTÉ CHARGÉE DE DOCUMENTER LA VIE DES ENFANTS À LA FRONTIÈRE. ELLE A RÉALISÉ CE CLICHÉ DANS L'AVION DE L'AIDE MÉDICALE. (USA)

▲ 303 LES CROISIÈRES AUX CARAÏBES, TEL ÉTAIT LE THÈME DE CETTE CAMPAGNE POUR LA COMPAGNIE ROYAL VIKING LINES. (USA)

PHOTOGRAPHER:

ANDRE BARANOWSKI

CAMERA:

NIKON F3

FILM:

KODAK PLUS-X

CLIENT:

GOLDEN CAPRICORN

PUBLICATION

ART DIRECTOR:

ANDRE BARANOWSKI

◄■ 304

PHOTOGRAPHER:

CHRIS WIMPEY

CLIENT:

DELEO CLAY TILE

ART DIRECTOR:

SCOTT MIRES

DESIGNER:

SCOTT MIRES

■ 305

■ 304 VIEW OF THE SCULPTURE GARDEN OF THE METROPOLITAN MUSEUM OF ART. THE PHOTOGRAPH BELONGS TO A SERIES OF FORTY ON THE SUBJECT OF NEW YORK'S CENTRAL PARK. (USA)

■ 305 A CORNUCOPIA OF AMERICAN KITSCH UNITED IN A SINGLE PHOTOGRAPH. A TYPICAL AMERICAN LANDSCAPE SEEN THROUGH THE FRONT WINDOW OF A CAR, ITS DASHBOARD ADORNED BY CULTURAL ICONS—PIN-UPS, A PHOTOGRAPH OF MARYLIN MONROE, THE STARS AND STRIPES, THE COCA COLA LOGO, A PACK OF CAMEL CIGARETTES, AND A KEY TAG FROM A HOLIDAY INN MOTEL. THE PHOTOGRAPH DECORATES A CALENDAR FROM A ROOFING TILE COMPANY. (USA)

● 304 BLICK AUF DEN SKULPTUREN-GARTEN DES METROPOLITAN MUSEUM OF ART. DIE AUFNAHME GEHÖRT ZU EINER REIHE ÜBER DEN NEW YORKER CENTRAL PARK. (USA)

● 305 EINE AMERIKANISCHE LANDSCHAFT, DURCH DIE FRONTSCHEIBE EINES AUTOS GESEHEN. AUF DEM ARMATURENBRETT IST EINE GANZE REIHE AMERIKANISCHER CLICHÉS VERSAMMELT: PIN-UP-PHOTOS, EINE PHOTOGRAPHIE VON MARYLIN MONROE, DAS STERNENBANNER, DAS COCA COLA-MARKENZEICHEN, EINE PACKUNG CAMEL-ZIGARETTEN UND EIN SCHLÜSSELANHÄNGER VOM HOLIDAY INN. DIESES PHOTO WURDE IM KALENDER EINES DACHZIEGELHERSTELLERS VERWENDET. (USA)

▲ 304 PHOTO TIRÉE D'UNE SÉRIE DE 40 IMAGES SUR LE THÈME DU CENTRAL PARK À NEW YORK. ICI UNE VUE DU JARDIN DES SCULPTURES DU METROPOLITAN MUSEUM OF ART. (USA)

▲ 305 CETTE PHOTO RASSEMBLE TOUS LES CLICHÉS TYPIQUES DU KITSCH AMÉRICAIN. AU TRAVERS DU PARE-BRISE, ON DÉCOUVRE UN PAYSAGE CARACTÉRISTIQUE DE CE PAYS. SUR LE TABLEAU DE BORD, ON PEUT VOIR DES PHOTOS DE PIN-UP ET DE MARYLIN MONROE, LE DRAPEAU ÉTOILÉ, LE SIGLE COCA COLA, UN PAQUET DE CIGARETTES CAMEL ET LA PLAQUE D'UNE CLEF DU HOLIDAY INN. CETTE PHOTO ILLUSTRE LE CALENDRIER D'UNE TUILERIE. (USA)

ARCHITECTURE

ARCHITEKTUR

ARCHITECTURE

PHOTOGRAPHER:

ANDREAS SÜSS

CAMERA:

SINAR F1

ART DIRECTOR:

ANDREAS SÜSS

DESIGNER:

ANDREAS SÜSS

◀■ 306

PHOTOGRAPHER:

ALAIN JANSSENS

CAMERA:

HASSELBLAD 50MM

FILM:

KODAK T-MAX 400

EXPOSURE:

1" À 22

CLIENT:

ORCHESTRE PHILHAR-

MONIQUE DE LIEGE

ART DIRECTOR:

AGENCE A3

■ 307, 308

■ 306 (PRECEDING SPREAD) FROM A SERIES OF SIX PHOTOGRAPHS CREATED AS A PERSONAL PROJECT BY PHOTOGRAPHER ANDREAS SÜSS ON THE SUBJECT "LIGHT-SHADOW-ARCHITECTURE." THE ENTIRE SERIES WAS TAKEN DURING THE SUMMER IN A BANK BUIDLING IN DARMSTADT, GERMANY. (GER)

■ 307, 308 TWO INTERIOR VIEWS OF THE ROYAL CONSERVATORY IN LIEGE, SHOT FOR THE 1989/90 PROGRAM OF THE PHILHARMONIC ORCHESTRA. THE ASSIGNMENT WAS TO EMPHASIZE THE RELATIONSHIP BETWEEN THE HUMAN BEING AND THE ARCHITECTURE. THE PASSION OF THE MUSICIANS, THE TRADITION OF THE BUILDING, AND THE IMMORTALITY OF THE MUSIC ARE CAPTURED HERE. (BEL)

● 306 (VORHERGEHENDE SEITE) BEISPIEL AUS EINER SERIE VON SECHS FREIEN AUFNAHMEN DES PHOTOGRAPHEN ANDREAS SÜSS UNTER DEM TITEL «LICHT-SCHATTEN-ARCHITEKTUR». DIE PHOTOS SIND IN EINEM BANKGEBÄUDE IN DARMSTADT IM SOMMER ENTSTANDEN. (GER)

● 307, 308 ZWEI SPEZIELLE INNENANSICHTEN DES KONSERVATORIUMS VON LÜTTICH FÜR DAS PROGRAMM 1989/90 DES PHILHARMONISCHEN ORCHESTERS. AUFGABE WAR ES, EINE VERBINDUNG ZWISCHEN MENSCH UND ARCHITEKTUR HERZUSTELLEN. LEIDENSCHAFT DER MUSIKER, DIE TRADITION DES BAUWERKS UND DIE UNVERGÄNGLICHKEIT DER MUSIK SOLLTEN ZUM AUSDRUCK KOMMEN. (BEL)

▲ 306 (PAGE PRÉCÉDENTE) L'UNE DES SIX PHOTOS QUE LE PHOTOGRAPHE ANDREAS SÜSS A RÉALISÉES POUR UN TRAVAIL PERSONNEL SUR LE SUJET: «LUMIÉRE/OMBRE/ARCHITECTURE». ELLES ONT ÉTÉ PRISES DANS UNE BANQUE DE DARMSTADT AU COURS DE L'ÉTÉ DERNIER. (GER)

▲ 307, 308 DEUX VUES DE L'INTÉRIEUR DU CONSERVATOIRE ROYAL DE MUSIQUE DE LIÈGE RÉALISÉES POUR LE PROGRAMME DE LA SAISON 89/90 DE L'ORCHESTRE PHILHARMONIQUE DE CETTE VILLE. LE BÂTIMENT EST PRÉSENTÉ SOUS LA FORME D'UN PARCOURS SUBJECTIF, ESTHÉTIQUE, GRAPHIQUE ET SURTOUT MUSICAL, DE MANIÈRE À UNIR L'HOMME ET LE LIEU. (BEL)

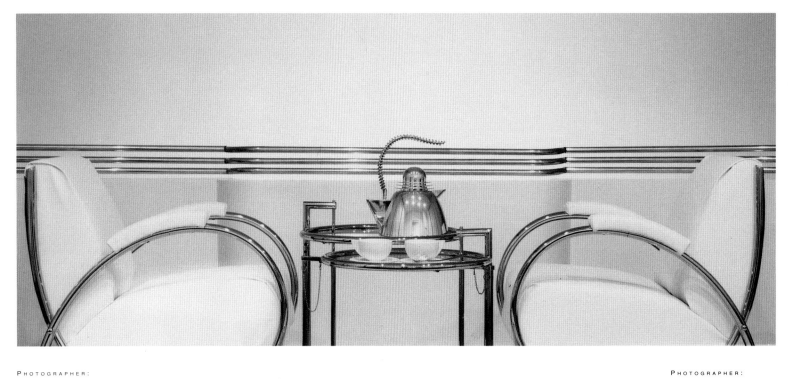

PHOTOGRAPHER:

MICHEL DUBOIS

REPRESENTATIVE:

PAULE FRIEDLAND

CAMERA:

SINAR P 4X5

FILM:

T-MAX 100 ISO

PHOTO EDITOR:

EDITION LOUISE

CLIENT:

SOCIÉTÉ DAMANN

ART DIRECTOR:

MICHEL DUBOIS

DESIGNER:

MICHEL DUBOIS

STYLIST:

CAROLINE CHAMPENOIS

■ 309

PHOTOGRAPHER:

JIANJUN SUN

CAMERA:

NIKON F4

FILM:

FUJICHROME VELVIA

50/18

EXPOSURE:

F 16, 1/4

▶■ 310

■ 309 *HOLLYWOOD 1932*, FROM A SERIES OF PHOTOGRAPHS DEPICTING TEA IN FAMILIAR SETTINGS. IN THIS CASE, THE FURNITURE IS USED TO ESTABLISH THE MOOD. THE STYLIST WAS CAROLINE CHAMPENOIS. (FRA)

● 309 «HOLLYWOOD 1932» – DIESE AUFNAHME GEHÖRT ZU EINER SERIE, IN DER DAS THEMA TEE DURCH CLICHÉS DARGESTELLT WIRD. DER PHOTOGRAPH MICHEL DUBOIS WURDE VON DER STYLISTIN CAROLINE CHAMPENOIS UNTERSTÜTZT. (FRA)

▲ 309 «HOLLYWOOD 1932». PHOTO TIRÉE D'UNE SÉRIE PRÉSENTANT DES CLICHÉS TYPIQUES SUR LE THEME DU THÉ. LE PHOTOGRAPHE MICHEL DUBOIS A ÉTÉ ASSISTÉ PAR LA STYLISTE CAROLINE CHAMPENOIS. (FRA)

■ 310 THE IRVINE BUSINESS CENTER IN CALIFORNIA SEEN FROM AN UNUSUAL PERSPECTIVE. THE PHOTOGRAPH IS A PERSONAL PROJECT OF PHOTOGRAPHER JIANJUN SUN. (USA)

● 310 DAS IRVINE BUSINESS CENTER IN KALIFORNIEN, AUS EINER UNGEWÖHNLICHEN PERSPEKTIVE GESEHEN. DIE AUFNAHME IST EINE FREIE ARBEIT DES PHOTOGRAPHEN. (USA)

▲ 310 LE CENTRE COMMERCIAL IRVINE BUSINESS CENTER EN CALIFORNIE VU DANS UNE PERSPECTIVE INHABITUELLE. LA PHOTO EST UN PROJET PERSONNEL DU PHOTOGRAPHE. (USA)

■ 311 THE NAT WEST BUILDING IN LONDON, SHOT IN THE DRAMATIC ATMOSPHERE OF THE NIGHT. THIS PHOTOGRAPH BELONGS TO AN ESSAY BY THE PHOTOGRAPHER ON THE CITY OF LONDON. (GBR)

● 311 DAS NAT WEST GEBÄUDE IN LONDON, DRAMATISCH, MIT NÄCHTLICHER BELEUCHTUNG AUFGENOMMEN. DIE AUFNAHME IST TEIL EINES ESSAYS DES PHOTOGRAPHEN ÜBER LONDON. (GBR)

▲ 311 LE NAT WEST BUILDING DE LONDRES, PRIS DANS UNE ATMOSPHÈRE NOCTURNE DRAMATIQUE. ÉTUDE PERSONNELLE FAISANT PARTIE D'UN PROJET SUR LA VILLE DE LONDRES. (GBR)

■ 312 AS PART OF AN ANNUAL, ONGOING PROJECT SPONSORED BY THE *CINCINNATI POST*, ALL OF THE BUILDINGS IN DOWNTOWN CINCINNATI OPEN THEIR DOORS TO PHOTOGRAPHERS ON A SINGLE NIGHT. GORDON BAER SEIZED THE OPPORTUNITY AND TOOK THIS APPROACH TO SHOW WHAT HAPPENS IN THIS BUILDING EVERY NIGHT OF THE YEAR. (USA)

● 312 JEDES JAHR SIND DIE GEBÄUDE IN CINCINNATI HELL ERLEUCHTET UND FÜR PHOTOGRAPHEN IM RAHMEN EINES WETTBEWERBS ZUGÄNGLICH. FÜR DIESE AUFNAHME BEKAM GORDON BAER VON DER *CINCINNATI POST* FREIE HAND. ER MACHTE SICH GEDANKEN DARÜBER, WAS IN ALL DEN ANDEREN NÄCHTEN HIER VOR SICH GEHT. (USA)

▲ 312 CHAQUE ANNÉE, LES BÂTIMENTS DE CINCINNATI SONT PENDANT TOUTE UNE NUIT ACCESSIBLES AUX PHOTOGRAPHES. A LA DEMANDE DE LA *CINCINNATI POST*, GORDON BAER DONNA SA VISION PERSONNELLE DE CE BÂTIMENT, QUI PEUT SE RÉSUMER AINSI: QUE SE PASSE-T-IL DANS CE LIEU TOUTES LES AUTRES NUITS DE L'ANNÉE? (USA)

PHOTOGRAPHER:

HERB SCHMITZ

REPRESENTATIVE:

PAT DOYLE

CAMERA:

HASSELBLAD 500 ELX/

CARL ZEISS

DISTAGON F4/50MM

FILM:

KODAK PLUS-X

EXPOSURE:

F 8, 1/250

PHOTO EDITOR:

ROBERT

MARCOTULLIO

◀■ 311

PHOTOGRAPHER:

GORDON BAER

CAMERA:

NIKON FM2

PHOTO EDITOR:

BRUCE CRIPPEN

CLIENT:

CINCINNATI POST

ART DIRECTOR:

GORDON BAER

■ 312

PHOTOGRAPHER:
DIETMAR HENNEKA
CAMERA:
SINAR P 8X10
FILM:
EKTACHROME 200
EXPOSURE:
FLASH
CLIENT:
LEITNER GMBH
DESIGNER:
SABINE MESCHER
■ 313-315

■ 313-315 PHOTOGRAPHS FROM A BROCHURE ADVERTISING EXHIBITION SYSTEMS MADE BY LEITNER. ALTHOUGH THE ASSIGNMENT WAS GIVEN TO EMPHASIZE THE SPECIFIC CHARACTERISTICS OF EACH PRODUCT, PHOTOGRAPHER DIETMAR HENNEKA WAS ALLOWED *CARTE BLANCHE* FOR THE REST. KEEPING IN MIND THE TARGET MARKETS FOR THE BROCHURE, HE WORKED WITH SPACE, LIGHT, AND ACCESSORIES TO HIS OWN SATISFACTION. (GER)

● 313-315 AUFNAHMEN AUS EINER BROSCHÜRE FÜR AUSSTELLUNGSSYSTEME DER FIRMA LEITNER. IN PRODUKTPORTRÄTS SOLLTE DER SPEZIFISCHE CHARAKTER JEDES EINZELEN AUSSTELLUNGS-SYSTEMS ZUM AUSDRUCK KOMMEN. DER PHOTO-GRAPH DIETMAR HENNEKA HATTE FREIE HAND IN DER UMSETZUNG DER IDEE. ER ARBEITETE MIT RAUM, LICHT, ACCESSOIRES UND VISUALISIERUNG DER ZIELGRUPPEN. (GER)

▲ 313-315 PHOTOS D'UNE BROCHURE PRÉSENTANT LES SYSTÈMES D'EXPOSITION DE LA FIRME LEITNER. IL S'AGISSAIT DE PRÉSENTER CHAQUE PRODUIT DANS SA SPÉCIFICITÉ. LE PHOTOGRAPHE DIETMAR HENNEKA REÇUT CARTE BLANCHE ET MIT EN SCÈNE CHAQUE SYSTÈME DANS UN ENVIRONNE-MENT SUGGESTIF. EN TRAVAILLANT AVEC L'ESPACE, LA LUMIÈRE ET DES ACCESSOIRES, IL RÉUSSIT À ÉVOQUER CHAQUE GROUPE D'INTÉRÊT. (GER)

PHOTOGRAPHER:

SHIGEO ANZAI

CAMERA:

HASSELBLAD 50CM

FILM:

KODAK PLUS-X

CLIENT:

ISAMU NOGUCHI

GARDEN MUSEUM

ART DIRECTOR:

WOODY PIRTLE

■ 316-320

■ 316-320 PHOTOGRAPHS FROM A SMALL BOOK ON THE ISAMU NOGUCHI GARDEN MUSEUM IN LONG ISLAND CITY, A MUSEUM DEDICATED TO JAPANESE SCULPTOR ISAMU NOGUCHI AND DESIGNED BY THE ARTIST HIMSELF. *316:* THE SECOND FLOOR GALLERY IN THE BUILDING ADDITION DESIGNED BY NOGUCHI IN 1980; *317:* THE CORNER GALLERY WITH VIEW OF MANHATTAN; *318:* GALLERY WITH NOGUCHI'S EARLIEST WORKS DATING FROM 1928; *319:* GALLERY CONVERTED FROM THE ORIGINAL FACTORY BUILDING PURCHASED BY NOGUCHI FOR STUDIO SPACE IN 1974; *320:* MARBLE SCULPTURES IN GALLERY ADJACENT TO THE GARDEN. (USA)

● 316-320 AUFNAHMEN AUS EINEM KLEINEN BUCH ÜBER DAS ISAMU NOGUCHI GARDEN MUSEUM IN LONG ISLAND CITY, DAS DEM JAPANISCHEN BILDHAUER ISAMU NOGUCHI GEWIDMET IST UND VON IHM SELBST ENTWORFEN WURDE. *316:* DIE GALERIE IM ZWEITEN STOCK IN EINEM ANBAU, DEN NOGUCHI 1980 ENTWARF; *317:* GALERIE MIT BLICK AUF MANHATTAN; *318:* GALERIE MIT NOGUCHIS FRÜHWERK AUS DEM JAHRE 1928; *319:* DIE AUS DEM EHEMALIGEN FABRIKGEBÄUDE ENTSTANDENE GALERIE, VON NOGUCHI 1974 ALS ATELIER ERWORBEN; *320:* MARMORSKULPTUREN IN DER GALERIE NEBEN DEM GARTEN. (USA)

▲ 316-320 PHOTOGRAPHIES ILLUSTRANT UN PETIT LIVRE SUR LE ISAMU NOGUCHI GARDEN MUSEUM SITUÉ À LONG ISLAND CITY. CE MUSÉE EST CONSACRÉ À L'ŒUVRE DU SCULPTEUR JAPONAIS ISAMU NOGUCHI, DONT IL A LUI-MÊME DESSINÉ LES PLANS. *316:* LA GALERIE DU SECOND ÉTAGE DANS L'AILE RAJOUTÉE PAR NOGUCHI EN 1980; *317:* VUE SUR MANHATTAN D'UN ANGLE DE LA GALERIE; *318:* PREMIÈRES SCULPTURES DATANT DE 1928; *319:* NOGUCHI TRANSFORMA LES SALLES D'UNE ANCIENNE USINE EN ATELIER EN 1974; *320:* SCULPTURES DE MARBRE DANS LA SALLE QUI DONNE SUR LE JARDIN. (USA)

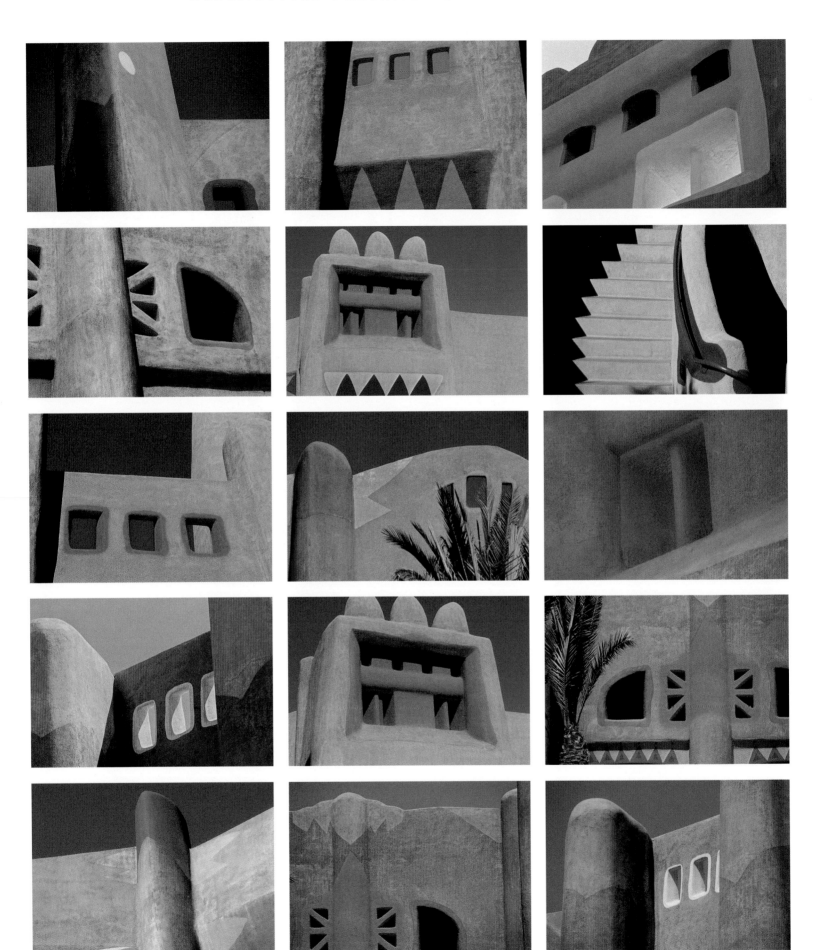

PHOTOGRAPHER:

ROY RITOLA

CAMERA:

LEICA R4

FILM:

KODACHROME 25

CLIENT:

NEOGRAPHIQUE

ART DIRECTOR:

ROY RITOLA

DESIGNER:

ROY RITOLA

◄■ 321-335

PHOTOGRAPHER:

ARTHUR MEYERSON

CAMERA:

NIKON F3

FILM:

KODACHROME 64

CLIENT:

VINSON ELKINS

DESIGNER:

MILLER, JUDSON &
FORD

■ 336

■ 321-335 *PAINTED WINDOWS* IS THE TITLE OF THIS SERIES OF STUDIES BY PHOTOGRAPHER ROY RITOLY OF A NEW BUILDING LOCATED IN THE SOUTHWESTERN DESERT OF THE UNITED STATES. WHILE THE ENTIRE PORTFOLIO IS AVAILABLE AS LIMITED EDITION CIBACHROME PRINTS, THREE (*321, 333* AND *335*) HAVE ALSO BEEN PUBLISHED AS POSTERS. (USA)

■ 336 FROM A BROCHURE, WHICH PROMOTES THE SERVICES OF A LAW FIRM THAT HAS OFFICES ACROSS THE UNITED STATES, FEATURING PORTRAITS OF THE VARIOUS PARTNERS IN THEIR WORKING ENVIRONMENTS. SHOWN HERE THE HEAD OF THE WASHINGTON, D.C. OFFICE. (USA)

● 321-335 DIESE *PAINTED WINDOWS* (BEMALTE FENSTER) GEHÖREN ZU EINEM NEUEN GEBÄUDE IN EINER WÜSTE, DIE IM SÜDWESTEN DER VEREINIGTEN STAATEN LIEGT. DER PHOTOGRAPH ROY RITOLY WAR FASZINIERT VON DEN STRUKTUREN. DIE PHOTOS SIND ALS CIBACHROME-DRUCKE IN LIMITIERTER AUFLAGE ERSCHIENEN, *321, 333* UND *335* AUCH ALS PLAKATE. (USA)

● 336 DIESE AUFNAHME STAMMT AUS DER BROSCHÜRE EINER ANWALTSFIRMA. ES WERDEN VERSCHIEDENE PARTNER AN IHREM ARBEITSPLATZ IN VERSCHIEDENEN STÄDTEN DER VEREINIGTEN STAATEN VORGESTELLT. HIER DER PARTNER AUS WASHINGTON, D.C. (USA)

▲ 321-335 *PAINTED WINDOWS*: ÉTUDES PERSONNELLES DU PHOTOGRAPHE ROY RITOLY. IL PHOTOGRAPHIA CETTE SÉRIE DANS LE DÉSERT DU SUD-OUEST. LES FENÊTRES SONT CELLES D'UN NOUVEAU BÂTIMENT. CES PHOTOS ONT ÉTÉ IMPRIMÉES EN ÉDITION LIMITÉE, TROIS D'ENTRE ELLES (DONT *321, 333* ET *335*) SOUS FORME D'AFFICHES. (USA)

▲ 336 PHOTO FIGURANT DANS LA BROCHURE D'UN CABINET JURIDIQUE IMPLANTÉ DANS UN GRAND NOMBRE DE VILLES AMÉRICAINES. LES DIVERS COLLABORATEURS Y SONT PRÉSENTÉS DANS LEUR CADRE DE TRAVAIL. ICI, LE REPRÉSENTANT DU SIÈGE DE WASHINGTON. (USA)

WILDLIFE

TIERE

ANIMAUX

WILDLIFE

TIERE

PHOTOGRAPHER:

HIRO

REPRESENTATIVE:

NOB HOVDE

CAMERA:

MAMIYA RZ67

FILM.

KODACHROME

PROFESSIONAL

PHOTO EDITOR:

THOMAS MCWILLIAM

CLIENT:

HOUSE & GARDEN

ART DIRECTOR:

KAREN GRANT

DESIGNER:

DEREK UNGLESS

◀■ 337

PHOTOGRAPHER:

HUGO A.

LAMBRECHTS

CAMERA:

MINOLTA XD7

PHOTO EDITOR:

RICHARD V. BRYANT

CLIENT:

MINOLTA CAMERA

CO. LTD.

ART DIRECTOR:

FRED O. BECHLEN

■ 338, 339

■ 337 (PRECEDING SPREAD) "CHANTECLAIR." THE
UNOFFICIAL NATIONAL BIRD OF FRANCE, WAS USED
TO ILLUSTRATE AN ARTICLE ON FRENCH CUISINE IN
HOUSE & GARDEN MAGAZINE. (USA)

■ 338, 339 THESE TWO PHOTOS WERE SHOT IN
NAMIBIA BY HUGO A. LAMBRECHTS ON SELF-
ASSIGNMENT. *338*: AN ELEPHANT ON HIS WAY TO A
WATER BOREHOLE AS THUNDERHEADS APPROACH IN
THE NAMIBIAN DESERT. *339*: A BARN OWL ALIGHTS
AT NIGHT WITH ITS PREY. (USA)

● 337 (VORANGEHENDE SEITE) «CHANTECLAIR»,
DAS INOFFIZIELLE NATIONALSYMBOL FRANKREICHS,
ALS ILLUSTRATION EINES ARTIKELS ÜBER DIE
FRANZÖSISCHE KÜCHE IN *HOUSE & GARDEN*. (USA)

● 338, 339 DER PHOTOGRAPH HUGO A. LAMBRECHTS
MACHTE BEIDE AUFNAHMEN IN NAMIBIA. *338*: EIN
ELEFANT AUF SEINEM WEG ZUM WASSERLOCH,
WÄHREND AM HIMMEL GEWITTERWOLKEN AUFZIE-
HEN; *339*: EINE EULE, HELL ANGESTRAHLT, MIT
IHRER BEUTE. (USA)

▲ 337 (PAGE PRÉCÉDENTE) «CHANTECLAIR», LE
COQ GAULOIS: PHOTO ILLUSTRANT UN ARTICLE SUR
LA CUISINE FRANÇAISE PUBLIÉ DANS LE MAGAZINE
HOUSE & GARDEN. (USA)

▲ 338, 339 CES ÉTUDES PERSONNELLES DE HUGO
A. LAMBRECHTS, ONT ÉTÉ RÉALISÉES EN NAMIBIE.
338: UN ÉLÉPHANT S'APPROCHE D'UN TROU D'EAU
TANDIS QU'À L'HORIZON SE PROFILE UNE TÊTE
D'ORAGE, ANNONCIATRICE DE PLUIE; *339*: L'ENVOL
D'UNE CHOUETTE EFFRAIE LA NUIT. (USA)

■ 340-348 THIS SERIES OF PHOTOGRAPHS WERE PUBLISHED IN A SMALL FOLD-OUT BROCHURE ENTITLED *A BOOK OF CHICKENS*, AND USED AS A SELF-PROMOTION BY THE PHOTOGRAPHER. PROVIDED AS A "THANK YOU" TO HIS CUSTOMERS, IT OFFERS US AN ENTERTAINING LOOK AT THE FOWL POPULATION, WHILE DEMONSTRATING NEWTON'S TALENTED EXPLORATIONS OF THE UNEXPECTED. IT IS THE PHOTOGRAPHER'S WAY OF SHOWING US THAT ONE LOOK IS WORTH A THOUSAND WORDS. (CAN)

● 340-348 DIESE AUFNAHMEN ILLUSTRIEREN EIN KLEINES EIGENWERBUNGSBUCH ÜBER DAS THEMA HÜHNER. DER PHOTOGRAPH VERSCHENKTE ES ALS DANKESCHÖN AN SEINE KUNDEN. DIESE SPEZIELLEN BILDER DER SELTSAMSTEN VERTRETER DER GATTUNG SIND EINE ERNSTGEMEINTE DEMONSTRATION DER MÖGLICHKEITEN, DAS UNERWARTETE ZU ERGRÜNDEN. DER PHOTOGRAPH WILL AUSSERDEM BEWEISEN, DASS EIN BILD MEHR ALS 1000 WORTE SAGEN KANN. (CAN)

▲ 340-348 CES PHOTOS ONT ÉTÉ RÉUNIES DANS UN PETIT LIVRE DÉPLIANT AUTOPROMOTIONNEL INTITULÉ «UN LIVRE DE POULES» QUE LE PHOTOGRAPHE RALPH NEWTON DISTRIBUE À SES CLIENTS EN GUISE DE REMERCIEMENT. L'ASPECT ÉTRANGE DE CES VOLATILES EST L'OCCASION POUR LUI DE DÉMONTRER QUE L'ON PEUT EXPLORER L'INATTENDU SELON DES MÉTHODES TOUT À FAIT UNIQUES ET QU'UNE PHOTO EN DIT SOUVENT PLUS QUE DES MILLIERS DE MOTS. (CAN)

PHOTOGRAPHER:
RALPH NEWTON
CAMERA:
HASSELBLAD
FILM:
KODAK VPS 6006
CLIENT:
RALPH NEWTON
ART DIRECTOR:
THE SPENCER
FRANCEY GROUP
DESIGNER:
PAUL HODGSON/
GARY TAUGHER
■ 340-348

BEST WILDLIFE

PHOTOGRAPHER:

TEIJI SAGA

CLIENT:

LIFE MAGAZINE

ART DIRECTOR:

TOM BENTKOWSKI

■ 349, 350

■ 349, 350 WILD SWANS CAUGHT IN A SNOW STORM IN NORTHERN JAPAN. SWANS ARE TEIJI SAGA'S ONLY SUBJECT AND FOR MORE THAN TWO DECADES HE HAS SPENT FIVE MONTHS EACH YEAR WITH THE GREAT WHITE MIGRATING BIRDS THAT COME FROM SIBERIA. TEIJI SAGA RECEIVED THE SPECIAL AWARD OF THE GRAPHIS 91 COMPETITION FOR OUTSTANDING ACHIEVEMENTS IN THE FIELD OF ANIMAL PHOTOGRAPHY, MADE POSSIBLE BY THE PROFESSIONAL PHOTOGRAPHY DIVISION OF THE EASTMAN KODAK COMPANY. (JPN)

■ 349, 350 WILDE SCHWÄNE IM NORDEN JAPANS VON EINEM SCHNEESTURM ÜBERRASCHT. DER JAPANER TEIJI SAGA PHOTOGRAPHIERT AUSSCHLIESSLICH SCHWÄNE, UND SEIT ÜBER 20 JAHREN VERBRINGT ER JEDES JAHR FÜNF MONATE MIT DIESEM ZUGVOGEL, DER AUS SIBIRIEN NACH JAPAN KOMMT. TEIJI SAGA ERHIELT DEN VON DER PROFESSIONAL PHOTOGRAPHY DIVISION DER FIRMA EASTMAN KODAK GESTIFTETEN PREIS FÜR HERVORRAGENDE TIERPHOTOGRAPHIE DES GRAPHIS-WETTBEWERBS 1991. (JPN)

▲ 349, 350 CYGNES PRIS DANS UNE TEMPÊTE DE NEIGE AU NORD DU JAPON. TEIJI SAGA PHOTOGRAPHIE EXCLUSIVEMENT DES CYGNES ET VOILÀ PLUS DE 20 ANS QU'IL PASSE CHAQUE ANNÉE CINQ MOIS AUPRÈS DE CES OISEAUX MIGRATEURS VENUS DE SIBÉRIE. IL A REÇU LE PRIX SPÉCIAL DU CONCOURS GRAPHIS PHOTO 91, SPONSORISÉ PAR LA SECTION PHOTOGRAPHIE PROFESSIONNELLE DE LA FIRME EASTMAN KODAK, POUR RÉCOMPENSER SON ŒUVRE EXCEPTIONNELLE DANS LE DOMAINE DE LA PHOTOGRAPHIE ANIMALE. (USA)

BEST OF SHOW

PHOTOGRAPHER:

JAMES BALOG

■ 354-358

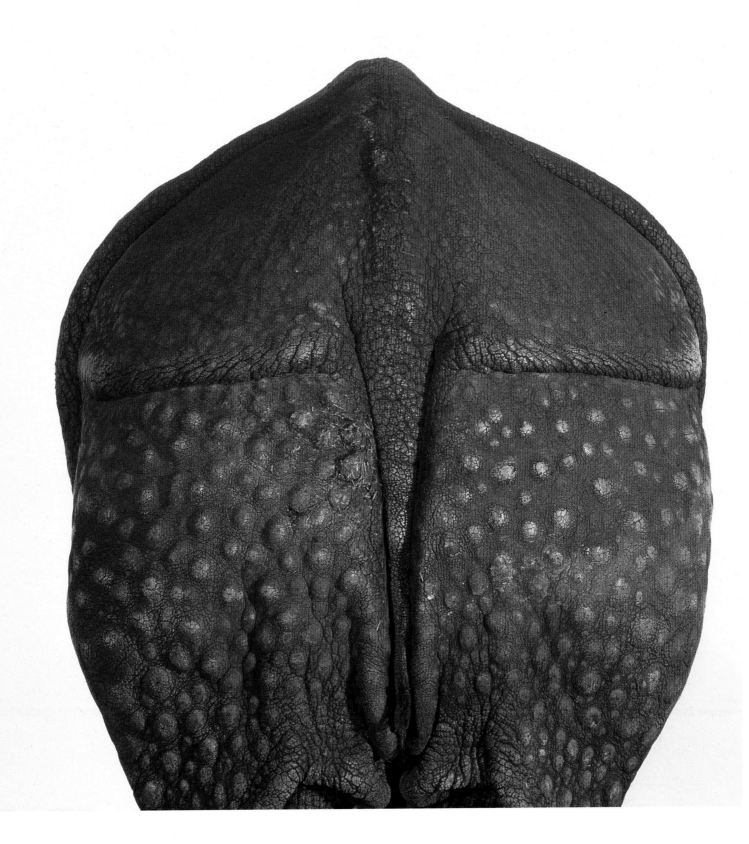

■ 354-358 FROM THE COLLECTION *SURVIVORS*, PUBLISHED BY ABRAMS, THESE PHOTOGRAPHS BY JAMES BALOG ARE BOTH A DOCUMENT OF AND A PLEAD FOR THE PROTECTION OF WILD ANIMALS. BECAUSE ALL OF THE ANIMALS SHOWN IN THE BOOK ARE ENDANGERED OR NEAR EXTINCTION, THEY WERE PHOTOGRAPHED IN ZOOS OR OTHER CONTAINED ENVIRONMENTS. TO EMPHASIZE THE LOSS OF THEIR NATURAL HABITAT, BALOG CREATED STUDIO-TYPE PORTRAITS OF HIS SUBJECTS. *354:* "NEW DEHLI DOLLY", GREATER INDIAN HORNBILL; *355:* FLORIDA PANTHER; *356:* "CHUKA", THE DRILL; *357:* MALE DAMA GAZELLE; *358:* "JORDY", THE GREAT INDIAN RHINOCEROS. THIS SERIES WAS AWARDED *BEST OF SHOW* IN THE GRAPHIS PHOTO 1991 COMPETITION, WHICH IS SPONSORED BY EASTMAN KODAK. (USA)

● 354-358 DIESE AUFNAHMEN DES PHOTOGRAPHEN JAMES BALOG, DIE IN DEM BEI ABRAMS ERSCHIE-NENEN BUCH *SURVIVORS* VERÖFFENTLICHT WUR-DEN, SIND SOWOHL EIN DOKUMENT ALS AUCH EIN AUFRUF ZUM SCHUTZ DER WILDTIERE: ALLE SIND VOM AUSSTERBEN BEDROHT. DER PHOTOGRAPH PHOTOGRAPHIERTE SIE IN ZOOS ODER WILD-TIERGEHEGEN, UND ZWAR IN DEN MEISTEN FÄLLEN VOR EINER EINFACHEN LEINWAND. 354: «NEW DEHLI DOLLY», EIN INDISCHER DOPPELHORNVOGEL; 355: FLORIDA-PANTHER; 356: «CHUKA», DER DRILL; 357: DAMA-GAZELLE; 358: DAS GROSSE INDISCHE RHINO-ZEROS «JORDY». JAMES BALOG ERHIELT FÜR DIESE AUFNAHMEN DEN VON DER PROFESSIONAL PHOTO-GRAPHY DIVISION DER FIRMA EASTMAN KODAK GESPONSERTEN PREIS «BEST OF SHOW» DES GRAPHIS PHOTO-WETTBEWERBS 1991. (USA)

▲ 354-358 CETTE SÉRIE DE PHOTOS DE JAMES BALOG, TIRÉE DU LIVRE «SURVIVANTS», EST À LA FOIS UN DOCUMENT ET UN MANIFESTE POUR LA PROTECTION DES ANIMAUX SAUVAGES: TOUS LES ANIMAUX PRÉSENTÉS SONT DES ESPÈCES EN VOIE D'EXTINCTION OU MENACÉES. LE PHOTOGRAPHE S'EST RENDU POUR CELA DANS LES PARCS ZOOLOGIQUES OU LES RANCHES D'ÉLEVAGE. LES ANIMAUX ONT ÉTÉ POUR LA PLUPART PHOTOGRAPHIÉS DEVANT UN SIMPLE RIDEAU. 354: «NEW DEHLI DOLLY», LE GRAND CALAO D'ASIE; 355: LA PANTHÈRE DE FLORIDE; 356: «CHUKA», LE DRILL; 357: LA GAZELLE DAMA; 358: «JORDY», LE GRAND RHINOCÉROS INDIEN. JAMES BALOG A REÇU LE «BEST OF SHOW» DU CONCOURS GRAPHIS PHOTO 91, SPONSORISÉ PAR LA SECTION PHOTOGRAPHIE PROFESSIONNELLE DE EASTMAN KODAK. (USA)

SPORTS

SPORT

SPORT

PHOTOGRAPHER:
ALAIN ERNOULT
REPRESENTATIVE:
ERNOULT FEATURES
CAMERA:
NIKON
FILM:
EKTA 100 PLUS
EXPOSURE:
F 4, 1/1000
CLIENT:
LIFE MAGAZINE
ART DIRECTOR:
B.B. BURROWS
◀■ 359

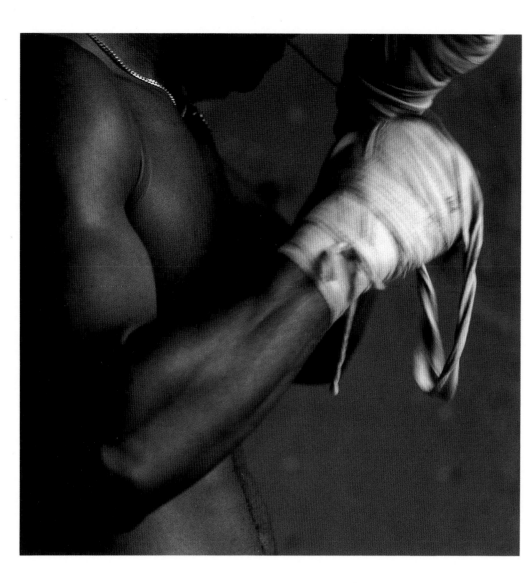

BEST SPORTS
PHOTOGRAPHER:
LACI PERÉNYI
CAMERA:
NIKONOS V
35MM/2.5
FILM:
FUJI 100
EXPOSURE:
F 5.6, 1/30
PHOTO EDITOR:
M. RABANUS
CLIENT:
SPORTS
▶■ 361

PHOTOGRAPHER:
MARK FERRI
REPRESENTATIVE:
KEVIN SCHOCHAT
CAMERA:
HASSELBLAD 250MM
CLIENT:
MARK FERRI
DESIGNER:
HEWSON BERLIN
ASSOCIATES, INC.
■ 360

■ 359 (PRECEDING SPREAD) THE FRENCH FOUR-MAN BOB PHOTOGRAPHED AT THE OLYMPIC GAMES IN CALGARY. THE PHOTOGRAPH HAS BEEN SHOWN IN *LIFE* MAGAZINE. (USA)

■ 360 *THE BOXER*, ONE OF A SERIES OF SIX PHOTOGRAPHS ON THE SUBJECT PUBLISHED IN A SELF-PROMOTIONAL BROCHURE BY THE PHOTOGRAPHER. THIS IMAGE WAS TAKEN IN THE WORLD-FAMOUS GLEASON'S GYM IN BROOKLYN. (USA)

■ 361 IT TOOK LACI PERÉNYI SEVERAL ROLLS OF FILM TO CAPTURE THIS SHOT OF EUROPEAN WOMEN'S FREESTYLE CHAMPION STEPHANIE ORTWIG ENTERING THE WATER. THE PHOTOGRAPHER WAS IN POSITION AT THE BOTTOM OF THE POOL, EQUIPPED WITH A NIKONOS UNDERWATER CAMERA AND HER FLASH FOCUSED ON THE SWIMMER'S KNIFE-STRAIGHT DIVE. ORIGINALLY PUBLISHED IN *SPORTS* MAGAZINE, THIS PHOTOGRAPH HAS RECEIVED THE BEST IN CATEGORY, SPORTS, AWARD FOR THE GRAPHIS PHOTO 91 COMPETITION, WHICH IS SPONSORED BY EASTMAN KODAK. (GER)

● 359 (VORHERGEHENDE SEITE) DER FRANZÖSISCHE VIERERBOB, AUFGENOMMEN BEI DER WINTEROLYMPIADE IN CALGARY. DAS PHOTO WURDE IN DER ZEITSCHRIFT *LIFE* VERÖFFENTLICHT. (USA)

● 360 «DER BOXER», EINE VON SECHS AUFNAHMEN ZU DIESEM THEMA, DIE IN EINER EIGENWERBUNGSBROSCHÜRE DES PHOTOGRAPHEN GEZEIGT WERDEN. SIE ENTSTAND IN DER BEKANNTEN BOXSCHULE «GLEASON'S GYM» IN BROOKLYN, NEW YORK. (USA)

● 361 LACI PERÉNYI VERBRAUCHTE MEHRERE ROLLEN FILM, UM DIESE AUFNAHME DES STARTSPRUNGS DER EUROPAMEISTERIN IM FREISTIL, STEPHANIE ORTWIG, ZU MACHEN. ER BEFAND SICH AUF DEM GRUND DES SCHWIMMBADES, AUSGERÜSTET MIT EINER NIKONOS-KAMERA UND EINEM UNTERWASSERBLITZ, ALS DIE SCHWIMMERIN DIREKT AUF IHN ZUSPRANG. DIE AUFNAHME WURDE IN DER ZEITSCHRIFT *SPORTS* GEZEIGT. AUSSERDEM WURDE SIE MIT DEM «BEST OF CATEGORY AWARD» FÜR DIE KATEGORIE SPORT VON GRAPHIS PHOTO 91 AUSGEZEICHNET. (GER)

▲ 359 (PAGE PRÉCÉDENTE) LE BOBSLEIGH DE L'ÉQUIPE FRANÇAISE LORS DES JEUX OLYMPIQUES DE CALGARY AU CANADA. CETTE PHOTO A ÉTÉ PUBLIÉE DANS LE MAGAZINE *LIFE*. (USA)

▲ 360 «LE BOXEUR»: L'UNE DES SIX PHOTOS PUBLIÉES SOUS FORME DE LIVRET AUTOPROMOTIONNEL. ELLE A ÉTÉ RÉALISÉE DANS UNE SALLE D'ENTRAÎNEMENT DU CÉLÈBRE GLEASON'S BOXING GYM DE BROOKLYN. (USA)

▲ 361 POUR RÉALISER CET INSTANTANÉ DU PLONGEON DE LA NAGEUSE STEPHANIE ORTWIG, LE PHOTOGRAPHE ALLEMAND LACI PERÉNYI ÉTAIT LUI-MÊME SOUS L'EAU, ÉQUIPÉ D'UN APPAREIL DE PHOTO SOUS-MARINE NIKONOS ET DE FLASH SPÉCIAUX. LA NAGEUSE PLONGEAIT DIRECTEMENT AU-DESSUS DE LUI. IL A FALLU PRENDRE DE NOMBREUX FILMS AVANT D'ARRIVER À CE RÉSULTAT. CETTE PHOTO A ÉTÉ PUBLIÉE DANS *SPORTS*. ELLE A REÇU LE «BEST OF CATEGORY AWARD/SPORT» DU CONCOURS GRAPHIS PHOTO 91 SPONSORISÉ PAR EASTMAN KODAK. (GER)

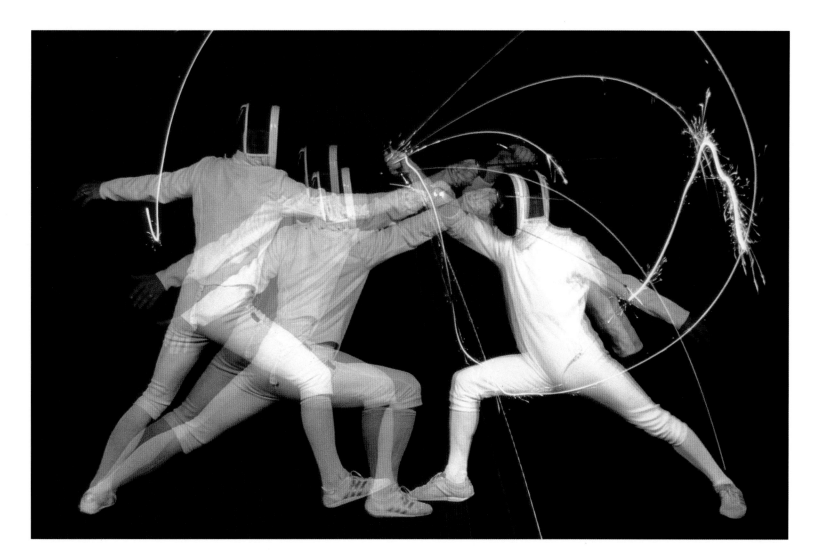

PHOTOGRAPHER:
KEVIN CRUFF
CAMERA:
HASSELBLAD 50MM
FILM:
KODAK PLUS-X
EXPOSURE:
F 11, 1/8
CLIENT:
KEVIN CRUFF
DESIGNER:
TIM FISHER
▲
◄■ 362

PHOTOGRAPHER:
KEVIN CRUFF
CAMERA:
HASSELBLAD 250MM
FILM:
KODAK PLUS-X
EXPOSURE:
F 8, 1/60
CLIENT:
KEVIN CRUFF
DESIGNER:
TIM FISHER
◄■ 363

PHOTOGRAPHER:
ALAIN ERNOULT
REPRESENTATIVE:
ERNOULT FEATURES
CAMERA:
NIKON
FILM:
EKTA 100 PLUS
PHOTO EDITOR:
FIGARO
CLIENT:
FIGARO
ART DIRECTOR:
ALAIN ERNOULT
■ 364

■ 362, 363 TWO EXAMPLES FROM A SERIES OF BLACK-AND-WHITE PORTRAITS OF ARIZONA ATHLETES LISA ANN JACQUIN AND JAY L. BARRS WHO PARTICIPATED IN THE SUMMER OLYMPIC GAMES IN SEOUL, SOUTH KOREA, 1988. PHOTOGRAPHER KEVIN CRUFF USES THEM FOR SELF-PROMOTION. (USA)

■ 364 THIS PHOTOGRAPH OF TWO FENCERS WAS TAKEN IN THE STUDIO WITH STROBOSCOPIC FLASH, A TECHNIQUE FIRST USED BY A COMPATRIOT OF THE PHOTOGRAPHER, E.J. MAREY, WHO LIVED FROM 1830 TO 1904. (FRA)

● 362, 363 ZWEI BEISPIELE AUS EINER REIHE VON SCHWARZWEISS-PORTRÄTS, DIE DER PHOTOGRAPH KEVIN CRUFF ALS EIGENWERBUNG VERWENDET. ER PHOTOGRAPHIERTE DIE ATHLETEN LISA ANN JACQUIN UND JAY L. BARRS AUS ARIZONA, DIE AN DEN OLYMPISCHEN SOMMERSPIELEN IN SEOUL 1988 TEILNAHMEN. (USA)

● 364 DIESE AUFNAHME DER BEIDEN FECHTER ENTSTAND IM STUDIO MIT HILFE VON STROBOSKOP-BLITZ, EIN VERFAHREN, DAS DER FRANZÖSISCHE PHOTOGRAPH E.J. MAREY (1830-1904).ERSTMALS FÜR DIE PHOTOGRAPHIE ANWANDTE. (FRA)

▲ 362, 363 CES DEUX EXEMPLES FONT PARTIE D'UNE SÉRIE AUTOPROMOTIONNELLE DE PORTRAITS EN NOIR ET BLANC DU PHOTOGRAPHE KEVIN CRUFF. ON Y TROUVE DES PORTRAITS DES ATHLÈTES LISA ANN JACQUIN ET JAY L. BARRS DE L'ARIZONA QUI PARTICIPÉRENT AUX JEUX OLYMPIQUES DE SÉOUL EN 1988. (USA)

▲ 364 PHOTO D'UN COMBAT D'ESCRIME PUBLIÉE DANS LE FIGARO MAGAZINE, RÉALISÉE EN STUDIO AVEC ÉCLAIRAGE STROBOSCOPIQUE. ELLE RAP-PELLE LES EXPÉRIENCES DE CHRONOPHOTOGRA-PHIE DE E.J. MAREY (1830-1904). (FRA)

PHOTOGRAPHER:
GREGORY HEISLER
CLIENT:
LIFE MAGAZINE
ART DIRECTOR:
TOM BENTKOWSKI
DESIGNER:
NORA SHEEHAN
■ 365

PHOTOGRAPHER:
ALAIN ERNOULT
REPRESENTATIVE:
ERNOULT FEATURES
CAMERA:
NIKON
FILM:
EKTA 100 PLUS
EXPOSURE:
Γ 0, 1/250
PHOTO EDITOR:
ALAIN ERNOULT
CLIENT:
FIGARO
ART DIRECTOR:
ALAIN ERNOULT
▶■ 366

■ 365 OLYMPIC CHAMPION CARL LEWIS IN THE STARTING BLOCK. THIS PHOTOGRAPH IS PART OF A SERIES FOR *LIFE* MAGAZINE ENTITLED "NO GOLD LIKE OLD GOLD," REFERRING TO LEWIS'S PAST ACHIEVEMENTS AND HIS FUTURE CHANCES—AT AN ATHLETICALLY RIPE AGE—IN A VARIETY OF TRACK-AND-FIELD EVENTS. (USA)

■ 366 THIS SPECTACULAR PHOTOGRAPH OF PARACHUTIST VIC NORMAN WITH THE BRITISH PLANE FORMATION WAS TAKEN ON THE OCCASION OF A FLIGHT SHOW IN FERTÉ-ALLAIS IN FRANCE AND PUBLISHED IN *FIGARO MAGAZINE*. THE CAMERA WAS ATTACHED TO ONE OF THE AIRPLANES. (FRA)

● 365 DER MEHRFACHE OLYMPIASIEGER CARL LEWIS IM STARTBLOCK. DIE AUFNAHME GEHÖRT ZU EINER REIHE FÜR EINEN ARTIKEL ÜBER LEWIS IN DER ZEITSCHRIFT *LIFE*. DER TITEL «NO GOLD LIKE OLD GOLD» BEZIEHT SICH AUF DIE ERFOLGE DER VERGANGENEN JAHRE UND DIE ZUKUNFTSAUS-SICHTEN DES RELATIV ALTEN ATHLETEN. (USA)

● 366 DIESE SPEKTAKULÄRE AUFNAHME DES FALL-SCHIRMSPRINGERS VIC NORMAN MIT EINER BRITI-SCHEN FLUGFORMATION ENTSTAND WÄHREND DER LUFTSCHAU IN FERTÉ-ALLAIS UND WURDE IM MAGA-ZIN DES *FIGARO* VERÖFFENTLICHT. DIE KAMERA WAR AN EINEM DER FLUGZEUGE BEFESTIGT. (FRA)

▲ 365 LE CHAMPION OLYMPIQUE CARL LEWIS DANS LE STARTING-BLOCK, AU DÉPART D'UNE COURSE. CETTE PHOTO EST TIRÉE D'UNE SÉRIE QUI A ÉTÉ PUBLIÉE DANS LE MAGAZINE *TIME* POUR UN ARTICLE INTITULÉ: «NO GOLD LIKE OLD GOLD» (JEU DE MOTS SUR LES ANCIENNES MÉDAILLES GAGNÉES PAR L'ATHLÈTE ET SES VICTOIRES FUTURES). (USA)

▲ 366 PHOTO SPECTACULAIRE DU CASCADEUR VIC NORMAN, AU COURS D'UNE EXHIBITION AÉRIENNE D'UNE PATROUILLE ANGLAISE LORS DU MEETING DE LA FERTÉ-ALLAIS. ELLE A ÉTÉ PUBLIÉE DANS LE *FIGARO MAGAZINE*. L'APPAREIL PHOTO EST FIXÉ SUR L'UN DES AVIONS. (FRA)

PHOTOGRAPHER:

CLINT CLEMENS

REPRESENTATIVE:

BECKY SANGSTER

(ART & COMMERCE)

CAMERA:

NIKON F4

FILM:

KODACHROME 200

CLIENT:

MOUNT GAY RUM

CORPORATION

ART DIRECTOR:

A.A. EL KAMMAS

DESIGNER:

A.A. EL KAMMAS

■ 367-371

■ 367-371 A SERIES OF PHOTOGRAPHS DOCUMENT-
ING HEAVY-WEATHER SAILING ON ASSIGNMENT FOR
THE MOUNT GAY RUM CORPORATION. PHOTOG-
RAPHER CLINT CLEMENS WAS ON BOARD THE YACHT
"COLT INTERNATIONAL," SAILING NEAR ANTIGUA IN
THE ANTILLES, WHEN THE CREW HAD TO TAKE IN
THE SAILS. AS SEEN HERE, THE CREW OF SEVEN
MEN FINALLY SUCCEEDED. (USA)

● 367-371 ALLE DIESE AUFNAHMEN FÜR DIE MOUNT
GAY RUM CORPORATION ENTSTANDEN BEI STURM.
DER PHOTOGRAPH CLINT CLEMENS BEFAND SICH AN
BORD DER SEGELJACHT «COLT INTERNATIONAL»
VOR ANTIGUA IN DEN ANTILLEN, ALS DIE MANN-
SCHAFT DIE SEGEL EINHOLEN MUSSTE. WIE MAN
SIEHT, GELANG ES DER SIEBENKÖPFIGEN BESAT-
ZUNG SCHLIESSLICH. (USA)

▲ 367-371 TOUTES CES PHOTOS PRISES EN MER
PAR GROS TEMPS ONT ÉTÉ RÉALISÉES POUR MOUNT
GAY RUM CORPORATION. LE PHOTOGRAPHE CLINT
CLEMENS SE TROUVAIT À BORD DU YACHT «COLT
INTERNATIONAL», PRÈS DE L'ÎLE D'ANTIGUA, DANS
LES ANTILLES LORSQUE LA TEMPÊTE CONTRAIGNIT
L'ÉQUIPAGE À BAISSER LES VOILES, CE QUI
FINALEMENT RÉUSSIT. (USA)

FINE ART

KUNST

ART

PHOTOGRAPHER:
GOTTFRIED HELNWEIN
CAMERA:
NIKON
FILM:
KODAK 64 372-376
KODAK 32 377
PHOTO EDITOR:
GOTTFRIED HELNWEIN

CLIENT:
EDITION BRAUS
ART DIRECTOR:
ERIK SPIEKERMANN
DESIGNER:
GOTTFRIED HELNWEIN
■ 372-377

PHOTOGRAPHER:
UWE SPOERING
CAMERA:
SINAR
FILM:
KODAK EPR
DESIGNER:
UWE SPOERING
►■ 378

■ 372-377 (PRECEDING AND THIS PAGE) PHOTO-GRAPHIC SELF-PORTRAITS BY GOTTFRIED HELN-WEIN FROM THE BOOK *DER UNTERMENSCH* ("THE UNDERDOG"), PUBLISHED BY BRAUS. LIKE HIS PAINTINGS, THE PHOTOGRAPHS ARE MARKED BY BANDAGES AND SURGICAL INSTRUMENTS. THE TRIPTYCH SHOWN AT TOP IS CALLED "THE QUIET GLOWING OF THE AVANT-GARDE"; IN THE CENTER ONE RECOGNIZES THE PAINTING "SHIP CAUGHT IN THE ICE" BY GASPAR DAVID FRIEDRICH (GER)

■ 378 PERSONAL STUDY BY PHOTOGRAPHER UWE SPOERING. (GER)

● 372-377 (VORHERGEHENDE UND DIESE SEITE) PHOTOGRAPHISCHE SELBSTPORTRÄTS DES KÜNST-LERS GOTTFRIED HELNWEIN AUS DEM BUCH »DER UNTERMENSCH«, ERSCHIENEN BEI BRAUS. WIE IN SEINEN BILDERN, PRÄSENTIERT SICH HELNWEIN IN ENTSTELLENDEN INSZENIERUNGEN MIT VERBANDS-MULL UND CHIRURGISCHEN INSTRUMENTEN. DAS TRIPTYCHON OBEN HEISST »DAS STILLE LEUCHTEN DER AVANTGARDE«; IN DER MITTE ERKENNT MAN GASPAR DAVID FRIEDRICHS »SCHIFF IM EIS«. (GER)

● 378 FREIE ARBEIT DES PHOTOGRAPHEN UWE SPOERING. (GER)

▲ 372-377 (PAGE PRÉCÉDENTE ET CETTE PAGE) AUTOPORTRAITS DE GOTTFRIED HELNWEIN TIRÉS DU LIVRE »UNTERMENSCH« (ÉDITIONS BRAUS). COMME DANS SES PEINTURES, IL SE PRÉSENTE DANS UNE MISE EN SCÈNE INQUIÉTANTE, SE DÉFI-GURANT À L'AIDE DE BANDES VELPEAU ET D'INS-TRUMENTS DE CHIRURGIE. EN HAUT, LE TRIPTYQUE «LA LUEUR TRANQUILLE DE L'AVANT-GARDE»; AU CENTRE, ON RECONNAÎT «LA BATEAU PRIS DANS LES GLACES» DE GASPAR DAVID FRIEDRICH (GER)

▲ 378 RECHERCHE PERSONNELLE DU PHOTOGRAPHE UWE SPOERING. (GER)

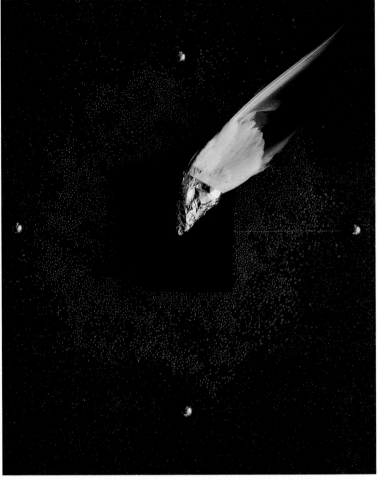

PHOTOGRAPHER:
RAPHAEL SENZAMICI
REPRESENTATIVE:
MANDRILL
CAMERA:
VIEW CAMERA 4X5/
VIEW CAMERA 8X10
FILM:
KODAK 228 4X5/
KODAK 205 8X10
■ 379-382

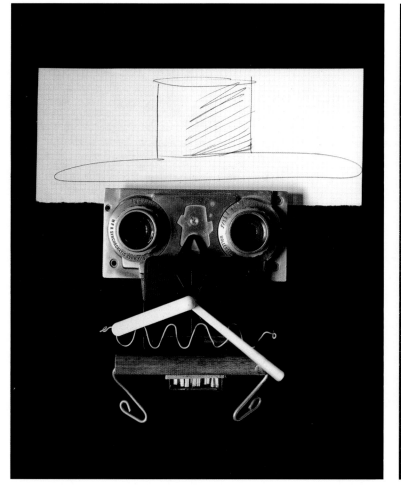

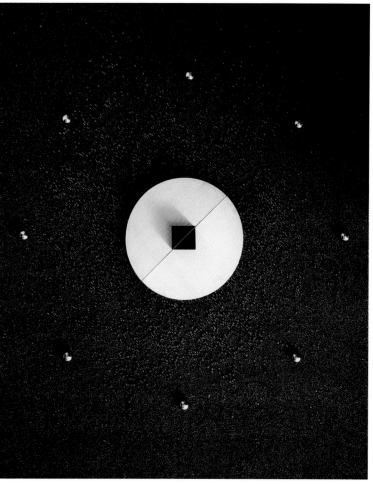

■ 379-382 PERSONAL STUDIES USED AS SELF-PROMOTION BY PHOTOGRAPHER RAPHAËL SENZAMICI. FROM LEFT TO RIGHT "ARCH," "STEEL FEATHER," "NIGHT ON THE TOWN," AND "SILENT CLOCK." THE PHOTOGRAPHER USES AN EIGHTY-YEAR-OLD CAMERA AND SHOOTS IN DAYLIGHT, WITH EXPOSURE TIMES OF UP TO THIRTY MINUTES. THE PHOTOS WHERE SHOWN IN AN EXHIBITION AT THE VIA GALLERY IN PARIS. (FRA)

● 379-382 FREIE ARBEITEN, DIE DER PHOTOGRAPH RAPHAËL SENZAMICI ALS EIGENWERBUNG VERWENDET. VON LINKS NACH RECHTS: «DER BOGEN», «STAHLFEDER», «NACHT ÜBER DER STADT» UND «STILLE UHR». DER PHOTOGRAPH ARBEITET MIT EINER 80 JAHRE ALTEN KAMERA. ER BENUTZT TAGESLICHT, WOBEI ER BELICHTUNGSZEITEN BIS ZU 30 MINUTEN HAT. DIE AUFNAHMEN WURDEN IN DER PARISER GALERIE VIA GEZEIGT. (FRA)

▲ 379-382 ÉTUDES PERSONNELLES UTILISÉES COMME AUTOPROMOTION PAR LE PHOTOGRAPHE RAPHAËL SENZAMICI. DE GAUCHE À DROITE: «L'ARC», «PLUME D'ACIER», «NUIT SUR LA VILLE», ET «HORLOGE SILENCIEUSE». LE PHOTOGRAPHE TRAVAILLE AVEC UN APPAREIL VIEUX DE 80 ANS, À LA LUMIÈRE DU JOUR; LES TEMPS DE POSE PEUVENT ATTEINDRE 30 MINUTES. CES PHOTOS ONT ÉTÉ EXPOSÉES GALERIE VIA, À PARIS. (FRA)

PHOTOGRAPHER:

DOLORES METZNER

CAMERA:

SINAR F+ 4X5/90MM

AND 210MM

FILM:

KODAK EKTACHROME

64T/

KODAK VERICOLOR

II, TYPE H

PHOTO EDITOR:

NANCY GLASSMAN

CLIENT:

LEAR'S MAGAZINE

ART DIRECTOR:

RON ALBRECHT

DESIGNER:

JEANNE ARNOLD

■ 384

PHOTOGRAPHER:

ALAN DAVID-TU

REPRESENTATIVE:

SANDEE ASHTON

ASSOC.

CAMERA:

SINAR

FILM:

KODAK 6117

CLIENT:

INTERNATIONAL

FLAVOURS +

FRAGRANCES

ART DIRECTOR:

PETER BRISTOW

►■ 385

■ 384 THIS PHOTOGRAPH BELONGS TO A SERIES OF ASSEMBLAGES THAT EMBODY THE PARADOXES OF BEAUTY AND SADNESS, LIFE AND DECAY. THEY WERE DONE FOR AN ARTICLE ON THE ENDANGERED RAINFORESTS WHICH APPEARED IN *LEAR'S* MAGAZINE. (USA)

■ 385 *BLUE HEAD* WAS ORIGINALLY COMMISSIONED BY A FRAGRANCE COMPANY WITH THE ASSIGNMENT CALLING FOR A PORTRAIT OF A WOMAN THAT EVOKED THE ERA OF THE 1930'S AND AN OVERALL FEELING OF "BLUE". (GBR)

● 384 DIESE AUFNAHME GEHÖRT ZU EINER REIHE VON ASSEMBLAGEN MIT GEGENSTÄNDEN, IN DENEN SCHÖNHEIT UND TRAUER, LEBEN UND ZERSTÖRUNG ZUM AUSDRUCK KOMMEN. SIE ENTSTANDEN FÜR EINEN ARTIKEL IN *LEAR'S* MAGAZIN ÜBER DIE ZERSTÖRUNG DER REGENWÄLDER. (USA

● 385 DIESE AUFNAHME MIT DEM TITEL *BLUE HEAD* ENTSTAND IM AUFTRAG EINES HERSTELLERS VON DUFTSTOFFEN. STICHWORTE FÜR DEN PHOTOGRA-PHEN WAREN DIE FARBE BLAU UND DER STIL DER 30ER JAHRE. (GBR)

▲ 384 PHOTO D'UNE SÉRIE MONTRANT DES ASSEM-BLAGES D'ÉLÉMENTS QUI SYMBOLISENT LA VIE ET LA DÉGRADATION, QUI ILLUSTRAIENT UN ARTICLE SUR LA DISPARITION DES FORÊTS TROPICALES, PARU DANS *LEAR'S* MAGAZINE. LES IMAGES ONT ÉTÉ SUGGÉRÉES PAR LE TEXTE. (USA)

▲ 385 CETTE PHOTOGRAPHIE A ÉTÉ RÉALISÉE POUR LA PUBLICITÉ D'UN FABRICANT DE PARFUMS. LE TITRE, «BLUE HEAD» A INSPIRÉ LES TONALITÉS DE BLEU DE CETTE IMAGE QUI ÉVOQUE L'ATMOSPHÈRE DES ANNÉES 1930. (GBR)

G R A P H I S D E S I G N 9 3

Entry Deadline: November 30, 1991

ADVERTISING: Newspaper and magazine. **DESIGN**: Promotion brochures, catalogs, invitations, record covers, announcements, logos and/or corporate campaigns, calendars, books, book covers, packaging (single or series, labels and/or complete packages). **EDITORIAL**: Company magazines, newspapers, consumer magazines, house organs, annual reports. **ILLUSTRATION**: All categories, black and white or color. **ELIGIBILITY**: All work produced between December 1, 1990 through November 30, 1991, as well as unpublished work from this period by professionals and students.

A N N U A L R E P O R T S 4

Entry Deadline: April 30, 1992

All annual reports, capability brochures, public interest reports, and other corporate public relations material produced in a brochure format. **ELIGIBILITY**: All work published between April 30, 1991 and April 30, 1992.

G R A P H I S P O S T E R 9 3

Entry Deadline: April 30, 1002

Cultural Posters: exhibitions, film, music theater, etc. Advertising Posters: consumer goods, self-promotion, etc. Social posters: education, conferences, and meetings, political, etc. **ELIGIBILITY**: All work produced between May 1, 1991 and April 30, 1992.

G R A P H I S P H O T O 9 3

Entry Deadline: June 30, 1992

Advertising Photography: Ads, promotional brochure, catalogs, invitations, announcements, record covers, and calendars on all subjects. Editorial Photography: for press media (journalism and feature stories), books, corporate publications, etc. on all subjects. Fine Art Photography: Personal studies on all subjects. Unpublished Photography: Experimental and student work on all subjects. **ELIGIBILITY**: All work produced between July 1, 1991 and June 30, 1992.

R U L E S

By submitting work to **GRAPHIS**, the sender grants permission for his or her publication in any **GRAPHIS** book, as well as any article in **GRAPHIS** magazine, or any advertisement, brochure, or other printed matter produced specifically for the purpose of promoting the sale of these publications.

E L I G I B I L I T Y

All work produced in the 12-month period previous to the submission deadlines, as well as rejected or unpublished work from this period, by professionals and students.

W H A T T O S E N D

Please send the printed piece (unmounted but well protected). Do not send original art. For large, bulky or valuable pieces, please submit color photos or (duplicate) slides. **Entries cannot be returned.** Only in exceptional cases and by contacting us in advance will material be sent back.

H O W A N D W H E R E T O S E N D

Please tape (do not glue) the entry form provided (or copy)–with full information–on the back of each piece. Entries can be sent by air mail, air parcel post or surface mail. Please do not send anything by air freight. Declare, "No Commercial Value" on packages, and label "Art for Contest." The number of transparencies and photos should be indicated on the parcel. (If sent by air courier, please mark "documents, Commercial Value 00.00.")

E N T R I E S

SINGLE ENTRY: North America: US $10.00 Germany: DM 10.00 All other countries: SFr. 10.00
FOR EACH CAMPAIGN ENTRY OF 3 OR MORE PIECES: North America: US $25.00 Germany: DM 25.00 All other countries: SFr 25.00

Please make checks payable to **GRAPHIS PRESS CORP. ZURICH** and include in parcel. These fees do not apply to students, if copy of student identification is included. (For entries from countries with exchange controls, please contact us.) A confirmation of receipt will be sent to each entrant, and all entrants will be notified whether or not their work has been accepted for publication. By submitting work you qualify for a 25% discount on the purchase of the respective book. Thank you for you entry.

GRAPHIS PRESS CORP. 107 DUFOURSTRASSE CH-8008 ZURICH, SWITZERLAND

EINLADUNG
. . . .

GRAPHIS DESIGN 93

EINSENDESCHLUSS: 30. NOVEMBER 1991

WERBUNG: In Zeitungen und Zeitschriften. **DESIGN**: Werbeprospekte, Kataloge, Einladungen, Schallplattenhüllen, Anzeigen, Signete und/oder Image-Kampagnen, Kalender, Bücher, Buchumschläge, Packungen. **REDAKTIONELLES DESIGN**: Firmenpublikationen, Zeitungen, Zeitschriften, Jahresberichte. **ILLUSTRATION**: Alle Kategorien, schwarzweiss oder farbig. **IN FRAGE KOMMEN**: Alle Arbeiten von Fachleuten und Studenten - auch nicht publizierte. Arbeiten -, die zwischen Dezember 1990 und November 1991 entstanden sind.

ANNUAL REPORTS 4

EINSENDESCHLUSS: 30. APRIL 1992

Alle Jahresberichte einer Firma oder Organisation (Tabellen und Diagramme, Illustrationen und Photos). **IN FRAGE KOMMEN**: Alle Jahresberichte und ähnliche Firmenpublikationen für Öffentlichkeitsarbeit in Form von Broschüren von 1991 bis 1992.

GRAPHIS POSTER 93

EINSENDESCHLUSS: 30. APRIL 1992

KULTUR: Plakate für Ausstellungen, Film-, Theater- und Balletaufführungen usw. **WERBUNG**: Plakate für Konsumgüter, Eigenwerbung usw. **GESELLSCHAFT**: Plakate für Ausbildung, die Ankündigung von Tagungen usw. **IN FRAGE KOMMEN**: Alle Arbeiten, die zwischen Mai 1991 und April 1992 entstanden sind.

GRAPHIS PHOTO 93

EINSENDESCHLUSS: 30. JUNI 1992

Werbephotographie: Anzeigen, Prospekte, Kataloge, Einladungen, Bekanntmachungen, Schallplattenhüllen, Kalender. Redaktionelle Photographie: Pressephotos, Firmenpublikationen usw. In den Bereichen Mode, Architektur, Kunst, Natur, Wissenschaft und Technik, Alltag, Sport, Porträts, Stilleben usw. Künstlerische Photographie: Persönliche Studien. Unveröffentlichte Aufnahmen: Experimentelle Photographie und Arbeiten von Studenten und Schülern. **IN FRAGE KOMMEN**: Alle Arbeiten, die zwischen Juli 1991 und Juni 1992 entstanden sind.

TEILNAHMEBEDINGUNGEN

GRAPHIS erhält die Erlaubnis zur Veröffentlichung der eingesandten Arbeiten sowohl im entsprechenden Jahrbuch als auch in der Zeitschrift **GRAPHIS** oder für die Wiedergabe im Zusammenhang mit Besprechungen und Werbematerial für **GRAPHIS**-Publikationen.

IN FRAGE KOMMEN

Alle Arbeiten von Fachleuten und Studenten - auch nicht publizierte Arbeiten -, welche in den zwölf Monaten vor Einsendeschluss entstanden sind.

WAS EINSENDEN

Bitte senden Sie uns das gedruckte Beispiel (gut geschützt). Senden Sie keine Originale. Bei unhandlichen, umfangreichen und wertvollen Sendungen bitten wir um Farbphotos oder Duplikat-Dias. **Bitte beachten Sie, dass Einsendungen nicht zurückgeschickt werden können** (Ausnahmen möglich).

WIE SCHICKEN

Bitte befestigen Sie das vorgesehene Etikett (oder Kopie) - vollständig ausgefüllt - mit Klebstreifen (nicht mit Klebstoff) auf der Rückseite jeder Arbeit. Bitte per Luftpost oder auf normalem Postweg einsenden. **Keine Luftfrachtsendungen**. Deklarieren Sie «ohn jeden Handelswert» und «Arbeitsproben für Wettbewerb». Die Anzahl der Dias und Photos sollte auf dem Paket angegeben werden (bei Luftkurier-Sendungen vermerken Sie «Dokumente, ohne jeden Handelswert»).

GEBÜHREN

SFR. 10.--/DM 10.-- FÜR EINZELNE ARBEITEN
SFR. 25.--/DM 25.-- FÜR KAMPAGNEN ODER SERIEN (MEHR ALS 3 STÜCK)
Bitte senden Sie uns einen Scheck (SFr.-Schecks bitte auf eine Schweizer Bank ziehen) oder überweisen Sie den Betrag auf PC Zürich 80-23071-9 oder PSchK Frankfurt 3000 57-602. Diese Gebühren gelten nicht für Studenten. Senden Sie bitte eine Kopie des Studentenausweises. (Für Einsendungen aus Ländern mit Devisenbeschränkungen bitten wir Sie, uns zu kontaktieren.) Jeder Einsender erhält eine Empfangsbestätigung und wird über Erscheinen oder Nichterscheinen seiner Arbeit informiert. Durch Ihre Einsendung erhalten Sie 25% Rabatt auf das betreffende Buch. Herzlichen Dank für Ihre Mitarbeit.

GRAPHIS VERLAG AG, DUFOURSTRASSE 107 CH-8008 ZURICH, SCHWEIZ

GRAPHIS DESIGN 93

DATE LIMITE D'ENVOI: 30 NOVEMBRE 1992

PUBLICITÉ: journaux, magazines. **DESIGN:** brochures de promotion, catalogues, invitations, pochettes de disques, annonces, emblèmes, en-têtes, campagnes de prestige, calendriers, livres, jaquettes, emballages (spécimen ou série, étiquettes ou emballages complets). **DESIGN ÉDITORIAL:** magazines de sociétés, journaux, revues, rapports annuels. **ILLUSTRATION:** toutes catégories en noir et blanc ou en couleurs. **ADMISSION:** Tous les travaux réalisés entre décembre 1990 et novembre 1991 par des professionnels ou étudiants, ainsi que les travaux refusés ou non publiés durant cette période.

ANNUAL REPORTS 4

DATE LIMITE D'ENVOI: 30 AVRIL 1992

Tous travaux publiés en relation avec le rapport annuel d'une entreprise ou d'une organisation. **ADMISSION:** Tous les rapports annuels et autre rapports destinés au grand public publiés sous forme de brochure en 1991 ou en 1992.

GRAPHIS POSTER 93

DATE LIMITE D'ENVOI: 30 AVRIL 1992

AFFICHES CULTURELLES: expositions, film, théâtre, ballet, concerts etc. **AFFICHES PUBLICITAIRES:** produits de consommation, autopromotion, etc. **AFFICHES SOCIALES:** formation, conférences et annonces de manifestations ou de réunions politiques, etc. **ADMISSION:** Tous les travaux réalisés entre mai 1991 et avril 1992.

GRAPHIS PHOTO 93

DATE LIMITE D'ENVOI: 30 JUIN 1992

PHOTO PUBLICITAIRE: annonces, brochures de promotion, catalogues, pochettes de disques, calendriers. **PHOTO RÉDACTIONNELLE:** reportages, livres, publications d'entreprises, etc. dans les domaines suivants: mode, arts, architecture, nature, sciences, techniques, vie quotidienne, sports, portraits, nature morte, etc. **PHOTO D'ART:** études personnelles. **PHOTOS NON-PUBLIÉES:** travaux expérimentaux et projets d'étudiants. **ADMISSION:** Les travaux réalisés entre juillet 91 et juin 92.

MODALITÉS D'ENVOI

Par votre envoi, vous donnez expressément à **GRAPHIS** l'autorisation de reproduire les travaux reçus aussi bien dans le livre en question que dans le magazine **GRAPHIS**, ou dans tout imprimé concernant des comptes rendus ou du matériel publicitaire sur les publications **GRAPHIS**.

ADMISSION

Sont acceptés tous les travaux de professionnels et d'étudiants - même inédits - réalisés pendant les douze mois précédant le délai limite d'envoi.

QUE NOUS ENVOYER

Veuillez nous envoyer un exemplaire imprimé. N'envoyez pas d'originaux. Pour les travaux de grand format, volumineux ou de valeur, veuillez nous envoyer des photos ou des duplicata. **Veuillez noter que les travaux ne peuvent pas être retournés,** sauf dans des cas exceptionnels et si vous nous en avisez à l'avance.

COMMENT ET OÙ ENVOYER

Veuillez scotcher (ne pas coller) au dos de chaque spécimen les étiquettes ci-jointes (ou photocopies) dûment remplies. Envoyez les travaux de préférence par avion, ou par voie de surface. **Ne nous envoyez rien en fret aérien.** Indiquez «Sans aucune valeur commerciale» et «Echantillons de spécimens pour concours». Le nombre de diapositives et de photos doit être indiqué sur le paquet. (Pour les envois par courrier, inscrire «Documents, sans aucune valeur commerciale».)

DROITS D'ADMISSION

SFR. 10.00 pour les envois concernant un seul travail
SFR. 25.00 pour chaque série de 3 travaux ou davantage
Veuillez joindre à votre envoi un chèque tiré sur une banque suisse ou verserez ce montant au compte chèque postal Zurich 80.23071.9. Les étudiants sont exemptés de cette taxe. Prière de joindre une photocopie de la carte d'étudiant. (Si vous résidez dans un pays qui connaît le contrôle des changes, veuillez nous contacter préalablement.) Nous vous ferons parvenir un accusé de réception. Vous serez informé par la suite de la parution ou non-parution de vos travaux. Votre envoi vous vaudra une réduction de 25% sur l'annuel en question. Veuillez faire parvenir vos travaux à l'adresse suivante:

ÉDITIONS GRAPHIS, DUFOURSTRASSE 107 CH-8008 ZURICH, SWITZERLAND

SUBSCRIBE TO GRAPHIS: USA AND CANADA

MAGAZINE	USA	CANADA

☐ NEW ☐ RENEW
☐ TWO YEARS (12 ISSUES)   US$149.00   US$166.00
☐ ONE YEAR (6 ISSUES)   US$ 79.00   US$ 88.00
☐ 25% DISCOUNT FOR STUDENTS WITH COPY OF VALID,
DATED STUDENT ID AND PAYMENT WITH ORDER
FOR CREDIT CARD PAYMENT:
☐ VISA ☐ MASTERCARD

ACCT. NO   EXP. DATE

SIGNATURE

☐ CHECK ENCLOSED ☐ BILL ME
CHECK THE LANGUAGE VERSION DESIRED:
☐ ENGLISH ☐ GERMAN ☐ FRENCH

SUBSCRIBE TO GRAPHIS: EUROPE AND WORLD

MAGAZINE	BRD	WORLD	U.K.

☐ NEW ☐ RENEW
☐ TWO YEARS (12 ISSUES)   DM305,-   SFR262.-   £102.00
☐ ONE YEAR (6 ISSUES)   DM162,-   SFR140.-   £ 54.00
☐ 25% DISCOUNT FOR STUDENTS WITH COPY OF VALID,
DATED STUDENT ID AND PAYMENT WITH ORDER
SUBSCRIPTION FEES INCLUDE POSTAGE TO ANY PART OF THE
WORLD. AIRMAIL AVAILABLE EVERYWHERE EXCEPT EUROPE
AND NORTH AMERICA.
☐ AIRMAIL SURCHARGE (6 ISSUES)   SFR 58.-
FOR CREDIT CARD PAYMENT:
(ALL CARDS DEBITED IN SWISS FRANCS):
☐ AMERICAN EXPRESS ☐ DINER'S CLUB ☐ EURO/MASTERCARD
☐ VISA/BARCLAY/CARTE BLEUE

ACCT. NO   EXP. DATE

SIGNATURE   CARDHOLDER NAME

☐ CHECK ENCLOSED ☐ BILL ME
CHECK THE LANGUAGE VERSION DESIRED:
☐ ENGLISH ☐ GERMAN ☐ FRENCH

PLEASE PRINT

NAME   DATE

TITLE

COMPANY

ADDRESS

CITY   POSTAL CODE

STATE/PROVINCE

COUNTRY

PLEASE PRINT

NAME   DATE

TITLE

COMPANY

ADDRESS

CITY   POSTAL CODE

STATE/PROVINCE

COUNTRY

PLEASE SEND ORDER FORM AND MAKE CHECK PAYABLE TO:
GRAPHIS US, INC.,
P.O. BOX 3063 SOUTHEASTERN, PA 19398-3063
SERVICE WILL BEGIN WITH ISSUE THAT IS CURRENT
WHEN ORDER IS PROCESSED (LETTERHEAD 1)

REQUEST FOR CALL FOR ENTRIES

PLEASE PUT ME ON THE "CALL FOR ENTRIES" LIST FOR THE
FOLLOWING TITLES:

☐ GRAPHIS DESIGN   ☐ GRAPHIS ANNUAL REPORTS
☐ GRAPHIS DIAGRAM   ☐ GRAPHIS CORPORATE IDENTITY
☐ GRAPHIS POSTER   ☐ GRAPHIS PHOTO
☐ GRAPHIS PACKAGING   ☐ GRAPHIS LETTERHEAD
☐ GRAPHIS LOGO

SUBMITTING MATERIAL TO ANY OF THE ABOVE TITLES,
QUALIFIES SENDER FOR A 25% DISCOUNT TOWARD PURCHASE
OF THAT TITLE.

PLEASE SEND ORDER FORM AND MAKE CHECK PAYABLE TO:
GRAPHIS PRESS CORP.,
DUFOURSTRASSE 107 CH-8008 ZÜRICH, SWITZERLAND
SERVICE WILL BEGIN WITH ISSUE THAT IS CURRENT
WHEN ORDER IS PROCESSED (LETTERHEAD 1)

REQUEST FOR CALL FOR ENTRIES

PLEASE PUT ME ON THE "CALL FOR ENTRIES" LIST FOR THE
FOLLOWING TITLES:

☐ GRAPHIS DESIGN   ☐ GRAPHIS ANNUAL REPORTS
☐ GRAPHIS DIAGRAM   ☐ GRAPHIS CORPORATE IDENTITY
☐ GRAPHIS POSTER   ☐ GRAPHIS PHOTO
☐ GRAPHIS PACKAGING   ☐ GRAPHIS LETTERHEAD
☐ GRAPHIS LOGO

SUBMITTING MATERIAL TO ANY OF THE ABOVE TITLES,
QUALIFIES SENDER FOR A 25% DISCOUNT TOWARD PURCHASE
OF THAT TITLE.

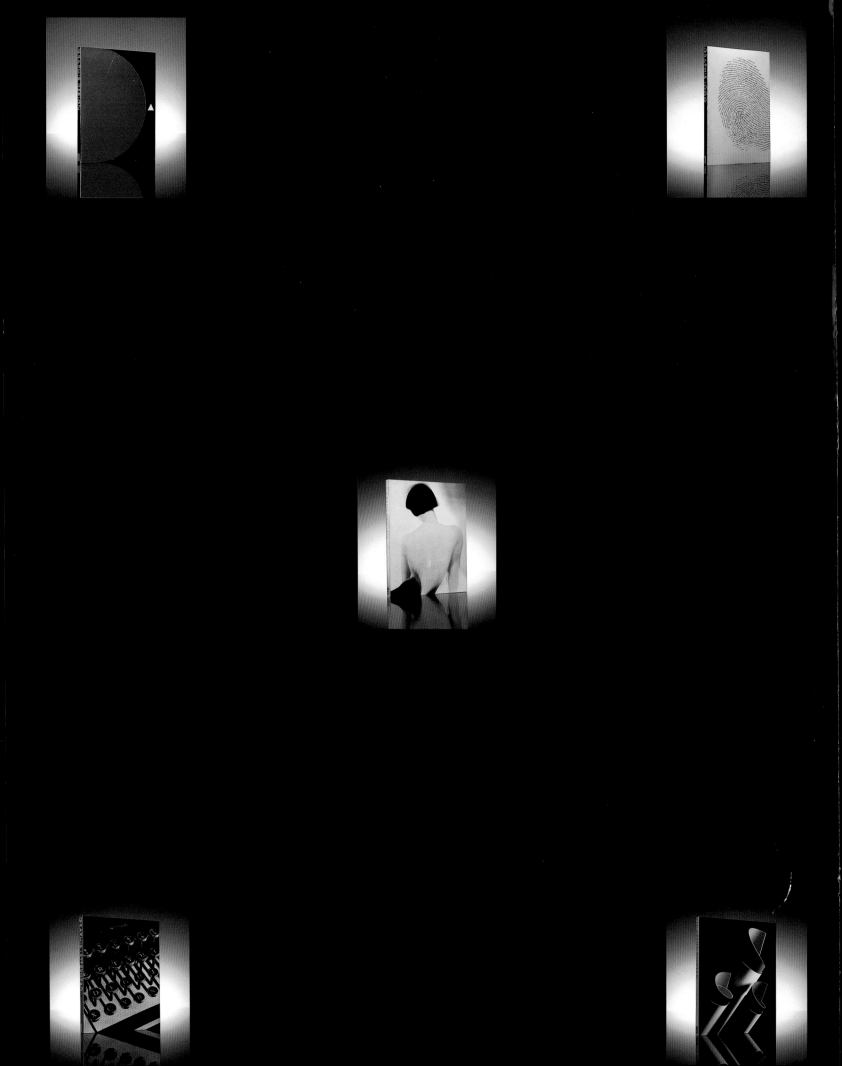

BOOK ORDER FORM: USA AND CANADA

BOOKS	USA	CANADA
☐ GRAPHIS PHOTO 91	US$69	US$ 94
☐ GRAPHIS POSTER 91	US$69	US$ 94
☐ GRAPHIS DESIGN 91	US$69	US$ 94
☐ GRAPHIS LETTERHEAD 1	US$69	US$ 94
☐ GRAPHIS LOGO 1	US$50	US$ 70
☐ THE GRAPHIC DESIGNER'S		
GREEN BOOK	US$25	US$ 41
☐ GRAPHIS PHOTO 90	US$69	US$ 94
☐ GRAPHIS ANNUAL REPORTS 2	US$75	US$100
☐ GRAPHIS POSTER 90	US$69	US$ 94
☐ GRAPHIS CORPORATE IDENTITY 1	US$75	US$100
☐ GRAPHIS PHOTO 89	US$65	US$ 91
☐ GRAPHIS PACKAGING 5	US$75	US$100
☐ GRAPHIS DIAGRAM 1	US$65	US$ 91
☐ GRAPHIS ANNUAL REPORTS 1	US$65	US$ 91

☐ CHECK ENCLOSED (GRAPHIS AGREES TO PAY MAILING COSTS)
☐ BILL ME (MAILING COSTS IN ADDITION TO ABOVE
BOOK PRICE WILL BE CHARGED, BOOK(S) WILL BE SENT
WHEN PAYMENT IS RECEIVED)

PLEASE PRINT

NAME   DATE

TITLE

COMPANY

ADDRESS

CITY   POSTAL CODE

STATE/PROVINCE

COUNTRY

SIGNATURE   DATE

PLEASE SEND ORDER FORM AND MAKE CHECK PAYABLE TO:
GRAPHIS US, INC.
141 LEXINGTON AVENUE, NEW YORK, NY 10016, USA

REQUEST FOR CALL FOR ENTRIES

PLEASE PUT ME ON THE "CALL FOR ENTRIES" LIST FOR THE
FOLLOWING TITLES:

☐ GRAPHIS DESIGN   ☐ GRAPHIS ANNUAL REPORTS
☐ GRAPHIS DIAGRAM   ☐ GRAPHIS CORPORATE IDENTITY
☐ GRAPHIS POSTER   ☐ GRAPHIS PHOTO
☐ GRAPHIS PACKAGING   ☐ GRAPHIS LETTERHEAD
☐ GRAPHIS LOGO

SUBMITTING MATERIAL TO ANY OF THE ABOVE TITLES,
QUALIFIES SENDER FOR A 25% DISCOUNT TOWARD PURCHASE
OF THAT TITLE.

BOOK ORDER FORM: EUROPE AND WORLD

BOOKS	BRD	WORLD	U.K.
☐ GRAPHIS PHOTO 91	DM149,-	SFR.123.-	£49.00
☐ GRAPHIS POSTER 91	DM149,-	SFR.123.	£49.00
☐ GRAPHIS DESIGN 91	DM149,-	SFR.123.-	£49.00
☐ GRAPHIS LETTERHEAD 1	DM149,-	SFR.123.-	£49.00
☐ GRAPHIS LOGO 1	DM108,-	SFR. 92.-	£36.00
☐ THE GRAPHIC DESIGNER'S			
GREEN BOOK	DM 54,-	SFR. 46.-	£18.00
☐ GRAPHIS PHOTO 90	DM149,-	SFR.123.-	£49.00
☐ GRAPHIS ANNUAL REPORTS 2	DM162,-	SFR.137.-	£52.00
☐ GRAPHIS POSTER 90	DM149,-	SFR.123.-	£49.00
☐ GRAPHIS CORPORATE IDENTITY 1	DM160,-	SFR.132.-	£48.00
☐ GRAPHIS PHOTO 89	DM148,-	SFR.118.-	£46.50
☐ GRAPHIS PACKAGING 5	DM160,-	SFR.132.-	£48.00
☐ GRAPHIS DIAGRAM 1	DM138,-	SFR.112.-	£45.00
☐ GRAPHIS ANNUAL REPORTS 1	DM138,-	SFR.112.-	£45.00

☐ CHECK ENCLOSED (FOR EUROPE, PLEASE MAKE SFR, CHECKS
PAYABLE TO A SWISS BANK)
☐ AMOUNT PAID INTO GRAPHIS ACCOUNT AT THE UNION BANK
OF SWITZERLAND, ACCT NO 3620063 IN ZÜRICH.
☐ AMOUNT PAID TO POSTAL CHEQUE ACCOUNT ZÜRICH 80-23071-9
(THROUGH YOUR LOCAL POST OFFICE)
☐ PLEASE BILL ME (MAILING COSTS IN ADDITION TO ABOVE
BOOK PRICE WILL BE CHARGED, BOOK(S) WILL BE SENT
WHEN PAYMENT IS RECEIVED)

PLEASE PRINT

NAME   DATE

TITLE

COMPANY

ADDRESS

CITY   POSTAL CODE

STATE/PROVINCE

COUNTRY

SIGNATURE   DATE

PLEASE SEND ORDER FORM AND MAKE CHECK PAYABLE TO:
GRAPHIS PRESS CORP,. DUFOURSTRASSE 107, CH-8008
ZÜRICH, SWITZERLAND

REQUEST FOR CALL FOR ENTRIES

PLEASE PUT ME ON THE "CALL FOR ENTRIES" LIST FOR THE
FOLLOWING TITLES:

☐ GRAPHIS DESIGN   ☐ GRAPHIS ANNUAL REPORTS
☐ GRAPHIS DIAGRAM   ☐ GRAPHIS CORPORATE IDENTITY
☐ GRAPHIS POSTER   ☐ GRAPHIS PHOTO
☐ GRAPHIS PACKAGING   ☐ GRAPHIS LETTERHEAD
☐ GRAPHIS LOGO

SUBMITTING MATERIAL TO ANY OF THE ABOVE TITLES,
QUALIFIES SENDER FOR A 25% DISCOUNT TOWARD PURCHASE
OF THAT TITLE.

PHOTOGRAPHER:
BRUNO J. ZEHNDER
CAMERA:
NIKON-F
FILM:
KODACHROME PKR 64
PHOTO EDITOR:
DIETER STEINER 352
METIN TILKI 353

CLIENT:
WIZARD & GENIUS
IDEALDECOR AG 351
STERN 352
ATHENA INT'L 353
ART DIRECTOR:
HANS H. KUNZ 351
WOLFGANG
BEHNKEN 352
TREVOR JONES 353
■ 351-353

■ 351 ADULT EMPEROR PENGUIN WITH CHICKS ON THE SEA-ICE OF THE ANTARCTIC. BRUNO J. ZEHNDER LIKES TO LOOK HIS SUBJECTS IN THE EYES. HERE, HE STOOD KNEE-DEEP IN SNOW TO CAPTURE THE RIGHT ANGLE. (USA)

■ 352 THIS PHOTOGRAPH ILLUSTRATED AN ARTICLE IN *STERN* MAGAZINE ON THE EXPLOITATION OF THE SOUTH POLE. THE PHOTOGRAPHER WANTED TO EMPHASIZE THE STRENGTH OF THE RUSSIAN PRESENCE AND, IN THIS PHOTOGRAPH, CONTRASTS THE VESSEL "AKADEMIK FEDOROW" WITH THE SINGLE EMPEROR PENGUIN. HE LAYED DOWN FLAT ON THE ICE, TWO INCHES AWAY FROM THE PENGUIN, TALKING TO HIM AS ONE WOULD TO A BEAUTIFUL MODEL. (GER)

■ 353 A U.S. COAST GUARD HELICOPTER LANDS ON THE SEA-ICE IN THE ANTARCTIC WHILE AN EMPEROR PENGUIN ,ESCAPES THE INTRUSION. TO ACHIEVE A PERSPECTIVE THAT WOULD SHOW THE PENGUIN AS THE NATURAL RULER OF THE REGION, THE PHOTOGRAPHER LAYED DOWN FLAT ON THE ICE. (USA)

● 351 ERWACHSENER KAISER-PINGUIN MIT JUNG-TIEREN IM ANTARKTISCHEN EIS. BRUNO J. ZEHN-DER, SPEZIALIST FÜR PINGUIN-PHOTOS, HAT GERN AUGENKONTAKT MIT IHNEN. BEI DIESER AUFNAHME STAND ER BIS ZU DEN KNIEN IM SCHNEE. (USA)

● 352 EIN KAISERPINGUIN IM EIS DER ANTARKTIS VOR DEM SOWJETISCHEN POLARSCHIFF «AKADEMIK FEDOROW». DER PHOTOGRAPH WOLLTE DIE STÄRKE DER SOWJETS IN DER ANTARKTIS DEMONSTRIEREN. BEI DIESER AUFNAHME LAG ER FLACH AUF DEM EIS, NUR WENIGE ZENTIMETER VON DEM PINGUIN ENTFERNT, SANFT AUF IHN EINREDEND, ALS SEI ER SEIN MODELL. DIE AUFNAHME ERSCHIEN IN EINEM *STERN*-ARTIKEL ÜBER DIE DROHENDE AUSBEUTUNG DES SÜDPOLS. (GER)

● 353 EIN HUBSCHRAUBER DER US-KÜSTENWACHE LANDET AUF DEM EIS DER ANTARKTIS. DER KAISER-PINGUIN KEHRT DEM EINDRINGLING DEN RÜCKEN. BRUNO ZEHNDER, FLACH AUF DEM EIS LIEGEND, WÄHLTE DIESE PERSPEKTIVE, UM DEN PINGUIN ALS WAHREN KÖNIG DER ANTARKTIS ZU ZEIGEN. (USA)

▲ 351 «LA CRÈCHE ROYALE»: UN MANCHOT ADULTE AVEC SES PETITS SUR LA BANQUISE DE L'ANTARC-TIQUE. BRUNO J. ZEHNDER, CONNU POUR CES PHOTOS DE MANCHOTS, PREND CONTACT AVEC EUX EN LES REGARDANT DANS LES YEUX. (USA)

▲ 352 UN MANCHOT ROYAL ADULTE DEVANT LE BATEAU SCIENTIFIQUE SOVIÉTIQUE «AKADEMIK FEDOROV». LE PHOTOGRAPHE ÉTAIT FASCINÉ PAR LE CONTRASTE ENTRE LA FORME PUISSANTE DE LA COQUE ET LE MANCHOT. IL DUT S'ALLONGER SUR LA GLACE POUR PRENDRE CE CLICHÉ, TOUT EN PARLANT À L'ANIMAL. CE REPORTAGE PHOTOGRA-PHIQUE ILLUSTRAIT UN ARTICLE SUR LE PÔLE SUD, OBJET DE CONVOITISES À CAUSE DE SES RI-CHESSES MINIÈRES, PUBLIÉ DANS *STERN*. (GER)

▲ 353 L'HÉLICOPTÈRE HH 52-AA DE LA GARDE CÔTIÈRE AMÉRICAINE ATTERRIT SUR LA BANQUISE DE L'ANTARCTIQUE, TANDIS QU'UN MANCHOT ROYAL S'ÉLOIGNE, FACE À CETTE INTRUSION MENAÇANTE DE L'HOMME ET DE LA TECHNIQUE. CETTE PHOTO A ÉTÉ PRISE À PLAT VENTRE. (USA)